B₂T 15.95

W9-BBN-122

THE PRIMORDIAL BOND

Exploring Connections between
Man and Nature through the
Humanities and Sciences

THE PRIMORDIAL BOND

Exploring Connections between Man and Nature through the Humanities and Sciences

Stephen H. Schneider
and
Lynne Morton

Plenum Press · New York and London

Library of Congress Cataloging in Publication Data

Schneider, Stephen Henry.
  The primordial bond.

  Bibliography: p.
  Includes index.
  1. Human ecology. 2. Humanities. 3. Science. 4. Philosophy of na-
ture. I. Morton, Lynne, joint author. II. Title.
GF50.S36   304.2   80-20376
ISBN 0-306-40519-9

304.2
S 359 p
1981

© 1981 Stephen H. Schneider and Lynne Morton

Plenum Press, New York
A Division of Plenum Publishing Corporation
227 West 17th Street, New York, N.Y. 10011

Printed in the United States of America

My interest is in the future because I am going to spend the rest of my life there.

—CHARLES F. KETTERING

PREFACE

Does the solution to our energy crisis depend upon the development of coal, nuclear, solar, or some other energy source? Are we better off because science and technology have made us less vulnerable to natural catastrophes? How, in fact, do we see ourselves now in relation to our natural world? The answers to these questions lie as much within the humanities as in the sciences.

Problems as seemingly unrelated as our vulnerability to OPEC oil price hikes or a smog alert in Los Angeles or Tokyo often have common, hidden causes. One of these causes is simply the way our society sees its place in nature. There are many reasons for the heavy demand for oil. Among these we can include desire for industrial growth, hopes for improved living standards, mobility through automobiles and rapid transportation systems, and, not least, an attempt to loosen the constraints on man imposed by nature. These constraints and man's concomitant dependence upon nature are examples of the intense and finely interwoven relationship between man and nature, a relationship that constitutes a primordial bond forged long before the era of modern technology. Similarly, man has explored this primordial bond through the humanities for all the centuries prior to our present technological age. As we will see in this exploration, the bond underlies many of the environmental and technological problems we have come to label the *ecological crisis*. It includes such now "classical" environmental issues as pollution, in addition to related technological problems of energy, health, transportation, hunger, and even war and peace. To be sure, how we see our place in nature is "only" one component of these issues, but it is a significant aspect.

It is of more than academic interest to trace the importance of our feelings about the primordial bond, for if they really are, as we intend to prove, among the main determinants of the "ecological crisis" (broadly defined), then *solutions* to the crisis will have to recognize and account for these feelings as well. In order to find solutions, we will need to search our artistic, literary, religious, and philosophical heritage for clues to how people have felt about the man/nature relationship. Then we will need the help of the sciences to demonstrate what is known about the physical, the biological, and even the social world in which we live. Finally, we will confront specific issues of conflict, whose resolution will involve choices and actions. Since choices and actions involve values, we must return again to the humanities, for it is here that we find numerous offerings to help us interpret our feelings and so crystallize our values. The varied disciplines of the humanities and the sciences will be tapped selectively to help us explore the connections among man, nature, art; science, and the ecological crisis. Our approach is to combine technical and ethical judgments into a search for solutions to pressing environmental and related technological problems.

ACKNOWLEDGMENTS. We deeply appreciate the close working relationship we have enjoyed with our editor, Linda Greenspan Regan. Her philosophical, substantive, and other editorial suggestions leave a major imprint on the book. We also wish to thank Robert Chervin, Robert Chen, Randi Londer, Richard Shields Redman, Richard Regan, Allyn Shaloff, Deborah Feigenbaum, and, in particular, Samuel and Doris Schneider, and Leonard and Barbara Morton. Cheryl K. Schneider not only offered timely editorial comments on various manuscript drafts, but also provided considerable typing help when deadlines were tight. Finally, we appreciate the efforts of the graphics and photographics people at the National Center for Atmospheric Research in preparing some of the illustrations and the general help from Mary Rickel in tying up a number of loose ends in the process of delivering the completed manuscript.

CONTENTS

Chapter 1 / MAN APART?   3

Chapter 2 / POETRY AND PLUTONIUM   21

Chapter 3 / HUMANISTIC EXPRESSIONS OF CYCLES IN NATURE   43

Chapter 4 / REACTIONS TO THE PRIMORDIAL BOND EXPRESSED IN THE HUMANITIES   75

Chapter 5 / ANCIENT GREEK NATURAL PHILOSOPHY: THE BRIDGE TO SCIENCE   123

Chapter 6 / WHAT IS SCIENCE?   147

Chapter 7 / THE GLOBAL CYCLES OF LIFE   177

Chapter 8 / HUMAN DISRUPTIONS OF THE GLOBAL CYCLES OF LIFE   243

Chapter 9 / THE SOCIAL TITHE   283

REFERENCE NOTES   303

BIBLIOGRAPHY   313

INDEX   317

The first mistake is to think of mankind as a thing in itself. It isn't. It is part of an intricate web of life.
—ISAAC ASIMOV

Chapter 1 / MAN APART?

Energy. Ecology. Conservation. Old issues now become "new" issues. The unpleasant soot and dirt of the factories in large industrial cities were a major complaint in the 19th century, as they also are today. What's "new" now is not the issues themselves but their magnitude. Behind the banter of technical experts and the polemics of industrial, environmental, and political advocates lurks a fundamental enigma. We are increasingly concerned about the environment, even though we are increasingly "separating" ourselves from Nature. This concern raises a key question, one that should be obvious but is more often sensed than asked. What is man's place in Nature?

3

We are told that the trouble with modern man is that he has been trying to detach himself from nature. He sits in the topmost tiers of polymer, glass and steel, dangling his pulsing legs, surveying at a distance the writhing life of the planet. In this scenario, man comes on as a stupendous lethal force, and the earth is pictured as something delicate, like rising bubbles at the surface of a country pond, or flights of fragile birds. . . .

Man is embedded in nature.

The biologic science of recent years has been making this a more urgent fact of life. The new, hard problem will be to cope with the dawning, intensifying realization of just how interlocked we are. The old, clung-to notions most of us have held about our special lordship are being deeply undermined.[1]

The words are those of Dr. Lewis Thomas in his award-winning *The Lives of a Cell*, a book that discusses not a single cell in a human body but a much larger metaphorical cell, the earth. He reemphasizes connections between man and the natural world by applying the terminology of the human body to its surroundings. Man and Nature must surely be closely allied if the same language may be used to describe each. And if this is so, then how can man actually detach himself from Nature, as Lewis Thomas says he is trying to do? Must it be a futile attempt?

It is just such a question that lies at the heart of the "environment" versus "economic development" debate in the 20th century. Are we decoupling ourselves from the natural world, substituting instead the emoluments of a technologically "advanced" culture? Our mechanical and electronic gadgets are some of the more obvious symbols of this attempt at separation. But are they merely new symbols in a futile, old pattern in which other "objects"—gods to be placated, for example—had the central role? Are we attempting the impossible by trying to extricate ourselves from a bond in which we are inextricably bound? And will we degrade the quality of our environment in the attempt? Might we even threaten our own survival?

Questions like these about man's relationship with Nature are not unique to contemporary society. A glance back through history can add perspective to our present dilemmas. It is of more than intellectual interest to ask about a culture's views of its place in Nature, for those beliefs can strongly influence its actions—which affect the quality of both human life and the natural environment. For example, global pollution is, in part, a consequence of the belief that man can use technology to overcome Nature and, in part, a willingness to accept some degradation of the environment for material improvements. Similarly, the reaction against those with these beliefs has fostered the environmentalism that is a major political force today. Of course, none of this is unique to our time.

To gain perspective on the dimensions of the modern "ecological crisis," a brief look at evolving beliefs about the man/Nature bond is helpful. In the 18th century in Europe, for example, the perfectability of man, as expressed by many in that age of "enlightenment." meant active efforts to overcome Nature and flaunt human inventions. Ecologist Rene Dubos writes of the great English parks built in the 18th century:

> The English landscape architects transformed the humanized land of East Anglia by taking their inspiration from bucolic but imaginary landscapes painted by Claude Lorrain, Nicholas Poussin, and Salvatore Rosa. They obviously did not believe that "nature knows best," but instead tried to improve it by rearranging its elements. They eliminated vegetation from certain areas and planted trees in others; they drained marshes and channeled the water into artificial streams and lakes; they

FIGURE 1-1. This quaint house is located on a man-made stream. It is one of a maze of beautiful tree-lined streams with shoreline houses and small lakes that comprise the Wroxham Broads near the city of Norwich in East Anglia, England. In the 18th century the English landscape architects transformed much of East Anglia into a visually pleasing series of open areas, woodlands, and waterways. Their inspiration was not from unrestrained nature but from the imaginary landscapes of artists such as Claude Lorrain or Nicholas Poussin. Those 18th-century men believed that nature could be improved upon, and they worked hard to create a new landscape that was a blend of the best of man and Nature (*Photo by Stephen H. Schneider*).

organized the scenery to create both intimate atmos-
pheres and distant perspectives. In other words, they
invented a new kind of English landscape based on local
ecological conditions but derived from the images provided by painters.[2]

The formal gardens of Versailles provide further symbolic
evidence of the 18th-century taste to restrain Nature. Other
examples abound. In his *Essay on Criticism*, first published in
1711, Alexander Pope wrote:

> Those Rules of old discovered, not devised
> Are Nature still, but Nature methodized:
> Nature, like liberty, is but restrained
> By the same laws which first herself ordained.[3]

In contrast to those who would see Nature restrained,
a century later a number of Romantic poets, Utopian philosophers, and naturalists reacted with disgust and sometimes
anger at man's efforts to control Nature. They were offended
by the dirt, smoke, and pall of the 18th-century industrial
centers. They relished the natural forest and saw beauty and
truth in *imitating* nature, not overwhelming it. Typical of their
work is the famous "Lines, Composed a Few Miles Above
Tintern Abbey," by William Wordsworth. These often-quoted
verses not only exult the majesty of the natural world but also
go beyond to show Nature as a model, an inspiration for man:

> These beauteous forms,
> Through a long absence, have not been to me
> As is a landscape to a blind man's eye;
> But oft, in lonely rooms, and 'mid the din
> Of towns and cities, I have owed to them,
> In hours of weariness, sensations sweet,
> Felt in the blood, and felt along the heart;
> And passing even into my purer mind,
> With tranquil restoration—feelings too
> Of unremembered pleasure; such, perhaps,
> As have no slight or trivial influence

FIGURE 1-2. Versailles—the town, the palace, and the gardens—a testament to what the French monarchy believed to be its ultimate power. In the 17th century, and on into the 18th century, the arts in France often expressed the pleasures of life; in 17th-century France, civilization and its pleasures centered around the Sun King. Few churches were built in France during the 16th and 17th centuries. Instead, tremendous amounts of time and money were spent creating lavish country estates for the nobility and the monarch. The Loire Valley was turned into a romantic landscape of majestic chateaus. But Louis XIV, the ultimate ruler, wanted the ultimate estate. He therefore gave architect André Le Nôtre (1613–1700) the task of creating such an estate. The result was Versailles, and it revolutionized French garden design, for Versailles was a totally organized space. It maintained a baroque quality of unity with sky and surroundings and had many rhythms in its design. Yet it also represented—and this is what is important for our purposes—man's subjugation of nature, as symbolized in these formal gardens, clearly fashioned by man:

> His [Le Nôtre's] brief for the grand country-house was simple: to organize the landscape into one mighty scene that would express the dignity and elegance of man and delight his senses. All nature should conform. . . . The concept of comprehensive landscape-planning, apparent at Richelieu, was fully realized in the gardens, palace and town of Versailles, which came to symbolize the power of a united nation. (From G. Jellicoe and S. Jellicoe, *The Landscape of Man: Shaping the Environment from Prehistory to the Present Day*, Viking, New York, 1975, p. 179.)

(Photo by Cheryl K. Schneider.)

> On that best portion of a good man's life,
> His little, nameless, unremembered acts
> Of kindness and of love.[4]

These sentiments were shared by the American Romantic Henry David Thoreau, who sought a more complete communion with Nature and made this attempt the very structure of his life. He removed himself from society to live the life of a semirecluse at Walden Pond in New England. In his poetry and essays (particularly his *Walden*) we sense his total commitment to the inspirational qualities and divine guidance of Nature. He writes of Nature in especially tender terms:

> I awoke to an answered question, to Nature and daylight. The snow lying deep on the earth dotted with young pines, and the very slope of the hill on which my house is placed, seemed to say, Forward! Nature puts no question and answers none which we mortals ask. She has long ago taken her resolution. 'O Prince, our eyes contemplate with admiration and transmit to the soul the wonderful and varied spectacle of the universe.' The night veils without doubt a part of this glorious creation; but day comes to reveal to us this great work, which extends from earth even into the plains of the ether.[5]

Sentiments of today's "environmentalists" are not dissimilar to those of their counterparts of a century earlier.

In the 20th century, views of our place in Nature have been changing. Seemingly, the first half of the century,* at least in the industrial world, has concerned itself less with being "pro" or "con" Nature than the preceding two centuries. Rather, it has stressed, as Lewis Thomas suggested, human developments separate from Nature.

---

* Dubos, commenting on the transition in "psychological attitudes" from disregard of Nature to stewardship, wrote: "I take the middle of the twentieth century as a watershed in the social view of the relationships between human beings and the earth."

FIGURE 1-3. *Fernand Léger, The City, 1919.* Fernand Léger was a painter of the industrial era. He understood the nuances of contemporary life and incorporated the images of the modern, mechanized world into his works of art. In *The City*, as in his other paintings, there is a new awareness of modern reality, an awareness that encompasses new materials and a new intensity, all of which he chose to represent visually. Through his special, then revolutionary, use of flat color and line, he was able to make visual order out of the chaos of the modern city. Man, as he had created his natural world, was part of it. Here Léger used symbols of the contemporary era—traffic lights, telephone poles, steel structures—as if they were parts of Nature, for they are actually Nature as we now know it in the city, as we have made it. As life has become mechanized, so has art. The abstract, mechanistic art of Léger captures the strident quality of the modern metropolis. His use of man-made motifs, dramatically symbolized by vibrant colors, greatly influenced advertising and shop-window layouts. It is interesting to speculate on whether Léger meant to condemn the new values of technology that merged man and Nature or whether he wished to record them. It is clear, though, that his industrial world is now one aspect of Nature. As such, it is just as appropriate a subject for the artist as the idealized landscapes painted in earlier centuries (*Philadelphia Museum of Art: The A. E. Gallatin Collection*).

Once again Rene Dubos provides an interesting example:

> In 1933, the city of Chicago held a World's Fair to cel-
> ebrate its hundredth anniversary. The general theme of
> the fair was that the increase in wealth and in the stan-
> dard of living during the "Century of Progress" has been
> brought about by scientific technology. The guidebook
> to the exhibits had a section entitled "Science discovers,
> Industry applies, Man conforms," and the text pro-
> claimed "Individuals, groups, entire races of men fall
> into step with . . . science and technology." There could
> not be a more explicit statement of the then prevailing
> belief that the real measure of progress is industrial de-
> velopment, regardless of consequences.[6]

Man apart from Nature. Indifference to Nature, and of the
consequences to Nature of our developmental activities, appears to remain a major part of our attitudes. Earlier we noted
that a recent backlash to indifference toward Nature is emerging, once again. The new environmentalism is one such reaction. For example, the conservation group Friends of the
Earth publishes a newsletter with the very title: "Not Man
Apart." Their concern for man's affinity with Nature directs
attention to the preservation/expansion of life on earth. Ex-
pansions beyond the bounds of our planet would be more
than interesting experiments—in fact they may prove necessary if man abuses his planet too much. Adverse impacts
on what R. Buckminster Fuller called "spaceship Earth" have
even led some to propose escape from earthly Nature: witness
the recent movement for space colonization.[7]

The notion of colonization is, of course, quite traditional.
Many times in the past, colonists have risked the unknown
to escape from old difficulties to "new worlds." And often,
over time, they merely re-created the sorts of difficulties from
which the first waves of their settlers had originally fled. It
is unlikely that the colonists of space will prove more suc-

cessful than, say, the colonists of North America, in eliminating those malevolent or destructive attributes of human behavior that remain widespread on earth. On the other hand, at least the colonization of space offers a chance for the continued survival of humanity in the event of a catastrophe wiping out life on earth. This may well be the strongest justification for such colonization. It remains to be seen the extent to which space colonies will be able to match the diversity of options for biologic and economic life support still available on Earth.

This discussion suggests that the spectrum of human behavior and values experienced throughout history is unlikely to be rapidly altered, even in space. Today, an often bitter debate rages over the extent to which such human behavior is inherited or learned: the classical question of "nature versus nurture."

E. O. Wilson[8] of Harvard University has popularized the term *sociobiology* to encompass the study of genetically coded behavior. To the extent that human behavior is governed by "genetic determinism," we are certainly inextricably embedded—like it or not—in Nature. Shakespeare has provided an example. In *The Tempest*, Prospero describes the monster Caliban as "A devil, a born devil, on whose nature nurture can never stick, on whom my pains, humanely taken, all, all lost, quite lost."[9] If we are genetically preprogrammed, then Nature determines our behavior—unless technologies like genetic engineering allow us to alter the genetic coding of our inheritance. Yet many feel that most human actions are based on "cultural determinism"—that our personality traits and behavior are primarily acquired by environmental factors inherent in social experience.

Examples can be given to support both points of view. Behavioral traits like sleeping, walking upright, and sexual reproduction largely fall in the "nature" category of genetic preprogramming. On the other hand, it would be hard to make a purely biological case for social habits such as vegetarianism or women's wearing skirts. But for a constellation of human characteristics, like fear, love, compassion, loyalty, aggression, or self-sacrifice, the relative importance of nature or nurture is less straightforward. So the debate goes on. As of now, at least, genetic engineering is in its infancy, and the nature/nurture debate remains unresolved, suggesting that this avenue of approach cannot yet shed much light on the question we are trying to answer: What is the place of man in nature?

Religion has become involved in the debate. Some members of the clergy have expressed opposition to any human experimentation with our genetic inheritance. In this connection, a recent book on the subject has appeared bearing the very title: *Who Should Play God?* Interestingly, a historian at UCLA, Lynn White, has traced the basis of present-day cultural attitudes about the man/Nature relationship to religion itself. In his 1967 article, "The Historical Roots of Our Ecologic Crisis," White argues that the Judeo-Christian tradition fosters a disregard for environmental preservation. He notes that in Aristotle's time, "intellectuals of the ancient West denied that the visible world had a beginning. Indeed, the idea of a beginning was impossible in the framework of their cyclical notion of time."[10] White contends that there is a sharp contrast between the Greek concept and the biblical concept (expressed in the Book of Genesis). He says:

> Christianity inherited from Judaism not only the concept of time as nonrepetitive and linear but also a striking story of creation. By gradual stages a loving and all-powerful God had created light and darkness, the heavenly bodies, the earth and all its plants, animals, birds, and

fishes. Finally, God had created Adam and, as an after-thought, Eve to keep man from being lonely. Man named all the animals, thus establishing his dominance over them. God planned all of this explicitly for man's benefit and rule: no item in the physical creation had any purpose save to serve man's purposes. And, al-though man's body is made of clay, he is not simply part of nature; he is made in God's image.[11]

This structure of the natural world places man within Nature and yet atop the hierarchy of being. Unfortunately, man most often accepts his special place in Nature, while ignoring that he is also part of it. Prior to the widespread acceptance of this Judeo-Christian interpretation, Nature her-self reigned supreme. Pagan religions were based on natural personifications and animism: "in antiquity every tree, every spring, every stream, every hill had its own *genius loci*, its guardian spirit."[12] Before any act harmful to any part of Na-ture could be carried out, great care was taken to placate the appropriate spirit.

Eastern religion and philosophy, White contends, led to attitudes less destructive of Nature: "nature was conceived primarily as a symbolic system through which God speaks to men: the ant is a sermon to the sluggards; rising flames are the symbol of the soul's aspiration."[13] White cites contra-dictions to his own argument. For example, there are modern environmental disruptions, such as air pollution in Japan, or soil erosions in some Islamic and Marxist Eastern countries. These, he argues, reflect the basic Western roots of Marxism, the Judeo-Christian influence on Islam, and the adoption of a Western technological culture by Japan, not indigenous Eastern values.

Other scholars, like University of Minnesota geographer Yi-Fu Tuan, have disagreed. Tuan says that there is a large gap between Eastern ideals and Eastern practices with regard to their treatment of Nature. He writes:

> Sensitive Westerners are wont to contrast their own ag-
> gressive, exploitative attitude to nature with the har-
> monious relationships of other times and other places.
> This view should be commended for generosity, but it
> lacks realism and fails to recognize inconsistency and
> paradox as characteristic of human existence.[14]

When Eastern practices have been to tread lightly on
Nature, then the motivation, Tuan believes, has been largely
rooted in practical experience, not religion. There have been,
for example, numerous Chinese leaders throughout history
who warned against massive deforestation, despite the pressures for fuel and timber created by swelling populations. He
goes on to say that they deplored the indiscriminate cutting
of trees in the mountains not only because of its harmful effects on the quality of the soil in the lowland but also because
"they believed that forested mountain ridges slowed down
the horse-riding barbarians." Practical reasons indeed.

Nonetheless, White concludes that without recognizing
the roots of those value sets that lead us to disregard Nature,
we are unlikely to change our attitudes:

> The fact that most people do not think of these attitudes
> as Christian is irrelevant. No new set of basic values has
> been accepted in our society to displace those of Chris-
> tianity. Hence we shall continue to have a worsening
> ecologic crisis until we reject the Christian axiom that
> nature has no reason for existence save to serve man.[15]

Regardless of the actual mix of causes that determine
human attitudes about Nature, it is clear that people try to
use or modify their environment to minimize their vulnerability to outside forces—both natural and man-made. In this
process we sometimes find that the modifications we impose
on Nature can cause unanticipated problems that may be

FIGURE 1-4. Few symbols of man's effort to push the restraints of Nature are more appropriate than the jet airplane. We can carry people and cargo today at heights and speeds that were virtually unimaginable even earlier in our own century. Our new-found mobility, provided by aviation technology and the social organizations that sustain it, is evidenced by these condensation trails or contrails, seen over Aspen, Colorado. But the very fact that they are visible is a sign that we have left a "footprint" on Nature. Since the Earth's climate depends on the brightness of the planet, and since human activities (like those which produce contrails) alter that brightness, we can begin to see the emergence of a conflict: Our inventions provide benefits (such as jet travel) that are often accompanied by undesirable side effects (such as the pollution of the sky and waters). The trade-off between these risks and benefits is at the core of the "economic development versus environmental quality" debate that is heard so often today. Resolution of this debate is both a technical matter, necessitating data from scientists, and a value trade-off issue, suggesting a role for humanists. Indeed, we believe that solutions to what is popularly called the "ecological crisis" can be effective only if *both* scientists and humanists participate in the process of ameliorating the crisis (*Photo by Stephen H. Schneider*).

more troublesome to us than the conditions that motivated the modifications in the first place.

Whether the risks of such modifications are "acceptable" in view of their benefits, however, is a value judgment. Before we can make value judgments, though, we need to have some information, the kinds of information offered by our artists and scientists. It takes scientific information to estimate both risks and benefits, and it takes elucidation of our feelings and values to help us translate these estimates into acceptable action. Providing data is a speciality of scientists. Interpretation of our feelings and values is a pursuit of artists and other humanists. Let us turn, then, to the humanities and the sciences. We want to find out how artists and scientists have viewed the structure of Nature; and even more importantly, we will hope to find out what is man's place in Nature.

If the most unrelated things share a place, time, or odd similarity, there develop wonderful unities and peculiar relationships—and one thing reminds us of everything.

—NOVALIS

Chapter 2 / POETRY AND PLUTONIUM

Along with the attempt to separate himself from Nature, man has also separated himself from his fellow man. We have subdivided ourselves into groups: professions, nationalities, religions, sexes, and even intellectual sectors like artists and scientists.

THE "TWO CULTURES" FISSION

Except for a common first letter, poetry and plutonium seem as unrelated as the arts and the sciences. Artists and scientists often place themselves at opposite ends of the intellectual spectrum. Artists have been known to proclaim that "science" is only a mechanical effort to collect sterile facts and translate them into dehumanizing theories. On the other hand, scientists have sometimes characterized "artists" as self-indulgent, undisciplined speculators, whose descriptions of man or Nature are replete with personal biases and punctuated by disdain for verification based on measured observations.

The polarization of the arts and sciences was understood by English essayist C. P. Snow. As a writer and a physicist, Snow, in 1956, coined the phrase "the two cultures": "Literary intellectuals at one pole—at the other scientists. Between the two [exists] a gulf of mutual incomprehension—sometimes (particularly, among the young) hostility and dislike."[1]

Snow's article caused quite a stir among intellectual circles in the late 1950s. Critics argued that there were more than two cultures. Among scientists, for example, physicists and sociologists are often as far removed from mutual comprehension as the most distant groups of scientists or poets. Others argued that, indeed, Snow was right, but that one of the "two cultures" was better than the other. Nobel laureate physicist Francis Crick, co-discoverer of the double-helix shape of the DNA molecule, wrote that although Snow correctly noted the different cultures,

> The mistake he made, in my view, was to underestimate the difference between them. The old, or literary culture, which was based originally on Christian values, is clearly dying, whereas the new culture, the scientific one, based on scientific values, is still in an early stage of development, although it is growing with great rapidity. It is not possible to see one's way clearly in the modern world unless one grasps this division between these two cultures and the fact that one is slowly

dying and the other, although primitive, is bursting into life.[2]

Crick applied his beliefs to the area of university education, chiding academic administrators for "propping up an aging and dying" culture rather than seeing that "Universities become centers" for the new culture. Of course, we can find opposite opinions.

Finally, it must be said that no matter how many mutually exclusive intellectual groupings or "cultures" there really are, there is also an additional one, and it is probably the "culture" with the greatest following. It is comprised of all of those unaware of or little concerned with the squabbles of intellectual factions. It is also the greater bulk of humanity, concerned primarily with day-to-day living and dying. Although this mass lives with the technical and intellectual products of the other cultures, it hardly participates in their debates. Despite this irony, and the refinements one could add to the "two cultures" portrayed by Snow, they will serve an important purpose here: to represent the role of humanists and scientists in the building—and sometimes the destroying—of society and its relationship to Nature.

Snow's contemporary, Jacob Bronowski (known to our generation as the author and narrator of the public-television series "The Ascent of Man") also wrote of the two cultures:

> The literary man. . .has been taught that science is a large collection of facts. . .he pictures them, the colorless professionals of science, going off to work in the morning into the universe in a neutral, unexposed state. They then expose themselves like a photographic plate. And then in the darkroom or laboratory they develop the image, so that suddenly and startlingly it appears, printed in capital letters, as a new formula for atomic energy.[3]

Doubtless, each of us has heard, or could ourselves create, similar invectives to describe either humanists or scientists. But how many of us are equally able to list ways (other than by mutual derision) in which the "two cultures" are *related*?

Both Bronowski and Snow acknowledge that these stock images of humanists or scientists, as is true of all stereotypes, are "not entirely baseless." However, Snow feels that such an approach is all destructive. He, and Bronowski, have stated that much of this type of generalization is based on misinterpretations that are dangerous.

One of our purposes will be to help de-emphasize such stereotypes. We have two reasons. One is, simply, that these stereotypes are often wrong. The other is our belief that a fissioning of intellect into "two cultures" is depriving each of an extra measure of influence needed to solve problems of common interest. We will explore one specific problem in which both humanists and scientists have mutual interests: the "quality of life," as determined by man's relationship with Nature. In order to do this, we will examine similarities in the *process* by which humanists and scientists create their works. Then, we shall look for *concepts* that practitioners from both cultures have uncovered through their examinations of Nature. The structure of Nature as revealed by the humanities and by science, it turns out, will contain remarkable similarities. Finally, we will demonstrate how the contributions of humanists and scientists need to be *taken together* if we are to hope to solve the evolving "ecological crisis."* With this purpose in mind, then, let us return to poetry and plutonium, tangible symbols for the humanities and the sciences.   At the

---

* In *ecological crisis* we mean to encompass a number of problems related to technology. These include urban decay, environmental pollution, energy shortages, and the threats to world peace related to technological development.

simplest level, our symbols have at least one mutual feature: they are both man-made. Poetry is self-evidently so. Plutonium is, perhaps, less familiar than poetry. It is a radioactive chemical element man has created in the laboratory by bombarding some naturally occurring chemical elements with various forms of energy. It is used as fuel for some nuclear reactors and is an element used to power some atomic weapons. It is also a highly toxic substance. Thus plutonium has also come to serve as a symbol of the evils of science for opponents of the use (sometimes even the study) of nuclear energy.

It is patently unfair, then, to symbolize all of science by plutonium alone. We could easily have selected penicillin and maintained the alliteration with poetry as a symbol for the arts. This symbol is far less "loaded" emotionally than plutonium. Yet penicillin too has its detractors. They argue that death control—eliminating deadly diseases by drugs, for example—without birth control can create a dangerous increase in population. If population grows too fast, it can be potentially more lethal to society than the diseases penicillin has been used to prevent.[4]

No single word can fully represent "science," since none would be free from the context of individual interpretations of its social context. Likewise, poetry is not totally representative of the humanities. Nor is it universally appreciated. Economist and social critic Kenneth Boulding once quipped that "poetry can be more dangerous than plutonium."* He was referring to views expressed in some poetry that could be "dangerous" to the ideas held by others. Whether the con-

---

* Boulding offered this remark at a session of an American Association for the Advancement of Science annual meeting in Boston, February 1976. During this discussion of human catastrophes, energy expert John Holdren replied, "Yes, but we may have to ban plutonium to make the world safe for poets!"

sequences of some uses of poetry do indeed exceed the dangers of some uses of plutonium is not an issue we intend to confront—except to point out that any such judgment does not lie in a comparison between the arts and the sciences but is rooted in values.

Human value judgments, which we will explore later on, are a major link between the interests of humanists and scientists (and certainly among nonhumanists and nonscientists as well). Moreover, intelligent choices among alternative actions depend on the input of both knowledge and values to the decision-making process. Scientists can provide data and inferences upon which we can assess the potential consequences of some proposed set of alternative actions. Artists can provide insights on how we might feel about those consequences. These insights, in turn, can help us to make our values more explicit when the time comes to choose among alternatives. But making a choice is a value judgment, and value judgments are not the sole province of artists or scientists. Ignorance or misunderstanding by one "culture" about the workings or findings of the other can only reduce our knowledge of the facts and values surrounding an issue, thus rendering social decision-making less intelligent, to the probable detriment of everyone. This, we intend to prove, is the paramount and immediate danger from any art–science schism, a threat no less serious now than it was a few decades ago, when Snow and Bronowski popularized it.

Before we can expect to promote more tolerant interactions among the practitioners of the "two cultures," we should elaborate on their common ground. We begin by examining the process by which each "culture" works to achieve its creations. Here Bronowski's words serve to typify both his and Snow's thoughts on the similarities of art and science:

> When Coleridge tried to define beauty, he returned always to one deep thought: beauty, he said, is "unity in

variety." Science is nothing else than the search to discover unity in the wild variety of nature—or more exactly, in the variety of our experience. Poetry, painting, the arts are the same search, in Coleridge's phrase, for unity in variety. Each in its own way looks for likenesses under the variety of human experience. . . . It is wrong to think of science as a mechanical record of facts, and it is wrong to think of the arts as remote and private fancies. What makes each human, what makes them universal, is the stamp of the creative mind.[5]

How do artists or scientists express such creativity? To Bronowski, the act of creation lies "in the discovery of a hidden likeness. The scientist or the artist takes two facts or experiences which are separate; he finds in them a likeness which had not been seen before; and he creates a unity by showing the likeness."[6]

Thus, it is not the "facts" to the scientist nor the "experiences" to the artist that are the principal common links between the two cultures. Rather, they are bound more by the creation of unifying concepts derived from their respective observations. A concept in the arts, whether a poetic or musical or visual metaphor, and a concept in the sciences, whether a physical law, a theory of biological evolution or an organizational principle of social behavior, share a basic unifying element: each is a creative construct of a human mind.

The universality of enduring concepts is expressed when each of us discovers a unifying pattern that connects what had seemed to be disconnected experiences. The beauty in some act of art or science follows from this "discovery." As Bronowski says:

> We remake nature by the act of discovery, in the poem or in the theorem. And the great poem and the deep theorem are new to every reader, and yet are his own experiences, because he himself re-creates them. They are the marks of unity in variety; and in the instant when

the mind seizes this for itself, in art or in science, the
heart misses a beat.[7]

Concepts, of course, need not be static, whether in the
humanities or in the sciences. New physical data or new social
or psychological experiences may not be explained or represented satisfactorily by existing concepts. Creative minds,
which belong alike to artists and scientists, will then search
for new concepts to help connect the new observations with
existing experiences. The methods and symbols used in these
searches will often differ, contributing to the "gulf of mutual
incomprehension" across the "two cultures." The ability to
create the new concepts out of a variety of experiences is the
gift that creative artists and scientists share. This too is unity
in variety.

Unity in variety; order out of chaos; likeness within diversity; a solid comprised of atoms; a poem of images; a forest
made of trees; an animal comprised of organs; an organ filled
with cells; a galaxy full of stars; a society of individual people.
These phrases express the concept of structure, holism, or,
as anthropologist/philosopher Gregory Bateson has put it,
"the pattern which connects."[8] In these pages we look to both
humanities and science for examples of a "pattern which connects." We will examine various forms of artistic expression
in the humanities and even the occult. We will do the same
for selected works of natural philosophy and science.

We can sample only select segments of art or science in our
search for patterns that connect diverse aspects of human
experience. There is no global consensus on any such *single*
unifying concept, and, indeed, many could be proposed. As
with all things, we must be selective. We are interested in
defining, and perhaps defusing, the "ecological crisis." Thus,
our search for a unifying structure will be primarily focused
on the natural world, particularly the man/nature relationship

in this world. Even in this "restricted" domain, many such unifying patterns might be identified by different explorers. We believe that we can point to a major unifying pattern in nature, one that appears and reappears in the expressions of artists, philosophers, and scientists across diverse civilizations and throughout time. This is a very basic pattern: a cycle. And the chief symbol of cyclical behavior—indeed, the most perfect representation of a cycle—is simply a circle.

TALKING IN CIRCLES

Sometimes we move in cycles and don't even notice. How many of us notice that the earth follows a cyclical path about the sun? What do we see? The *effects* of these travels (i.e., the seasonal cycle or the day/night cycle, in these examples), not the cyclical paths themselves. It has taken humanists, philosophers, and scientists literally millennia to unravel the major *details* of these "noticeable" astronomical repetitions. Yet, long before they could observe or explain the details, there were humanists, philosophers, and early scientists who conceived of the natural world as structured in cycles.

The cycle has been a universal, unifying theme in artistic, philosophical, and religious expression about the natural world. Does *modern* science also find that this pattern is a major unifying structure in nature? Today's scientists, unlike the humanists, philosophers, and early scientists of history, are armed with a scientific method, as well as the powerful new logical and physical instruments it employs. When these tools are turned to look at Nature, the result is a startling array of new scientific findings and applications (i.e., technologies). We can now use telescopes and computers to chart the course of the stars, planets, Earth, and moon with precision sufficient to have successful manned space travel. Employing powerful microscopes, we now know enough of the basic structure of living things to alter the genetic codes that record and preserve our biological inheritance.

It is obvious that the style of modern life is dramatically dependent on recent scientific discoveries and technological inventions. We must ask: Do the findings of modern science revoke the concept that Nature is structured in cycles, a theme so often evoked in the past? One of our purposes will be to explore that basic question. And along the way, our inquiries will lead us into another related area: Is the human race, by the very application of its science and technology, altering not only these cyclical structures but also the man/Nature relationship itself? Finally two most important questions arise, for these are rooted in human values: (1) Does it matter if we are altering either the cyclical structures in Nature or the man/Nature relationship? And if so, (2) what should we do about it?

Before we begin to answer these questions, we need to define some terms. The terms *man, nature,* and *Nature* need clarification. We've indicated that man and Nature are separate, but we've also implied that man and Nature are inseparable. All living things are part of what is generally called the *natural world,* both man and his physical and biological surroundings. When we speak of this all-encompassing natural world, we'll be using the small *n, nature.* However, when we want to separate man from the rest of the natural world we'll be using the capital *N, Nature.* This device will prove convenient in examining man's place in Nature, and particularly the issue of human impacts on the environment.

Our use of the terms *cycles* and *circles* needs further clarification. *Cycles refers to repetitive patterns, but not necessarily exact duplications. The circle* is a symbol of cyclical motion, for it is an idealized path of cyclical travel. It may, depending on context, be used interchangeably with *cycle* in our text. We'll be discussing cycles as expressed in the humanities and science and as perceived in our daily experience. Exploring examples of cycles in each of these categories will further clarify the point.

Claude Monet, the 19th-century French Impressionist, created a series of paintings of the cathedral at Rouen. These paintings are good examples of the elements of a cyclic pattern of Nature expressed in the humanities. Although Monet painted the same subject, he did so at different times of the day. Consequently they are far from identical. He returned to the same subject, often from the same angle, only to find that the changes in time of day had altered the available light, which, in turn, had altered the colors. Each painting was the cathedral, yet substantially different in color and shadow: alike and different.

The creativity of the artist has captured a unifying concept, a pattern that connects. The collection of paintings becomes greater than the sum of its parts. Each painting is also an integral part of a familiar natural cycle. The special appeal of the ensemble, then, comes from our recognition of the morning, midday, or evening lighting expressed in each painting by the artist. We recognize these lighting patterns as "morning" or "evening" because we have seen such patterns so often. The lighting of one day is not an exact duplicate of every other day, but there is enough similarity among days so that changing patterns of light are familiar. Indeed, they are part of the normal daily cycle captured so strikingly by the artist.

Perhaps you've never visited the cathedral at Rouen. However, a "walk around the block" is a common experience.

FIGURE 2-1. Claude Monet was one of the greatest of the Impressionists, a 19th-century group of painters who felt constrained by the traditional approaches to both form and, especially, color. Their paintings of Nature were not idealized landscapes. In some cases, they were not even clearly defined constant areas but were presented as loosely formed shapes, loose because each individual's perception of that natural scene was different. Nature did have a form, but it was also determined, to some degree, by our perception of it. They allowed for individual interpretation of Nature. They also noticed that our perceptions of the same scenes differ under various conditions. Monet was particularly concerned with this perceptual difference.

(A) Beginning in about 1890, he painted the same scene in a series, showing the same subject under different conditions of light and atmosphere. The first of these series was the 40-odd paintings he did of the cathedral at Rouen. The subject changes so dramatically under the varied conditions that there is, in addition to a change of colors, a dematerialization into an almost blurred form. Although we "see" the same image, we could actually forget what the subject is, so different are the paintings. Monet's series of water lilies, done in the early 1900s, achieves the same effect. In both these series, Monet showed how Nature behaves in a cyclical manner. Although he returned to the same subject it was not the identical subject. Alterations had taken place (alterations caused by a natural condition—i.e., light) that made it alike and yet different (*Photo by Stephen H. Schneider, taken in 1967 at the Jeu de Pomme, Paris, where several of Monet's Cathedral at Rouen paintings were hung side by side*).

(B) *Claude Monet, Rouen Cathedral: Tour d'Albane, Early Morning, 1894.* A detail of the early morning painting (*Museum of Fine Arts, Boston: The Tompkins Collection*).

When we walk around the block, we repeat a pattern, a cycle. Yet each time the trip is made, the experience can be different, both physically and psychologically. We meet different people at different times; we hear different sounds; we walk in the rain or the sun or the snow. Each factor alters the *physical* experience of walking around the block. *Internal* factors, thoughts, or moods can be different on different trips, changing our observations and reactions. Physically and psychologically, each go-round is not exactly the same. Nevertheless, a repetitive pattern, a cycle emerges, despite the varying details of each trip.

Let's turn next to examples of cycles in nature as expressed in the findings of modern science. Reconsider the two cycles mentioned earlier: the revolution of the earth around the sun, causing the seasonal cycle, and the rotation of the earth on its axis, leading to the day/night cycles.

We have said that our definition of cycles does not require that each circuit be a perfect replica of every other. It might appear that these examples from astronomy are exceptions; they seem to be identical, perfectly circular repetitions. However, astronomers do not believe that these motions are perfect repetitions. The orbit of the earth around the sun is not a perfect circle. It is a flattened circle, an ellipse. The earth is a few million miles (a small percentage of the average earth–sun distance) closer to the sun in January than it is in July. Furthermore, the amount of flattening in the orbit (called its *ellipticity*) changes in a somewhat irregular cycle of about 100,000 years. In fact, some scientists believe that such alterations to the orbital cycles are related to the comings and goings of ice ages on earth.[9] This distortion of the orbit from a perfect circle is caused by the tug on the earth of the gravitational forces of the other planets in the solar system.

Consider next another scientific example: the earth's rotation. Here, it would seem, is an example of a fully repetitive cycle, where each 24-hour rotation is a perfect copy of all others. Not so—and the evidence for this is as noticeable as the tides. The tides are caused by the gravitational tug on the earth of other heavenly bodies, primarily the moon. It is also evident that a great deal of energy is expended as the tides rise and fall. Where does this energy come from? Astronomers now believe that the energy used to drive the tides comes partly from the energy contained in the rotation of the earth about its axis. The orbit and rotation of the moon on its axis are also involved, but these details are not important here. The conclusion we observe is that the earth's rotation period, the length of our day, is increasing very slowly (in human terms) as the kinetic energy contained in the earth's rotation is dissipated by tidal motions and gravitational forces. Of course, it takes very sensitive instruments to detect this inexorable, but infinitesimal drift. Nevertheless, it is there. Each daily cycle is not an identical duplication.

Our examples from art, science, and common experience show that not only may the concept of "cycle" be assigned to events whose repetitions are not perfect duplicates, but the cycles themselves may change. And it is of fundamental importance that cycles in nature may alter, for without change there can be no growth, and no decay. In an essay on the formation of DNA (the complex organic molecule that is a building block of life), Lewis Thomas notes that only by mutation, by change, has life evolved. If all future reproductions were flawless copies of their predecessors, evolution would never proceed. It has been "errors," mutations, that made man: "The capacity to blunder slightly is the real marvel of DNA. Without this special attribute, we would still be anaerobic bacteria and there would be no music."[10]

Thomas did not say, however, that if Nature—or man—

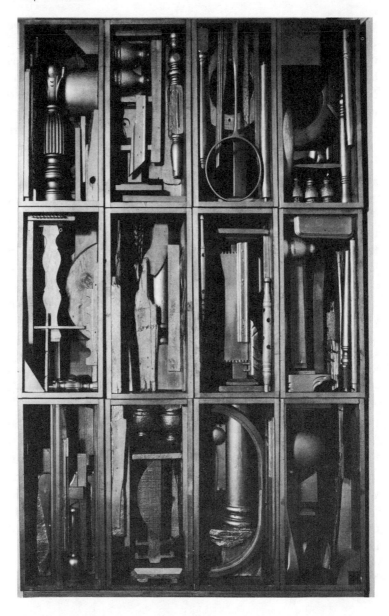

FIGURE 2-2.*Louise Nevelson, Night Music A, 1962.* "Unity in variety"—this phrase aptly describes both the art and the philosophy of a great contemporary artist, Louise Nevelson. Her sculptures are often comprised of odds and ends that she collects at random: wheels, mechanical parts, pieces of lumber, abandoned architectural elements. (There are, of course, other sculptures in which she shapes all the metal parts herself. This represents one facet of her work.) The diverse pieces are then put together in a design, to represent an image, and are united not only in the one larger work of art but also in the uniform color that they are painted. These large works of art are all one color, usually black or white, although a few have been done in gold. Her inspiration for these and for all her works of art come from Nature. As she herself states, "Whatever creation man invents, the image can be found in nature. We cannot see anything of which we are not already aware. The inner, the outer equal one" (Glimcher, Arnold B., *Louise Nevelson*, Dutton, New York, 1972, p. 79) *(Pace Gallery)*.

makes *too big* a blunder, music may once again cease to be. Whether changes to the structures in Nature are "good" or "bad," though, is a value issue.

With our basic definitions clarified, we can now chart our course. Our search for evidence of cyclical structures in Nature will begin with discussions of examples from the humanities, primarily from mythology, literature, art, and religion. This initial examination of perceptions by some humanists of cycles in nature will lead into an exploration of another area of the humanities: natural philosophy. Again, we will look for evidence of beliefs that nature is structured in cycles. We will also ask how some natural philosophers conceived of man's place in Nature. At that point, we'll be ready to leave the humanities for science, to see what modern science has learned of cycles within the natural world and what evidence exists to support or explain these cycles.

We have already spent considerable time showing that individual cycles are not necessarily exact duplications within unifying patterns, but that they do incorporate some degree of variability and change. Man can be a contributing factor to change in the cycles of nature. We'll be seeing just how man *chooses*—either by accident or on purpose—to create such change. We'll look, too, at potential consequences *to* nature of some of these changes. More importantly, we will see ways that these changes can boomerang.

While our explorations will largely be analyses of past findings about nature and man's place in it, we will also be looking at our present relationship with Nature. This exploration will put us in touch with a current political dilemma: the search for solutions to our environmental and related technological problems. With our background understanding of natural structures, how man is embedded in these structures, and how—and why—human activities are altering the environment, we'll be better able to confront the significant issue of what, if anything, we should do about these alterations. We'll find that contributions from each of the "two cultures" are necessary if we are to find workable solutions to these problems of the 20th century.

Nature influences everything I do. I see everything in a round shape, because nature is based on circles rather than on squares or triangles. And that's why in my choreography you often see a circular movement, a sweeping motion. If you look at a human body, it is all round. So much is—the earth, the moon, tree trunks. Everywhere you look in nature you see this roundness. It's strange because it's such an impractical shape. You can never fit circles together as you can squares. If you look around, notice how much of what is made by man is square, while most things in nature are round.

—JIŘÍ KYLIÁN
(artistic director and chief choreographer, Netherlands Dance Theatre)

Chapter 3 / HUMANISTIC EXPRESSIONS OF CYCLES IN NATURE

We believe there is a pervasive unifying concept among the common themes about Nature expressed in art cross-culturally and throughout time. Nature is cyclical. We all know that the sun will rise and set tomorrow, and that the cycle will go on. Modern American balladeer Tom Paxton sings of the cyclical aspect of Nature, not only as a physical entity but also in the affairs of man:

> This world goes round and round, green leaves will turn
>   to brown,
> what goes up must come down, it all comes back to you,
> and you find whatever you feel, you lose whatever you
>   steal,

just like a spinning wheel the world goes 'round and
'round.
Rainwater runs down to the sea, evaporation makes the
clouds free.
Then it all comes and rains on me, and the world goes
'round and 'round.[1]

There are countless clichés to this effect, as: "History re-
peats itself"; "The acorn will grow as the tree"; "Like father,
like son." These imply certain cycles or regularities of behavior: that one day follows another, that generations have
particular inherited characteristics, that good will evolve into
evil and vice versa. Similarly, biologists teach that each development of an individual fetus parallels the evolutionary
development of the same species. That is what every high
school biology text means by "ontogeny recapitulates phy-
logeny." A wide variety of people—farmers, sportsmen, va-
cationers—depend upon seasonal cycles for their livelihood
and for their entertainment. That Nature contains cycles
seems clear.

THE SPECULATIVE SCIENCES

Examples of cyclical themes are widespread within the
humanities: in the areas of mythology and religion (including
some from the occult); in literature and the visual arts; and
in natural philosophy. We will call these particular forms of
expression the *speculative sciences* when they offer "explanations" of Nature. By *explanations*, we do not mean to imply
that a rational explanation was necessarily the motive for
these humanistic examples, even if such a motive might seem
implicit. Like the "hard sciences," or, as we've come to call
it, *Science*, one of the recurring motifs in the speculative sci-

ences is this cyclical aspect of Nature. The manner of approach and, clearly, the *way* in which "conclusions" or "explanations" of Nature are formed are markedly different among these arts and sciences. But these "cultures" differ more in the manner in which they provide *details* of their "explanations" of natural phenomena than in the unifying concepts they find to explain man and Nature. An examination of the "hard" and "speculative" sciences will help to provide a perspective from which to view the current debate over the proper place of man in Nature. An introductory example to the speculative sciences can be found in Greek mythology.

The ancient Greeks tell of a young goddess named Demeter and her daughter, Persephone. Demeter was the goddess of fertility. She caused the flowers to bloom, the crops to grow, the earth to be rich. Her daughter, Persephone, was also a fertility goddess and was, in addition, a rare beauty, guarded carefully by her doting mother. Demeter's watchful eye, though, couldn't prevent word of Persephone's charms from spreading throughout the world. Even Hades, one of Zeus' brothers and the ruler of the underworld, heard of the beautiful Persephone. So enchanted was he by these tales that he decided to make Persephone his bride. To do this, he would have to circumvent Demeter's close hold on Persephone, and so he devised a careful plan. One day while Persephone was picking flowers in the fields, he made one of them look particularly dazzling and tempting. As she bent over to pluck this blossom, the earth opened wide and out sprang Hades. He swept up the surprised maiden and carried his prize away in a chariot.

At home, Demeter was awaiting the return of her daughter. When Persephone did not appear, her mother became alarmed. She searched the fields, but there was no sign of the vanished Persephone. Still Demeter continued the search. As she mourned for her daughter, the earth suffered her lack of attention; famine and desolation spread. Still Demeter continued the search. Her only clue was a noise coming from underground, a sound that she became sure was the cry of her daughter pleading for rescue. For ten days Demeter wandered the earth in mourning, until she came upon the Sun. The Sun told her that Persephone's abductor was Hades. Enraged, Demeter appealed to Zeus for the return of her daughter. She vowed that she would not set foot on Olympus, nor would crops spring forth from the earth again, until Persephone was returned. Zeus listened to the entreaties and threats of the earth goddess and decided to intervene in the dispute between Hades and Demeter.

When Zeus approached Hades to arrange for Persephone's return, he discovered that, while underground, Persephone had eaten of the pomegranate seed, a fruit sacred to the underworld. This constituted a bond between the maiden and the underworld; Persephone was tied to Hades. Zeus, in his wisdom, managed to arrange a compromise. Persephone would spend part of the year in the house of Hades and the remainder of time with her mother on earth. Demeter, faithful to her part of the bargain, restored fertility to the earth, but only when her daughter was with her.

In the tale of Persephone we find that, in addition to the "explanation" of the seasonal cycles, there is another cycle evident. A link is established between life and death. Both Demeter and Persephone are life-giving fertility goddesses, yet Persephone becomes the bride of the god of the underworld, Hades. There would seem to be a contradiction here. However, the life/death interaction (itself another cycle) is a widely accepted belief. In life there is death, and in death a variation on life, as some religions tell us. Whether or not we accept the various religious interpretations of the meaning of death, this would-be contradiction is one of the paradoxes of our daily existence. Life becomes death, then death breeds life, and so nature continues. This is a scientific as well as a mythological observation. What's more, it is an observation that has not only been immortalized in legend by the Greeks but also appears in the traditions and religious beliefs of other cultures.

That the continuity of Nature has a counterpart in the life/death cycle is seen, for example, in the contemporary beliefs of the U.S. Southern Baptists. They use the term *reborn* to refer to a spiritual reawakening. Although they don't believe this literally to be a bodily transfer or reincarnation, their choice of the term *reborn* does reflect the life/death cycle. There is also a coincidence between the modern Christian Easter celebration (which in the northern hemisphere is a springtime rite) of spiritual rebirth and the life/death cycle of the Persephone myth. We somehow choose to celebrate the union between life and death, which is clearly an aspect of the Resurrection, at the time of Nature's own reawakening, spring. Yet another example can be found in the Nordic civilizations, where there is a belief that one newly deceased is reborn in his descendants. Thus, the newly born one is given the name of the deceased. This custom is believed to have existed as late as the period of the migration, among the East Goths. There is a comparable tradition among Jews, whereby children are named for deceased relatives, implying a continuation of the chain. That is why Jews are seldom named for living parents. It would be tantamount to a death wish for one following this custom to name a child after a living relative.

Not only are there cross-cultural parallels to the cycles inherent in the myth of Persephone, but these themes also

FIGURE 3-1. *Dante Gabriel Rossetti, Persephone.* The Pre-Raphaelites were a group of 19th-century artists who reacted against what they thought was a frivolous Romantic school. In both literature and the visual arts, they used Nature as a guideline. Their approach, though, was not one of adoring an idealized Nature but the Gothic aim of searching for purity. Part of their search was in Nature. One of the foremost Pre-Raphaelite painters was Dante Gabriel Rossetti (who helped found the Pre-Raphaelite Brotherhood in 1848). He found inspiration not only in Nature, but in the myth that explains man's seasonal bond with Nature, the tale of Persephone. (The myth, you recall, "explains" the seasons: in spring Persephone is on the Earth, and in the winter she is in the underworld with Hades/Pluto.) Rossetti focused on the mystery of the myth, on the pomegranate seed, the surprising, binding element that holds Persephone to Hades. In his painting, Persephone looks as though she is trying to understand her plight, while not fully comprehending it, even though she holds it in her hand *(Tate Gallery, London).*

have provided the impetus for works of art throughout succeeding centuries. A similar theme, death in life, can be found in the well-known 20th-century poem by Dylan Thomas, "Fern Hill":

> Now as I was young and easy under the apple boughs,
> About the lilting house and happy as the grass was
>   green . . .
>   Time let me hail and climb
>   Golden in the heyday of his eyes . . .
> Nothing I cared, in the lamb white days, that time would
>   take me.
> Up to the swallow thronged loft by the shadow of my
>   hand . . .
> Oh as I was young and easy in the mercy of his means,
>   Time held me green and dying
> Though I sang in my chains like the sea.

The "Time" that the poet thanks for his carefree youth is also the "Time" that will ultimately claim his life. Celebratory youth is a part of oncoming old age. They are shared by each individual, just as Persephone is shared by the life-symbol Demeter and the death-symbol Hades. The poet, likewise, is held both "green and dying." These fundamental paradoxes remain a part of all our lives.

So far we've seen that, at least within the Western tradition, man believes that there are cycles in Nature. However, recognition of these cycles of seasonal rotations and life/death have roots that go farther back than the Greeks and that cross oceans and continents. From the Book of Common Prayer comes the familiar line, "Earth to earth, ashes to ashes, dust to dust." Similarly, in the Rig Veda, the Hindu counterpart of the Bible, is the line, "Creep back to the earth, thy Mother"[2] (Veda X,18,10). From yet another culture and time comes a further similar interpretation. In one of Confucius' Five Classics, the *I Ching*, there is the following observation,

> The sun goes and the moon comes; the moon goes and
> the sun comes;—the sun and the moon thus take the
> place of each other, and their shining is the result. The
> cold goes and the heat comes; the heat goes and the cold
> comes;—it is by this mutual succession of the cold and
> the heat that the year is completed.[3]

A brief quote from the Rig Veda isn't nearly enough to show the central role of cycles in Eastern thought, for the Hindu culture has an elaborate structure of natural life cycles. A principal tenet of Hinduism is belief in the transmigration of the soul. Upon death, the soul can be liberated from the body—by cremation for many Hindus—after which it can inhabit another being. Out of the destruction of one individual comes the creation of another, and so the cycle continues. Three gods take their part in these life cycles. They are Brahma, Vishnu, and Siva,* all actually forms of the one God. They have three distinct functions: Creator, Preserver, and Destroyer, respectively. All are part of the One; all take their turn. Hindu legend has it that Vishnu lies asleep upon a 1000-headed cobra. From his navel grows a lotus, out of which Brahma is born. Brahma, the god of the philosophers, creates the world. Vishnu's role is as preserver: the universe is absorbed in his body while he is asleep, and while he is awake, he serves as its ruler. Siva, the god of change, represents the darker side of Nature. He can be the destroyer of time, as with the devastating powers of Nature on man. He has many disguises, and his primary task is one of destruction and reintegration. All three gods are interdependent; without all, the universe wouldn't function. The rotation of the gods—the

* Pronounced "shé-vuh."

FIGURE 3-2. The flames being stoked by these Balinese Hindus on Sanur Beach, Bali, Indonesia, are believed by the faithful to be liberating the soul of the deceased, whose body lies in the coffin being consumed by the fire. Colorful, elaborate funerals of this sort are a regular feature of many Hindu cultures, which believe in the transmigration of the soul. The soul is liberated from the body in the flames. The dominance of cyclical themes in Eastern religions is exemplified by the ritual burnings, which are rooted in the belief of birth and rebirth *(Photo by Stephen H. Schneider)*.

FIGURE 3-3. Regardless of your beliefs about the existence or transmigration of the soul, one cyclical aspect of the life/death cycle is directly observable: the body participates. This thick bush has its roots in the fertile ground of a graveyard, whose soil is enriched by the nutrients of formerly living beings. (In Chapter 7, the physical, chemical, and biological characteristics of the cycling of nutrients between living and dead entities are explored in detail.) *(Photo by Stephen H. Schneider).*

fact that each must take his turn in the life process—is indicative of the cycle. After there is destruction, there is new creation; so the cycle continues. Life and Death are personified by gods that are then part of the one God, the sum total of the three parts.

The Hindus have also adopted this circularity into visual, religious symbolism, with their mandala. The *mandala*, a graphic symbol of the universe, is a circular form within which can be found geometric forms of triangles and squares. All over the Orient, it has become a symbol of unity and also a focal point for contemplative orientation. It is one of our earliest uses of the circle as a symbol of wholeness, and it has symbolic value in areas other than religion. The mandala has been psychologically linked with other figures composed of elements enclosed in a square or a circle, for example, the labyrinth, the zodiacal circle, and the clock. Ground plans of circular, square, or octagonal buildings are also mandalas. Temples have been constructed after the pattern of the mandala, with its balanced counterelements and its geometric forms. The *stupa* in Buddhism, a great dome-shaped structure, is perhaps the most characteristic of such temples.

Yet another adaptation of a mandalalike wheel or cyclical shape can be found in the symbol of the wheel of fortune. The tarot, an esoteric and now occult art, combining the mysticism of the East with the cabala system of numbers and letters found among some of the Jews, has as one of its symbols the wheel of fortune. It is believed that the affairs of men follow the rhythmic patterns of Nature, that not only the cyclical pattern is evident, but progress as well.[4] There is widespread appeal in stories of rags to riches and back to rags, where fate controls the outcome. The popular success of the Horatio Alger stories shows this appeal. The wheel serves multiple purposes: The ancients saw it as a symbol of the

FIGURE 3-4. The mandala is a Hindu or Buddhist graphic symbol of the universe. Its circular form is in keeping with the prominent place of cycles in Eastern thought *(Photo by Stephen H. Schneider)*.

FIGURE 3-5. The cross-cultural belief in cycles in Nature is strengthened by this Navajo Indian sand painting. This form, known as a *whirling rainbow*, is common in Navajo art and is said to be a symbol of healing *(Photo by Stephen H. Schneider)*.

FIGURE 3-6. The *stupa* is a mound or a towerlike structure that serves as a Buddhist shrine. The circular shape of the dome is another example of the importance of cycles in Eastern traditions. This *stupa*, located near Katmandu, Nepal, is a gigantic cement dome, more than 100 feet in diameter and many stories tall, with several smaller domes and towers along its perimeter. At the center of the giant cement dome is a golden tower, with searching eyes painted on its four sides and a large prayer wheel at the top. This *stupa* is an imposing structure, visible from miles away *(Photo by Samuel Schneider)*.

FIGURE 3-7. Many Buddhists believe that a prayer can be written on a piece of paper, placed on a wheel, and registered in heaven when the wheel spins. When this "prayer wheel" is rotated on its axis, the written prayer is counted, once for each rotation of the wheel. Built into the sides of giant *stupas*, like the Nepalese structure in Figure 3-6, are many prayer wheels. The faithful are often seen circling around and around the *stupa*, spinning with their hands the prayer wheels mounted in the walls of the massive structure. This worshiper is moving rhythmically around the periphery of the *stupa*, spinning the prayer wheel that can be seen in her right hand (*Photo by Stephen H. Schneider*).

cosmic forces, of creative individual expression, and of the natural components of the universe. Its cyclical symbolism thus functions on many levels—on the level of the natural world, of the individual, and of the way man fits into this natural world.

Astrology provides another example of belief in cycles, the cycle of the zodiac over a 12-month period. In Chinese tradition, there are 12 years, each named for an animal, that repeat in sequence. As a reward for heeding a summons from the Buddha, each of these 12 animals is sovereign for one year (e.g., year of the pig, year of the rooster, etc.) of the 12-year cycle. It is believed that people born in, say, the year of the snake will have different behavioral characteristics from those born in the year of some other animal. Even the compatibility of marriage partners can be foretold by these traditions. The sales figures of materials offering astrological interpretations are, to this day, undoubtedly huge, attesting to the widespread interest in these ancient cyclical beliefs.

Cycles involving animals are not evident only in astrology, of course. Changes of shape, reincarnations of a sort, are not uncommon in classical Western mythologies. Ovid's *Metamorphoses* offers many charming tales of changes from one form to another. Like the Greek myths, these Roman stories contain morals as well as observations of the natural world. One of our favorites is the tale of Baucis and Philemon, an old couple dwelling in the Phrygian hills. The story goes that Jupiter (the Roman equivalent of Zeus) went looking for food and shelter in the homes of the dwellers of this area. Disguised as a wandering mortal, he was turned away from one home after another. As his rage built, he came upon the poor dwelling of Baucis and her husband, Philemon. The old couple welcomed the traveler into their humble home and offered him whatever food and beverage they could provide. Jupiter decided to spare them the punishment he was about

FIGURE 3-8. The tarot, an occult art, has as one of its chief symbols a cyclical representation of life: the wheel of fortune. Writing about this symbol, tarot expert Paul Foster Case says, "Occult teaching emphatically asserts that what seems to be chance—whether absence of purpose or absence of design—is really the working of unalterable law. The rotation of circumstance appears to be accidental, but it is not really so: Every effect is the consequence of preceding causes, and the better we grasp this law of sequence and cyclicity, the greater our command over subsequent events. There is periodicity in everything." Thus, belief in cycles is further evidenced from the tradition of the tarot (*From Paul Foster Case, The Tarot: Key to the Wisdom of the Ages, Macoy Publishing, Richmond, Va., 1947, pp. 118–121*).

FIGURE 3-9. *Bramantino (Bartolomeo Suardi) (1455–1536), Baucis and Philemon.* The myth of Baucis and Philemon is found in Ovid's *Metamorphoses.* The tale speaks of transformations within Nature as they relate to the life/death cycle. Baucis and Philemon were an old couple who took pity on a begging, disguised Jupiter and offered him food and shelter. Although Jupiter punished the less kind-hearted inhabitants of the area with a familiar "blow" from Nature—a flood—he did save these two kind people. He granted their wish, that they die simultaneously, and he furthermore transformed them into two intertwining trees, an oak and a linden. Bramantino's painting is a very serious, almost religious scene of the meal shared by the couple and Jupiter. He made the center of the painting a large tree, symbolic of the trees into which they were transformed *(Museen der Stadt, Cologne, Federal Republic of Germany).*

to inflict on the less generous inhabitants of the area and also to reward them by granting whatever wish they made. Their request was simple: they wanted to die at the same time, so that neither would have to live a lonely life without the other. Jupiter then punished the cold-hearted inhabitants of the area by purging the land of them in a flood. As the waters enveloped all, Jupiter made the home of the two good souls into a temple, high on a hill overlooking the flooded area. Baucis and Philemon became priests of the temple. When death came to claim them, Jupiter remembered the remainder of his promise. Instead of dying, they were simultaneously transformed, one into an oak tree and the other into a linden tree, with their limbs arched and intertwining.

This particular myth extends the cyclical theme explored so far. Here the life/death cycle actually merges into a man/Nature interconnection, for the two old people are transformed through death into nonhuman living entities. Similarly, many Hindus believe that a human soul can, after death, transmigrate to an animal, for example, the sacred cow.

It is more than curious that these diverse cultures, without efficient means of communication in those pretelephone times, expressed comparable concepts of nature at different times. Such similar cross-cultural beliefs attest to the primacy—indeed, to the primordial quality—of the structure of a cycle. There may well be something in man's psyche that is touched by the recognition of natural cycles, directing human artistic expressions in similar ways, thus transcending cultural differences, language barriers, geography, and even time. Aniela Jaffe, in Carl Jung's *Man and His Symbols*, suggests that the need for wholeness in the human psyche takes comfort in such cyclical patterns. Indeed, she attributes the predominance of mandalalike forms to their comforting circularity. It is her feeling that the circle is the symbol of the psyche.

The remarkable cross-cultural similarities in the artistic and religious expressions of cycles in Nature could be interpreted as evidence that there is a "collective unconscious" across all of humanity. Moreover, worship of or myths about the natural world often share common elements in their structure as well as in the concepts they reveal (e.g., cycles). Other evidence of a collective unconscious might include the many cases in which some aspect of Nature is personified, and deified, as in the Hindu trinity of Creator, Preserver, and Destroyer, or in the Greek mythological "explanation" of the seasonal cycles.

Other examples of anthropomorphism that might indicate a collective unconscious include the Hindustani *Upanishads*. Their tales contain numerous personifications of natural elements interrelating, for example, fire talking to wind. And their observations sometimes bear close resemblance to the actual workings of nature. The early Egyptians, for example, had several predominant nature gods. They worshiped their river, the Nile, as a god. Their sovereign god was Ra (also called Re or Phra), the sun god. (Ra's principal sanctuary was at Heliopolis.) In Central America, the Toltec's god of fire, Huehueteotl, was one of their major deities, as was Thaloc, the god of rain and germination. Yet another example can be found among the African tribal customs. The Ashantis worshiped a god called Asase Yaa—literally translated to us, Mother Thursday.[5] Asase Yaa was the earth goddess, Mother Nature, whose holy day was Thursday. Her name became a combination of Mother Nature and the day of observance, Thursday. The Christian and Jewish religions have similar customs of the supreme god's ordaining a special day as holy. The Bible introduces the parallel concept of the Sabbath, the sacred day of rest in accordance with God's laws.

A more fascinating intercultural comparison can be made with the culture of the Pygmies in the forest regions of the Congo River. They believe in a great being of the sky, a lord of storms and of rain, who is similar to Zeus. And we can extend this comparison into the visual arts as well, for the Pygmies portray this god as an old man with a beard, the very same visual image also used in the Western tradition! It seems that not only have physically disconnected cultures noted the same observations and relationships, but they have even drawn on comparable visual imagery to convey their beliefs.

In the case of the Greek god Zeus, we can see two structural elements common to much of mythology—personification of natural elements and, concomitantly, man's interconnection with Nature—revealed in his persona. Zeus was originally the god of the sky; he seems to have been responsible for the phenomena of the sky, for the workings of the atmosphere. In particular, he has been presented as the god of thunder and of thunderbolts (a way in which he has often been portrayed in works of art) and as the god of rain.

Mythological stories, as well as the godlike personifications of the elements, convey the interconnection between man and Nature. We just mentioned that Zeus was the god of rain. An actual function of rain, as can be observed, is the watering of plants, a form of fertilization. And so, in Greek mythology, there is a direct—perhaps unconscious—transference of this observation into the behavior of their rain god, Zeus. We can find a preponderance of myths, among both the Greeks and Romans, in which Zeus—or his Roman equivalent, Jupiter—makes love to women who then give birth to subsequently famous mortals and gods. Quite literally, what Zeus is doing is "fertilizing" these women. A prime example of such a myth, among the Greeks, is the story of Leda and the swan (immortalized in verse by W. B. Yeats), in which

Zeus takes the form of a swan in order to trick Leda and make love to her (such trickery is behavior that is characteristically "human"). Out of this union came Helen, later to become Helen of Troy, the prize over which the Trojans fought. This story provides the core of Homer's *Iliad*. The Romans also have their mythology of Zeus, or Jove, as fertilizer of women. Ovid's *Metamorphoses* tells the tale of Europa, a woman to whom Jove came in the shape of a bull and so made love to her. Midas and Rhadamanthus were the products of Europa's union with Jove.

Zeus' personification of rain leads us into a fascinating cyclical structure, for his very behavior parallels that of Nature. If Zeus equals rain, and rain fertilizes the earth, and Zeus fertilizes women, then what further connections can we draw? We need to recall that the Earth, according to the Greeks, was a woman, whose name is given in several forms: Gaea/Gaia, Ge. Cultures have reused this particular association down through the centuries, and many continue to refer to nature as Mother Nature or the earth as Mother Earth. We can now complete the example. Since Zeus fertilizes women, and Earth is a woman, Zeus, who is the rain god, also fertilizes the earth—upon which we depend. The rain continues the cycles of life on earth, and Zeus, as the embodiment of Nature, participates in the process by which the cycles of human life are maintained:

FIGURE 3-10. *Titian, Leda and the Swan (16th Century)*. Titian's subject in this painting is the union of Leda, a mortal, with a swan, Zeus in disguise. Two of Zeus' many roles in mythology were as lover of both gods and, more often, of mortals, and father of half-mortal/half-god children. This particular metamorphosis and union have been the subject of numerous works of art, not only because of the striking visual image but also because the result of this union was the birth of the beautiful Helen, the Helen of Troy for whom the Trojan War was fought. The union of the divine with the "earthly" often breeds catastrophe *(National Gallery, London)*.

Here we have chosen for this example one of the many possible interpretations of the meaning or root of these personifications. But our purpose at this point is not to propose a general theory behind these personifications of Nature. Rather we are sharing the extent to which we are impressed by the similarities in motifs and concepts evident in mythology in very different cultures. The cycle is not the only motif or concept repeated in disparate cultures. It is, though, as our various examples illustrate, undoubtedly one of the most pervasive and enduring ones. If one were to argue, however, that these cross-cultural similarities shown so far are evidence to demonstrate the existence of a collective unconscious, we feel that more examples would still be needed to strengthen the case. Nevertheless, the ubiquitousness of the imagery, the frequent belief in cycles in Nature, and the common use of similar deity personifications across cultures are striking, whether or not we accept all this as evidence for the existence of a human collective unconscious. Let us assume that there is a psychological recognition—conscious or unconscious—of the primacy of cycles in Nature. To alter these cycles, then, would be an act against our own internal nature. Here we can return to the Greek myths to look at another story, which, although familiar, has not often been considered in such a context.

The tale is that of Sisyphus, the man who was bound for eternity to push a boulder up a hill, only to have it roll back down again. Many people know of the plight of Sisyphus, whose name is synonymous with futility, but fewer know the reason for this punishment. Sisyphus was the son of Aeolus, the god of winds, and is best known for his clever trickery and pranks. One day, Thanatos (Death) came to claim him, and Sisyphus' wiles were put to the test. The ploy almost succeeded. Clever Sisyphus deceived his captor and captured him in turn. He bound Thanatos so tightly that he would probably not have escaped had Zeus not intervened. Once placed in Hades, Death's lower region, Sisyphus still attempted various returns to earth. He so plagued the gods with his roguery that the best means of containing him was to keep him constantly busy. So Zeus devised a punishment—rolling a stone up a hill, only to watch it roll back and so again roll it up—that would leave him no time for further pranks or escape plans.

This is a bittersweet tale, for our sympathies are with Sisyphus in his attempts to elude Death's grasp. Yet we cannot escape noticing that he had attempted to intervene in the life/death cycle already established as an integral part of the natural world. He was prevented only by Zeus, the highest power, and so was punished. One inference from this myth is that it is futile to interfere with the established pattern of life and death. Furthermore, we—as a species, at least—should not fear death, for the cycle of human life is dependent upon it. (Even if we were to contemplate immortality, we would find ourselves faced with the life/death cycle. Our planet is finite; it can accommodate only a certain number of people. Either we would eventually have to have no more children, so as to keep our population size finite, or we must continue to make room by eliminating some of those already here. The physical law of the conservation of matter, then, tells us that immortality for a growing population on a finite planet is ultimately impossible.)

As we have already said, the Greek myths, and all these fundamental associations with Nature, often provide sound observations of the workings of Nature, as well as a set of motifs used in succeeding works of art. One final example of our observation of Nature as cyclical can be found 2000 years later in Percy Bysshe Shelley's poem "The Cloud"

FIGURE 3-11. *Titian, Sisyphus, 1548–1549.* Man's defying the gods—who are often symbolic of the natural order of the universe—forms the basis of several tales of mythology. In all cases, man was punished for daring to defy the natural order. Man as subordinate to Nature was a theme of these myths. Perhaps the tale that most conveys the sense of futility associated with such efforts is the myth of Sisyphus. Sisyphus, who tried many tricks to escape his turn in the life/death cycle, was the mortal condemned by Zeus to eternal torment for these acts of defiance, a torment itself based on the natural law of gravity: he was condemned eternally to roll a boulder up a hill, only to have it roll back down again. Titian was inspired by the Greek and Roman tales of defiance and completed a series of paintings entitled *The Four Condemned*, the "four" being Tityus, Tantalus, Ixion, and Sisyphus. Although Titian did preserve the sense of eternal damnation in the Sisyphus myth, he took some liberties with the iconography he used. The Sisyphus he painted is carrying the stone, rather than rolling it, up the hill. This same unique interpretation was reputed to have been found in an illustrated edition of Ovid's *Metamorphoses* printed in Venice in 1522 *(Prado Museum, Madrid, Spain).*

(1820):

> I am the daughter of Earth and Water,
>> And the nursling of the Sky;
> I pass through the pores of the Ocean and shores;
>> I change, but I cannot die.
> For after the rain when with never a stain
>> The pavilion of Heaven is bare,
> And the winds and sunbeams with their convex gleams
>> Build up the blue dome of air,
> I silently laugh at my own cenotaph,
>> And out of the caverns of rain,
> Like a child from the womb, like a ghost from the tomb,
>> I arise and unbuild it again.

Here Shelley took the theme of cycles in Nature and applied the concept to specific components of Nature itself. Clouds, earth, and water are all related, living and dying, all in a continuous cycle.

An intuitive statement of artists in culture after culture is that there are cycles in Nature. This theme is not fundamentally at odds with the observations of modern science, as we will see later. But it is ironic—perhaps tragic—that our generation, which, through its science, has so strongly confirmed the reality of the traditional theme of the continuity of cycles in Nature, may be the first in history to disrupt those cycles of life on a global scale.

All life is interrelated. To understand art, one must understand man. To understand man, one must understand all living things.
                    —ROMAN VISHNIAC
                    (*photographer, scientist*)

Chapter 4 / REACTIONS TO THE PRIMORDIAL BOND EXPRESSED IN THE HUMANITIES

The humanities convey (among other things) man's feelings about his place in Nature. When looking to the humanities for cycles in Nature, we were actually finding repeated patterns of feelings. A more complete understanding of these is essential before we move into the realm of hard science. We need to analyze our feelings about man's place in Nature before we can properly understand our present environmental and related technological crises, for these emotions are the driving force behind the changes that can create or alleviate such crises. The wide range of human feelings about our relationship with Nature can be seen if we look briefly at one of the Greek "elements," water.

Water both constrains and frees humanity, so our feelings about it are varied and complex. All would agree that our bond to water is fundamental. Most of our physical being is made up of it! Artistic expressions of the relationship between man and water down through the centuries have acknowledged that survival depends upon water, but that water also has the power to destroy us.

T. S. Eliot expressed a wide range of feelings about emotional reactions to water in "The Dry Salvages" (1941). This poem, one of his magnificent *Four Quartets*, opens with a lengthy passage on water:

I do not know much about gods; but I think that the river
Is a strong brown god—sullen, untamed and intractable,
Patient to some degree, at first recognized as a frontier;
Useful, untrustworthy, as a conveyer of commerce;
Then only a problem confronting the builder of bridges.
The problem once solved, the brown god is almost forgotten
By the dwellers in cities—ever, however, implacable,
Keeping his seasons and rages, destroyer, reminder,
Of what men choose to forget. Unhonored, unpropitiated
By the worshippers of the machine, but waiting, watching and waiting.
His rhythm was present in the nursery bedroom,
In the rank ailanthus of the April dooryard,
In the smell of grapes on the autumn table,
And the evening circle in the winter gaslight.
The river is within us, the sea is all about us;
The sea is the land's edge also, the granite
Into which it reaches, the beaches where it tosses
Its hints of earlier and other creation:
The starfish, the horseshoe crab, the whale's backbone;
The pool where it offers to our curiosity
The more delicate algae and the sea anemone.
It tosses up our losses, the torn seine,
The shattered lobsterpot, the broken oar
And the gear of foreign dead men. The sea has many voices,
Many gods and many voices.[1]

These opening lines (without our denying the beauty and uniqueness of their phrasing) are almost a listing of water images, some adoring, others fearful, many contradictory, yet all recognizable. Most of us who have been at sea in a storm could well proclaim such water to be "untamed" or "intractable," strong and potentially destructive, while those who love plants and flowers recognize water's essential and beneficial role in their life cycles, roles that are supportive and creative. Then there are the fishermen, to whom water is life; they live by its whims, eat by its bounty. Or the soldiers, to whom water may represent an obstacle, a territory to be conquered, a milestone in a campaign. Without elaborating on all the qualities mentioned in this one brief passage, we can sense the great variety of connotations of water. Man defines and, in some cases, manipulates one aspect of what we will be explaining as the "bounds" of Nature through his interaction with water.

Many of our great poets, such as T. S. Eliot, have drawn their images from the stockpile of "traditional" motifs, most of which refer to Nature. Such choice, of course, makes a work of art enduring, able to transcend the limits of a brief, contemporary readership. People in diverse cultures at all times have been able to relate to such imagery. This kind of appeal is "universal," but it is more than just that. It is primordial, like the bond between man and Nature. T. S. Eliot called his river "destroyer, reminder of what men choose to forget." We can cite both old and contemporary examples of rivers to fit his image, starting with the Bible.

The Old Testament tale of the flood is an obvious example of the destructive and instructive quality of water. The flood itself was punishment for what God felt to be improper behavior. The "bad" were destroyed and the "good" were saved on the Ark. The rainbow, furthermore, that postflood symbol of the covenant between man and God, is a regular reminder of the power and beauty of water. These are biblical lessons of the power of Nature—in this case, of water—in relation to man, and we are meant to learn from them. Such lessons, though, aren't confined to biblical history. A more recent example is the case of a Pennsylvania town called Johnstown, which was constructed on a floodplain. The residents and builders, in their haste to develop the land, ignored the natural history of the area. The town was destroyed by a flood in 1889. As is too often the case, unhappy history repeated itself. Another flood destroyed Johnstown in 1977. And it is rebuilding! (In this case, the people either did not learn sufficiently from the past or have accepted the risk.)

Literature is not the only form of the humanities in which such natural man/water imagery occurs. In the visual arts, scenes of dramatic tension are often portrayed on the ocean, with waves leaping and boats swaying. Géricault's *Raft of the Medusa*, one of his numerous historical paintings that use the sea as a setting, is one such example typical of this early 19th-century genre. An important moment in history is heightened by the dramatic visual effect of the leaping waves. The power of the sea was an important visual metaphor in historical and Romantic works of art. Here we see—and feel—the great power of the sea, a power that has destroyed all but these few survivors hanging onto life on this raft. In the latter part of the 19th century, the Impressionist artists saw other visual uses for water. In their experiments with the reflections and separations of color, they found that the sea served well as a reflective source of light and, hence, of color.[2] Thus, there are many Impressionist paintings of the sea, like those of Renoir and Monet.

At about the same time, Claude Debussy, one of the masters of Impressionism in music, chose water as a theme.

FIGURE 4-1. *Théodore Géricault, Raft of the Medusa, 1818–1819.* The power of Nature over man—in this case, the power of water—is the theme of a major painting by Théodore Géricault. The French frigate *Medusa* was wrecked in a storm off the west coast of Africa on July 2, 1816, and 149 passengers were put on a raft. When it was sighted, only 15 men had survived. The disaster attracted much attention, not only because of the high death toll but also because of the tales of hardship and cannibalism that emerged. Géricault used the story as the focus of a painting that shows the event in a contemporary way. Nature is not idealized, nor are the survivors. (In fact, the painting was considered by some at the time to be vulgar, for here were ordinary seamen painted with the same seriousness as gods.) The force of the wind and the water in this painting has clearly caused much suffering for those clinging desperately to the raft. Géricault's painting conveys the dramatic force of the situation as opposed to an idealized, purely Romantic scene of Nature *(The Louvre, Paris, France).*

FIGURE 4-2. *Arthur Rackham, "The Shipwrecked Man and the Sea."* The power of Nature over man is perhaps nowhere more poignantly portrayed than in Arthur Rackham's illustration. At one pole of human reactions to man's place in Nature is fear. The dominance of the sea over man is one of the most common artistic themes that expresses human fear of Nature *(From Aesop's Fables, William Heinemann, Ltd., 1912, reprinted in Arthur Rackham, edited by David Larkin, Peacock Press/Bantam Books, Toronto, 1975, Plate 12).*

One of his compositions is *La Mer*, with its undulations of melody, bounding and shimmering like the light in Impressionist paintings. Water, here, is not dangerous in quality, but soothing.

These few examples suggest the depths of emotional reactions to only one part of Nature.

Basic feelings include opposite emotions: happiness or contentment versus unhappiness or discontent. Both feelings, the favorable and the unfavorable, lead to values. By making a specific value judgment, we decide to act on what we like or dislike. This applies to our relationship with Nature. If we are happy—if we have decided that we like our relationship with Nature—then we will probably want to preserve that relationship exactly as it is. Maintenance of the status quo, or a disdain for alterations of Nature, is one reaction to the feeling of contentment or happiness. On the other hand, we could feel unhappy or be discontented with our place in Nature. Unhappiness is often caused by fear of Nature, in which case we might consider efforts to control Nature so as to alter the balance in our favor. We might try to diminish our vulnerability to Nature, for instance. These activities could take a wide variety of forms. For example, a religious reaction might be prayer to a god to provide calm seas. A more man-centered reaction would involve some attempt at physical control of Nature. This could entail some "harmless" actions, like the building of houses, or more disruptive alterations of Nature, like attempts at weather control. Technology has made many degrees of alteration possible. Alteration is not necessarily *control*, of course, unless an attempt at altering Nature produces precisely the desired result, and not a host of unwanted side effects.

Yet another reaction to our place in Nature might be an attempt to "live closer" to Nature; this kind of reaction, even though it suggests altering the present status of the man/ Nature bond, would not be based on a fear of Nature. It merely conveys a sense of discontent with the relationship as it now stands.

We've used the word *alteration* several times. What we would try to alter are the "bounds" that Nature imposes on human activities. Nature's bounds are what constrains man.

Without exception, it has been said, man lives within the "bounds of Nature." But the "bounds" of Nature within which we are constrained are not always fixed; they can, to a considerable extent, be manipulated by man. While we are ultimately bound by Nature in many cases (we can't, for instance, make the sun hotter), we can, at least, expand the immediate bounds of Nature through intelligent manipulation of the amenities Nature offers. That is, man's physical surroundings or his reach can be broadened. Some natural limitations, however, such as the available quantity of sunlight cannot be altered.

All this is easily comprehensible provided we agree on the meaning of *bounds*. If we take the *bounds of Nature* to include *all* our resources—not merely our nearby physical space or geographic situation—then we are essentially living in a fixed relationship with Nature. A case in point is the example we've just mentioned, the amount of available sunlight. The same holds true for what is called the *carrying capacity* of our land. There are only so many people who can live in a given area before the population exceeds what the land can support, its *ultimate* carrying capacity. But the carrying capacity can be increased by, for example, the use of fertilizer, up to some limiting value.[3]

In the case of agriculture, no matter how much we increase the efficiency by which green plants use sunlight to make plant tissues, the amount of land and sunlight available constitutes ultimate bounds to agricultural productivity.[4] These are the ultimate bounds, the fixed limitations that Nature imposes on Earth. However, long before these ultimate limiting bounds are reached, there is a plethora of changes, or manipulations, that can be made to expand the present bounds of Nature toward the limiting values. We could talk of a pretechnological civilization, for which the bounds of Nature were largely immediate environmental factors, such as temperature or land area, or of a highly developed technological culture, whose constraining limits are not often the environmental factors of geography but, more importantly, the natural abundance of raw materials (e.g., sunlight, iron, copper, oil). People in both of these stages of civilization, however, have to live within the bounds of Nature in force at their time. If they don't like the position, then they can try to alter the balance. Natural bounds, regardless of how close to ultimate limits they may be stretched by our inventive genius, will remain. Not only will they remain, but they have also always been a major factor in man's relationship with Nature. The power that Nature wields over man, in terms of both the limitations imposed and the opportunities offered, has shaped a bond that has held man to Nature for as long as we can determine. This primordial bond remains today, despite the struggles of many to break it.

Some cultures have struggled to break the bond, whereas others have been more content. When we looked for cycles in the humanities, we examined works from a variety of cultures. The same approach will be used here. Now, though, we are asking different questions: How do different people *feel* about Nature? And how do they respond to it? The first is an emotional reaction to our place in Nature, and the second is a course of action (or inaction) to alter (or maintain) our position. Clearly, different cultures—indeed different in-

FIGURE 4-3. The bounds of Nature are not always fixed. We can wear clothes or build shelters, thereby reducing the constraints Nature imposes on us. However, there are, as this photo symbolizes, ultimate bounds of Nature beyond which we cannot go. One example is the carrying capacity of the Earth for humans. The sheer limits to physical space and available sunlight put ultimate bounds on our food supplies—and human population. We use technologies and social organizations to push ourselves closer to the ultimate limits, but limits remain nonetheless *(Photo by Stephen H. Schneider).*

dividuals—will differ in reaction to their bond with Nature and thereby propose different actions in response. However, feelings—and ultimately actions—reflect values. Thus, common beliefs about the structure of Nature need not lead to common feelings and actions about our place in that structure. While reactions may vary from one particular culture to another, as well as from one individual to another, two general types of reactions are widespread.

For some, there is considerable comfort in the regular patterns, the cyclical aspects of Nature. Even the extreme variability of some aspects of Nature may not be perceived as threatening to people with these values. They accept what is with a feeling of adoration and wonder, entertaining few wishes to alter the outcome. They live within the primordial bond and flow with its variations. This reaction to Nature characterizes one absolute set of values about man's place in Nature. Affinity for Nature is their emotional reaction, and their policy of action is to preserve Nature, not to alter the primordial bond. Indeed, why alter a natural course of events with which they can live happily? They are patient with Nature and thoroughly at ease with its structure, as in the adage "Take the good with the bad." Both a deep appreciation of natural wonders and an acceptance of what life/Nature offers are expressed. Of course, few *totally* embrace this absolute set of values. Even the American Indians, probably the culture most congruent with this value set, live in shelters to protect themselves from the elements and have devised ceremonies to "control" Nature (e.g., the rain dance). Acceptance of *anything* Nature offers can be just as unacceptable to some as the need to preserve Nature held by others.

The desire for "progress" leads us, of course, to a second, polar opposite, set of values. While the first set of values describes those who find only comfort in the patterns and power of Nature, the second set describes those who react with uneasiness—often terror. People with these values would clearly prefer to tip the balance of power toward themselves and lessen their dependence on natural variations. They are impatient with the man/Nature bond as it stands. A second set of values, then, comes from the feeling of fear of Nature, coupled with its attendant action or policy: to control Nature, to bend it to our purposes. Some tend to think of the humanities—in particular, the visual arts and poetry—as celebrating Nature. This is too simple, for fear/control values are also prevalent in the humanities. Their roots can be found in early mythologies and can be traced throughout the succeeding generations in the arts.

Of course, there is a spectrum of values between the dichotomy of value sets we've drawn here. As in nature, we are determining bounds, but within these limits the possibilities are diverse. At a superficial level, we could associate the affinity/preservation values with a culture like that of the American Indians or Buddhists and the fear/control values with the culture of a highly organized and technologically "advanced" society like ours. However, there are aspects of both sets of values in every culture, as we shall see, and a deeper look is in order.

Although we have yet to bring in the thoughts of natural philosophers on the man/Nature relationship, it would be especially appropriate to discuss the work of one such philosopher here. Hesiod's *Theogony* contains the dichotomy of values—affinity versus fear—that we've presented. He introduces the principle of opposites, a philosophical basis of a polarity of values. There are natural tensions within the universe, Hesiod tells us. These can be found in his chronologies of the children of Zeus. Among them are Darkness and Light, the first among those created in the world order.

FIGURE 4-4. We have seen opposite emotional reactions to man's place in Nature as expressed in the visual arts: fear versus affinity. These emotional reactions are often the bases for concrete political actions either to preserve or alter that place in Nature, depending upon whether our emotional reaction was originally one of affinity or of fear. The photo is of Lake Dillon, a large reservoir in the Rocky Mountains west of Denver, Colorado. The fear of natural variability in precipitation, coupled with a desire for industrial, ag-

ricultural, and urban growth, dictated that a more reliable supply of water was needed each year than a fluctuating Nature normally provides. Thus, a dam was constructed by those fearing that variability in natural water supplies was too unpredictable to allow sustained growth in the region. However, this attempt to use technology to push back the bounds of Nature, the constraints that Nature imposes on us, is not without negative consequences. Those who feel an affinity with Nature argue that the development of the Denver metropolitan area should be kept within the uncontrolled bounds of Nature, and that dams merely disturb our affinity with Nature by altering the bounds. Here, though, such values were in the minority, and the reservoir was built to aid the development of the region. However, as this photo taken in the spring of 1978 (after two successive drought years) shows, the lake is not nearly filled to its capacity. In fact, the water shortage was so serious in the mid-1970s that the State of Colorado, faced with water insufficiency for an already well-developed society, undertook a controversial weather-modification program in the hopes of augmenting the winter snow pack in the mountains. Whether this very active step to control Nature is justified in order to maintain the growth of industry, agriculture, and urban development is a major political debate today. But it is more than a technical argument among experts on development or weather modification. It is an issue of values, which, at its core, is related to how each individual feels about his own place in Nature. Without a recognition of this value basis of "environment" versus "development" debates, the emotional and ethical components of which are found in the humanities, solutions to many related current problems may fall wide of the mark. These feelings lie at the center of many modern issues we call the *technological crisis (Photo by Stephen H. Schneider).*

Later, as the world becomes more clearly defined and structured, we find listed among the genealogies a wider range of elements: Memory, Law, Desire, Love, Distraction, Famine, Sorrow, Grief, and so on. Hesiod's world includes aspects that would apply to either of our polar-opposite value systems. There is much to be appreciated, Memory, Law, Desire, and Love being among these, and there is much to be feared: Distraction, Famine, Sorrow, and Grief, to name a few. He even goes so far as to make this polarity or duality of feelings—indeed, values—a natural part of the world order, by establishing such contrasts among the gods. In Hesiod's *Theogony*, there is divisiveness between the children of the two formative gods (who are themselves elements) of the universe: the Void and Earth. The children of Sky, the Void, are vastly different from the children of Earth.

Hesiod presents us with a world in which a variety of possibilities exists (choices of good and evil), but he does not direct our choice. Rather, he leaves that option to man. By so doing, he begins to establish another fundamental concept: the principle of free choice. To this day, we, when we are rational, are operating on this basis, aware of many of the options in regard to Nature, weighing the pros and cons of each decision, and then acting. Other philosophers and, as we will see, scientists have provided us with additional knowledge so that we can make decisions regarding our actions to preserve and/or control aspects of the natural world. While the scope of our knowledge has expanded, the basic principle of free will is still in operation. Therefore we might choose an option that would minimize our impact on Nature while, at the same time, permitting man to experience a lesser degree of vulnerability to the vagaries of Nature. At least, that is a goal.

Any reaction to Nature has complications. Total acceptance of the natural world leads us to the problem of adapting to things as they are. Similarly, attempts at controlling or altering Nature may lead to quite different, often unexpected troubles, like pollution. Unintended side effects of attempts to push back the bounds of Nature have been illustrated in the humanities. Consider Mary Shelley's novel *Frankenstein: The Modern Prometheus*, originally published in 1818, though still popular and more meaningful than ever. Millions of people are familiar with the story, so a plot summary is not necessary.

Prometheus, who is part of the title of Shelley's novel, was a Greek mythological figure who, by giving fire to man, dared to defy Zeus, the god of the natural order. Frankenstein defies the existing natural order by daring to create his own living being. He is plagued and tormented by what he has created, a monster rather than a human being. His own words convey the anguish of premature ventures into alterations of nature; they also highlight the tension between our value sets:

> Learn from me, if not by my precepts, at least by my example, how dangerous is the acquirement of knowledge, and how much happier that man is who believes his native town to be the world, than he who aspires to become greater than nature will allow.[5]

This story highlights our inability to foresee the outcome of some attempts to alter Nature. We must be aware that unintended consequences are possible; we must weigh the potential gains against the potential losses, recognizing the possibility of unpredictable outcomes, and then decide upon an action. And weighing risks and benefits is, of course, a value judgment.

There is no denying that man is able to do considerable damage—to himself and other species—with certain kinds of knowledge. For knowledge is power, the power to improve, but also the power to destroy. Knowledge remains separate from values, *until* it is applied. The Frankenstein story reiterates the trade-offs we must weigh when knowledge can lead to actions that will alter nature. Furthermore, "progress" itself is a series of value trade-offs. This is a central part of our current energy crisis or the limits-to-growth debates taking place in overcrowded areas. The debaters are questioning the relative disadvantages and benefits of energy or population growth versus conservation and contraception, for example. The choices have come largely from technologies developed through knowledge. Thus, this issue is not fundamentally different from those posed in mythological tales. But the scale of potential risks has been escalating—along with the benefits—since the time of the ancient Greeks. The current risk of "progress" is far greater than the risks faced by past generations. Indeed, to make a comparison, a modern-day Prometheus might well ask if humanity is better or worse off with the knowledge of the "fire" of the atom?

Unlocking the secrets of the natural world raises questions inherent in another well-known legend, that of Pandora's box. Part of Zeus' vengeance against Prometheus for granting man the knowledge of fire took the form of creating a woman whom he hoped would beguile Prometheus to his ruin. The lovely creature was taught by a variety of gods. Athena dressed her; Aphrodite gave her beauty and charm; Hermes taught her guile and treachery. Decked in flowers and jewels, she was sent to Prometheus' brother, Epimetheus. Epimetheus, whose name translates into "afterthought," was more easily deceived than his brother Prometheus, who was wary of any gifts from Zeus. Despite warnings from Prometheus, Epimetheus welcomed the woman, called Pandora (the "all-giver"), into his home. One day Pandora found (or revealed that she had—the myth is unclear) a box containing a variety of ills: diseases, evils, deceits, misery. Pandora opened the box and out flew the hateful spirits. Realizing her error, she closed the box as fast as she could, managing to keep one spirit inside. That was the spirit called Hope.

Just as Hope remained in Pandora's famous box, so it remains for us. There is hope that man will use knowledge wisely. There is also hope that Nature will have sufficient regenerative ability to withstand the drastic, destructive acts that man has inflicted and will increasingly inflict. The resilience of Nature to every abuse is not absolute, of course. Certainly, individuals, and even individual species, will not necessarily outlive every blow to their survival, whether dealt by man or Nature, as the fossils of countless extinct species bear witness. We need the Hope that Pandora has left us, but we need more than that. We need to choose to prevent final reliance just on hope.

VALUE SET ONE: AFFINITY/PRESERVATION

We have suggested that these value pairs (affinity/preservation and fear/control of Nature) are not wholly embraced by any individual or culture. We present them here as distinct entities primarily to bound common reactions to the man/Nature relationship. Now we can look more specifically at each set of value motifs, beginning with affinity/preservation. Man's appreciation of Nature and desire to preserve it can be seen in the very earliest artistic examples at our disposal: the cave paintings found in France and Spain. These paintings probably served a variety of purposes: religious value, an attempt at communication, a pictorial language, and sheer artistic value. The pictographs often portray objects of the natural world, such as animals and landscapes. The beauty of their artistic depiction quite possibly indicates a deep awareness—and very likely an appreciation—of that world. Part of artistic motivation is the desire to preserve the beauty of the object portrayed. It would seem, then, that the values of affinity/preservation were at work, to a considerable degree, in the creation of these early works of art.

Similarly, the predominance of gods who are personifications of natural elements—e.g., rain, wind, clouds—indicates both an awe and an appreciation of this natural world. The ultimate sign of respect in some cultures is to elevate these natural elements to the status of gods. As we've already seen, such personifications exist in a wide range of cultures, from the ancient Greeks to the Chinese to the American Indians. Through the act of making gods of these natural elements, not only are their powers appreciated, but it also becomes somewhat of a "sin" to interfere with their functions. One possible interpretation of these early anthropomorphic religions is that they bolstered the tradition of the sanctity and the need for the preservation of the natural world.

However the affinity/preservation motif or outlook began, it has certainly become a standard of the literary and visual arts. Within the genre of poetry, for example, the appreciation of Nature has been a constant theme. In fact, one of the major tenets of the 18th- and 19th-century Romantic school of poets was, simply, the appreciation of Nature and the desire to preserve it. To such Romantic poets as Wordsworth, Nature was divine. Romanticism in all the arts has been, to a large degree, a celebration of Nature. Earlier on, we looked at William Wordsworth's "Lines, Composed a Few Miles Above Tintern Abbey" of 1798. The passage quoted in Chapter 1 is a fine example of the affinity/preservation set of values, although we did not refer to it in those terms then. The reverence of Nature and comfort with its structure is truly typified by such Romantic words of poetry.

Many of us expect to find these values in poetry. Poetry is often stereotyped as being full of images of flowers and trees. The values of affinity with Nature, though, are hardly confined to poetry. The philosophies and religions of many early civilizations, for example, contain much about man's affinity with Nature. Two Chinese philosophies—Confucianism and Taoism—espouse man's deep relationship with Nature, holding up the workings of Nature as guidelines for man to follow. The *Hsun Tzu* of Confucianism states, "Nature [*t'ien*, "heaven"] operates with constant regularity. . . . Respond to it with disorder and disaster will follow."[6] Likewise, one of the Taoist beliefs, as expressed here by Chuang Tzu, is

> Know the action of nature and man, and follow nature as the basis and be at ease with one's situation, then one can expand or contract as times may require. This is the essential of learning and the ultimate of truth.[7]

Our main examples of the thought of early civilizations come from the Greeks and the Romans, and here, too, we can refer to them. Unlike the Chinese, in some of their axiomatic moral guidelines, the Greeks and Romans appreciated Nature in a less moralistic sense. They felt the regularity of the seasons as a major life-determining force, as in the story of Persephone. With Nature as the example, some found comfort in a comparison between the stages of Nature and the stages of man:

> Notice the year's four seasons: they resemble
> Our lives. Spring is a nursling, a young child,
> Tender and young, and the grass shines and buds
> Swell with new life . . .

And then comes summer
When the year is a strong young man, no better time
Than this, no richer, no more passionate vigor.
Then comes the prime of Autumn, a little sober,
But ripe and mellow, moderate of mood,
Halfway from youth to age, with just a showing
Of gray around the temples. And then Winter,
Tottering, shivering, bald or gray, and aged,
Our bodies also change.[8]

We've looked relatively little so far at our own American literary and artistic tradition, and this is an especially appropriate place to do so. For the American culture, while loudly proclaiming the ethic of material progress and the value in pursuit of knowledge, has always had artistic communities advocating restraints on such "progress"—or at least questioning the meaning of progress and the value of knowledge. To these various groups, Nature was the ideal and material or scientific progress a threat. In the 18th century, the French social philosopher Rousseau proposed the concept of the noble savage, that is, the idea that man in a "state of Nature" was basically a benign creature (in fact, this concept formed the basis of his democratic political philosophy). Americans have picked up on the theme of a benign nature. The American transcendentalist philosophy of the 19th century—as found, for example, in the works of Thoreau, who was quoted earlier—expresses (in fact, almost insists on) an appreciation of Nature and the need for communion with Nature. The writings of such other great American writers as Emerson and Dickinson bear similar testament to their belief in the sanctity of Nature. It is interesting to speculate on the possible transference of these emotional affinities with Nature into the philosophies of communal living. The communal groups, such as that of Owings Mill, that arose during the 19th century tried to live in harmony with Nature. So are many such recent "communes," as defended by Charles Reich's *The Greening of America*, and the back-to-Nature-oriented people he classified as "Consciousness III."[9] There are many contemporary artistic expressions of the back-to-Nature ethic, ranging from such revolutionary theatrical presentations as *Hair* to the stark, expressionistic visual portraits of Nature offered in the works of the artist Georgia O'Keeffe. Many of these are artistic manifestations of affinity with Nature. In a similar vein are changes in lifestyles, which encompass interest in "health-food" or "organic" farming.

The vast array of American artistic expressions of affinity with Nature have a spiritual as well as an intellectual component. Perhaps no other culture holds more steadfastly to the belief that man depends on Nature, and should both appreciate and preserve it, than that of the American Indians. They exemplify the belief that Nature watches over man, that Nature feeds and cares for man, under the watchfulness of what is called the Great Spirit. Man's closeness with Nature is the center of their beliefs. Man does not work the arts of agriculture on the land without the consent of the land. Young Chief, of the Cayuse Indians, speaks beautifully of this sense of his people's dependence upon Nature and, consequently, of the respect and admiration that should be felt in return for this Earth:

> The ground says, It is the Great Spirit that placed me here. The Great Spirit tells me to take care of the Indians, to feed them aright. The Great Spirit appointed the roots to feed the Indians on. The water says the same thing. The Great Spirit directs me, Feed the Indians well. The ground, water, and grass says, the Great Spirit has given us our names. We have these names and hold these names. The ground says, the Great Spirit has placed me

FIGURE 4-5. *Georgia O'Keeffe, The White Trumpet Flower, 1932.* Georgia O'Keeffe, one of our greatest living American artists, has devoted almost her entire life to painting Nature: flowers, stones, clouds, hills, skulls, and stars. The Nature that she paints, though, is not the Nature that we all see. Rather, it is her perception of it, often a purposely exaggerated perception so that our own senses and interests will be piqued. For she, an artist with an affinity for Nature, believes that they should be:

> A flower is relatively small. Everyone has many associations with a flower—the idea of flowers. . . . Still—in a way—nobody sees a flower—really—it is so small—we haven't time—and to see takes time, like to have a friend takes time. If I could paint the flower exactly as I see it no one would see what I see because I would paint it small like the flower is small.
>
> So I said to myself—I'll paint what I see—what the flower is to me but I'll paint it big and they will be surprised into taking time to look at it—I will make even busy New Yorkers take time to see what I see of flowers. (In *Georgia O'Keeffe*, Viking, New York, 1976, unnumbered pages)

(San Diego Museum of Art, San Diego, California.)

> here to produce all that grows on me, trees and fruit.
> The same way the ground says, It was from me man was
> made. The Great Spirit, in placing men on the earth,
> desired them to take good care of the ground and to do
> each other no harm.[10]

The spiritual significance of Nature isn't limited to native
Americans. Emerson's poem to a flower, "The Rhodora"
(1834), harks back to the more primitive, deified Nature discussed earlier. He suggests, as do the Indians, that Nature
and man share a spiritual unity through God:

> Why thou wert there, O rival of the rose!
> I never thought to ask, I never knew;
> But, in my simple ignorance, suppose
> The self-same Power that brought me there brought
> you.[11]

To return to the Greeks, our primary mythological reference point, we find that they, too, believed in the sanctity
of the world order and in the need for its preservation. Their
structure of gods included a group called the Eumenides,
whose job it was to preserve this natural order. They were
so merciless in their punishment, legend has it, that they went
by another name as well, the Erinyes or Furies. The role of
the Eumenides has been presented, most notably, in the trilogy of plays by Aeschylus called *The Oresteia*. *The Oresteia*
contains the intricate tale of the house of Agamemnon, a tale
of human sacrifice, murder, revenge, and curses. The last of
the three plays is *The Eumenides*. These Furies are presented
as figures of terror with snaky hair and blazing torches. They
relentlessly track down Orestes, who must pay for the un-
natural crime of murdering his mother, Clytemnestra—a revenge murder, since she murdered her husband—and for the
curse of his family. The Furies originally propose the kind of

justice we've come to call "an eye for an eye, a tooth for a tooth," a primitive form of punishment that is the epitome of revenge. However, the Furies, in the version of Aeschylus, change from defenders of the simple principle of revenge to more beneficent defenders of civil justice. The rule of law, of reason, becomes part of the natural order. Thus, the interpretation of the role of the Eumenides offered by Aeschylus includes a social component within natural order. That is, it includes not merely what we would now call the "law of the jungle" or natural selection, but the natural order of man, of reason, as well, and the preservation not merely of Nature, but of nature with man as a component. At this point, the Greeks went beyond mere appreciation of the beauty of the natural world to forge a union of natural order and human ethics.

So far, we've focused on artistic examples of the affinity/preservation values within the realm of literature. Even a brief look at its role in the visual arts will remind us that these values have served there as a similarly dominant motif. Once again, we can see this in a variety of cultures and at different times. In Japan, the popularization of Buddhism was enveloped in the fine arts of the 12th and 13th centuries. During this period, it was believed that a depiction of a marvel of Nature was visual evidence of the presence of gods in Nature. Actual personification of gods, handsome creatures in flowing robes, was not necessary. It was enough to show the splendor of a waterfall or a mountain skyline. Such renderings of the natural world were sufficient proof of the presence of the gods. (The concept is not unlike those later offered by Wordsworth or Emerson, who also felt the presence of God in Nature.) In Chinese tradition idealized landscapes are formulated. To this day, traditional Oriental art is known for the

FIGURE 4-6. Oriental art is often filled with tranquil scenes containing many flowers, trees, birds, streams, or other natural objects. Affinity with Nature, as expressed in works like this panel from the back side of a black, lacquered 6-foot-high wooden Chinese screen, is a common theme in Oriental art *(Photo by Stephen H. Schneider).*

beauty of its landscapes; single flowers or trees are presented with simple majesty, conveying a deep sense of appreciation and an inherent need for the preservation of such beauty.

Our examination of the values of affinity/preservation has taken us through a brief selection of diverse cultures throughout history. Even these examples, though, are only a select few. The emergence of such similar values in varied cultures and across time can only further emphasize the fundamental appeal of this motif in the man/Nature bond. Affinity/preservation values appear to be something inherent in man, because these values have consistently recurred under such different cultural conditions. To what extent does present society espouse these values? Should it? Or should we want to break with this cultural heritage? These are the kinds of questions that are implicit in decisions as practical as the development of nuclear power. They only seem to be modern, but they are also as primordial as our feelings about the proper place of man in Nature. We'll consider these kinds of issues later. First, to the opposite value set.

VALUE SET TWO: FEAR/CONTROL

Comparable questions, and a comparable breadth of evidence, can be found in the humanities in support of the opposing set of values: the fear of Nature and the desire to control it. We can even use some of the same artistic examples, in reverse. Earlier we discussed the anthropomorphization of Nature in primitive religions. We said (p. 93):

> Through the act of making gods of these natural elements, not only are their powers appreciated, but it also becomes somewhat of a "sin" to interfere with their functions. One possible interpretation of these early an-

FIGURE 4-7. (A) *Lan Ying (1578–1660), Landscape.* A deep appreciation for Nature is felt in Oriental works of art. Lan Ying, a Chinese artist of the 16th–17th centuries, painted this landscape using the traditional Chinese medium, washes of ink combined with broad brushstrokes. The landscape is not seen in detail but is conveyed almost as a total experience. Through this painting, we can sense what being a part of this setting would be like, provided we shared the artist's affinity for Nature. Even the misty quality of the fog is conveyed here *(The Art Institute of Chicago).*

(B) *Nachi Waterfall, Kamakura Period (1185–1333).* At an even earlier time, Japanese artists were celebrating the majesty of Nature, as in this *Nachi Waterfall.* They believed that there were natural gods and that their presence could be felt merely by looking at the beauties of Nature. It was believed that a local Shinto god lived in this waterfall, although no god-image is shown here. The nature veneration of Shintoism may well have been the driving force behind this work of art *(Nezu Art Museum, Japan).*

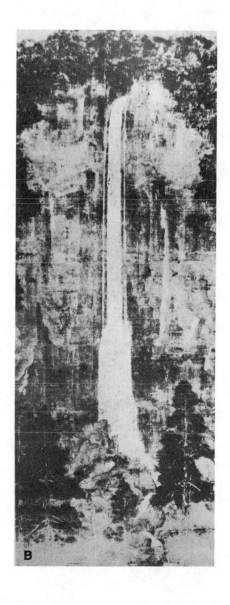

thropomorphic religions is that they bolstered the tradition of the sanctity and the need for the preservation
of the natural world.

An opposite interpretation of anthropomorphization is possible. That is, worship is not an affinity/preservation reaction
of the supplicants but a fear/control reaction. If the gods are
not appeased through prayer, sacrifice, and reverence, then
feared natural variability—storms, floods, drought, disease—
could well be visited upon the irreverent as punishment. In
essence, prayer can be, even if only unconsciously, a *control*
action. The act of prayer places one in touch with the source
of power, and thus, hopefully, he is able to sway and even
manipulate some of that power. So, the fear/control values
can be present even in religious structures.

Other, perhaps more accessible, examples can be found
in the arts. A classic of the Russian theater is Chekhov's *The
Cherry Orchard* (1904), a powerful drama of many themes. The
major focus of the play, though, the object from which all
actions and themes arise, is the cherry orchard itself. The
magnificent cherry orchard has been owned for generations
by a wealthy Russian family, the Ranevskys, and has become
a symbol of their comfortable position and status quo behavior. They are harmless but ineffective people, eventually
forced to sell their estate as a result of the mismanagement
of family money. A member of the rising middle class, a former peasant on their estate, ultimately buys the estate and,
of course, the cherry orchard along with it. Power over the
cherry orchard, a symbol of importance, is now in his hands;
but he values change, not the maintenance of the status quo
preferred by the leisure class. Consequently, he will not follow their preservationist and, to him, self-indulgent behavior.
He is a "modern" man with an emphasis on "progress."

Through his new-found power he expresses his values. He chops down the cherry orchard to replace it with commercial ventures on the property. Here is a clear artistic example of the dichotomous contrast between differing reactions to the place of man in Nature. The established leisure class expresses appreciation for and preservation of Nature (at least, the natural world in their own backyard), even at the cost of the maintenance of the status quo. The opposite reaction— Nature as an obstacle to progress, as something to be overcome and ultimately controlled (which in this case means the destruction of Nature)—is an acceptable price in the value system of those struggling for what they interpret as greater human status. There are, of course, no absolutes here, rather a balancing of value trade-offs. One's viewpoint often depends upon where one stands materially and how one defines the "quality of life." (A well-known "law" in political science suggests that "A politician usually stands very close to where he sits.") In his way, Chekhov points out the tragedy of those who blindly follow either extreme. The totally status-quo-oriented preservationists lose their land, and the ambitious developers of "progress" destroy their beauty. How to reconcile these value opposites is, of course, a major continuing political problem. We'll come back to it later.

Let's return to Greek mythology, where once again a legendary story exists that can serve to elucidate this point. This time our tale is that of Daedalus and his son, Icarus. Daedalus was a master craftsman summoned to Crete by King Minos to construct the labyrinth. Having completed it, Daedalus desired to return home. King Minos, though, would not allow the craftsman to leave. Petitions were made to Zeus for permission to leave. Meanwhile, Daedalus began to see his obstacles in a new light. Minos could control his travel by land and sea, leaving only one other option—which fell solely under the control of Nature—the air. A poor craftsman did not have the means to combat a king on land or sea, but as a master of his art, he believed himself sufficiently skilled to overcome this obstacle of Nature. Rather than waiting for Zeus' answer, Daedalus took the matter into his own hands. He studied the creatures of the sky and, by combining feathers, wax, and straps, fashioned a man-made replica of a part of Nature. He fastened one pair of wings onto himself and the other pair onto his son, Icarus, giving the young Icarus careful instructions: Do not fly too close to the water and be weighed down, and do not fly too close to the sun, which will melt the wax holding the wings together. He recommended flying at a moderate height to be safe. His handicraft worked, and they took flight. Icarus, though, exhilarated with flying, soared higher and higher in defiance of gravity, and heedless of his father's advice. Not surprisingly, his excursion was to be ill-fated, as the heat of the sun melted* the wax in the wings, after which gravity reclaimed its supremacy and plunged the young Icarus into the depths of the sea below. Where the boy landed is now called the Icarian Sea. As with other Greek myths, there is not just one interpretation. Part of the message lies in the son's disobedience of his father, the father's disobedience of the king, and his impatience in waiting for a judgment from Zeus. But surely a significant segment of the lesson of Daedalus and Icarus is a warning about the risks of attempting to alter man's place in Nature. Daedalus' defiance of Minos led to a defiance of Nature as well—or at least an attempt to overcome, or control, its influence. He tried to extend the bounds of Nature. Ovid says, of Daedalus,

---

* Actually, it gets colder, not hotter, as one goes from the Earth's surface up to the highest clouds, but the legend can be maintained even in the face of modern scientific knowledge—the wax could have frozen and cracked, and Icarus would have fallen anyway.

"He turned his thinking/Toward unknown arts, changing the laws of nature."[12] Man, says this Greek legend, is bound to suffer if he attempts to control or overextend the bounds of Nature. Of course it was his *lack of moderation* (flying too high) that doomed Icarus. His plan might have succeeded if he had flown at moderate heights. And so it is with any attempt to overcome Nature. There are limits beyond which Nature will yield little advantage. It will bring anguish to those who push too hard too fast. Drawing the line at what is "too fast" is, in essence, a value dilemma behind many of today's problems. Chief among them is the energy crisis.

The legend tells us that new knowledge—how to make and use wings, in this case—has benefits and risks, as is always the case when man tries to overcome Nature or push the bounds of Nature closer to its limits. The story of Daedalus and Icarus is, of course, part of our literary tradition, and its moral has been the repeated reality of human development. James Joyce, a major 20th-century author, used this old image of defiance in the main character of *A Portrait of the Artist as a Young Man* and *Ulysses*, Stephen Daedalus, one of the most well-known literary characters of modern times. Stephen Daedalus reacts to the totality of the limiting bounds of his own 20th-century Dublin. He too defies the ruling authority—in this case, the restraints placed upon him by the Catholic church. At one point, the narrative says about him that

> He burned to appease the fierce longings of his heart before which everything else was idle and alien. He cared little that he was in mortal sin, that his life had grown to be a tissue of subterfuge and falsehood. Beside the savage desire within him to realise the enormities which he brooded on nothing was sacred.[13]

There is also a literary tradition of man versus Nature, of man proving himself in a series of encounters with Nature.

FIGURE 4-8. *Pieter Brueghel, The Fall of Icarus, c. 1558.* The tale of Icarus and his father Daedalus is the only mythological subject that Brueghel chose to use as an artistic subject. It is curious that life goes on so casually in this pastoral scene, with the only actual trace of Icarus being his legs still visible above the water as he has come splashing down to his death (detail). By flying, Icarus and Daedalus chose to defy the existing natural order. Icarus' own defiance went one step further, for he also defied the warnings of his father about flying too close to the sun, which would melt the wax in his wings. There are many possible interpretations of Brueghel's visual presentation of the fall of Icarus. It is certainly not tragic, from the seemingly carefree scene. Nor is it even worthy of much attention. The ploughman continues leisurely to attend to what is important to his own survival. The shepherd, who does look up to notice what we assume is the still-flying Daedalus, has virtually no expression on his face (detail). It would seem that the fall of Icarus, to Brueghel, was merely an act of folly. The painting barely comments, though, on the significance of the effort *(Musées Royaux des Beaux-Arts, Brussels).*

This tradition stems from early civilizations. The term *trial by fire* suggests the passing of a test that is actually a confrontation with Nature, or with a natural element. In this case, the ability to withstand the power and the pain that Nature can inflict is indicative of strength and, often, of manhood. The Greeks, too, showed proof of manhood through direct confrontation with Nature. The labors of Hercules were a series of tests, of man pitted against natural obstacles, and were necessary thresholds that Hercules had to cross on his way to fulfilling what was his natural destiny, to become a hero. Similarly, the tale of Beowulf is the story of a man conquering a "natural" nonhuman being, a creature terrorizing the area. In various cultures, proof of manhood requires successful tests of the candidate's ability to overcome aspects of Nature. *Moby Dick* contains, among other themes, that of man versus Nature, with the emphasis on man's attempt to subjugate Nature—to his great peril in this work. Even in our modern era, examples of these control values abound. Ernest Hemingway's stories and novels are full of the theme of man versus Nature, with manhood won by conquering Nature.

Architecture is an art form that we have barely considered. While it is extremely difficult if not completely impossible to identify clear motives within this discipline, it is quite tempting to speculate on the extent to which a desire to control Nature contributed to the construction of certain structures. Earlier we discussed Versailles, the magnificent palace and grounds constructed at the direction of Louis XIV, as an example of Nature's subjugation by man. We did not then speculate (and speculate is all we can do) on Louis XIV's motives, or the values he employed. One of the splendors of the palace of Versailles is its hall of mirrors, a space with the power to create a dazzling reflection, almost as much "sun" as the sun itself. Perhaps such an opportunity to rival

Nature was part of the Sun King's desire to build the palace. Could it not also be possible that the soaring cathedrals of the Gothic architectural period reflect a desire not only to celebrate the heavenly powers by literally reaching up to their heights but also, by creating such towering masterpieces, to push back a little the constraints of Nature that keep man on the ground? It is even possible that the construction of the pyramids, whose circumstances are still a mystery to modern scholars, arose from a partial desire to overcome the accustomed limits of Nature (in addition to the religious significance we already attribute to them). Such interpretations, while little more than speculations, are possibilities in light of the extensive evidence for control of Nature as a basic reaction to the man/Nature bond.

We've now looked at some common divergent reactions that man has had to his relationship with Nature: on the one hand, a strongly felt affinity with Nature and a concomitant desire to preserve it and, on the other hand, a dread fear of Nature and a desire to control it or overcome it. The artistic examples we've selected show how man has expressed both kinds of strong feelings about Nature and how contradictory his reactions can be, even within individuals. Each individual has an initial emotional reaction that leads to values. These can drive actions to control or to preserve Nature. Rarely will either absolute value set be dominant in an individual or a culture. We can imagine, for example, a town that is threatened by a flooding river. A blending of values becomes clear as we consider what actions would be taken under such circumstances. It would clearly be wise to build dikes to hold back potential floodwaters. Construction of such devices is a control on Nature; in this case, it would seem necessary to preserve life. Unfortunately, after dikes are built, more people might then move into the floodplain, comforted that they are

FIGURE 4-9. The cathedral at Chartres is a masterpiece of the High Gothic style. The original cathedral dated from the early 12th century, but it was largely destroyed by fire. The second rebuilt version, 1194–1220, represents the mature Gothic style. The galleries and passageways are narrow, whereas the nave arcade opens up into a taller and narrower space. The thrust of our attention is definitely upward. As our eyes travel up, they encounter the magnificent stained glass windows, which diffuse light through the symbolic decorative patterns within the glass. The arches, ribs, and columns supporting the vaults show the harmony of elements at work here. They are not only supports but also bring light into the vast structure and once again emphasize the height of the cathedral. The impressive Gothic cathedrals were designed as places in which to celebrate the glories of God. Their magnificent construction also allows us to celebrate the glories of man's own abilities, which might even have been a motivating factor in their construction. In this interpretation, they can serve as symbols of man's desire to overcome some constraints imposed by Nature (Photo by Lynne Morton).

FIGURE 4-10. *Giorgione, The Tempest, 1505.* The mystery of Nature and how we react or do not react to it are aspects of Giorgione's fascinating painting. In the background of this painting, there is a storm brewing, and lightning is flashing. Yet, in the foreground are a young soldier and a nude mother nursing her baby, both seemingly unaware of, or unconcerned about, the oncoming storm. The landscape itself is one of idyllic, pastoral beauty. However, the mood remains one of mystery. Are these people so naturally a part of this beautiful world that they are not afraid of what Nature may hold in store for them? Are they fully at ease with Nature or merely unaware of the oncoming storm and ignorant of its destructive potential? Whereas later, the Romantic poets also captured this sense of nostalgic reverie connected with Nature, here there is an additional element of foreboding, unexplained characters and expressions. As Giorgione, a Venetian master of the High Renaissance, shows, reactions to our place in Nature are not readily understood and have various possible interpretations *(Academy of Fine Arts, Venice, Italy).*

safe, even though dikes have been known to fail.[14] A greater number, then, would be living at risk. Thus, control of Nature, if attempting to expand the bounds of Nature too far, can lead to worse consequences than learning to live within more realistic bounds.

An undue fear of Nature can lead to foolish and often premature attempts at controlling Nature. Fear of storms has led to programs to modify hurricanes, for example. Fortunately, so far these efforts have been experimental rather than operational and have been aimed at studying the feasibility of storm control. Such weather modification operations are, of course, attempts to control Nature. However, in this case, we do not understand the potential consequences of our actions very well, and operational programs at this stage of ignorance may do more harm than good, depending upon what unintended side effects result from the programs. Attempts to control Nature are potentially dangerous—at least, in their early stages—and need to be carefully considered before action is taken. The policy of attempting or not attempting to control Nature follows from a trade-off that must balance our two opposite sets of values. What tips the balance, making the application of one set of values more justified, changes with each situation and with each person.

The world of the ancient Greeks was not as technologically complicated as our modern world, but even their mythology reflects the conflict between these two sets of values over the preservation or control of Nature. As within their culture, so within ours: values determine public policy. Our next question, then, is: How are we to determine what is a just or unjust balance of each set of values? That is a much more difficult question than even those we've dealt with so far, for it requires an assessment of the collective values of our (and other) societies. Perhaps the best we can do is to be sure that each citizen learns how much and how little is known in each problem area. Then, individual values can be aggregated through the political process.

We must use modern science to help us learn the "facts." What to do about what we have learned is a more complicated issue. To decide this, we need *all* the available data. The humanities must be called upon to help us assess the range of human reactions and values concerning our place in Nature. Without contributions from both of the "two cultures," neither is likely to act wisely to solve problems common to both. It is a mistake to view modern environmental and related technological problems, for instance, as purely scientific issues. Science is indeed a major component. Ethics, however, is no less relevant to policymaking than is science. We proceed then toward science, passing through ancient natural philosophy. It is our bridge to modern science.

*He that knows not what the world is,
knows not where he is himself.*
        —MARCUS AURELIUS, *Meditations*

Chapter 5 / ANCIENT GREEK NATURAL PHILOSOPHY: THE BRIDGE TO SCIENCE

We began our search for an understanding of man's relationship with Nature with the Greeks. Their myths entertained, offered observations and "explanations"* of the natural world, and also laid the foundations for subsequent works of art. Many artistic motifs and images—not only those treating Nature or the man/Nature relationship—can trace their roots to the Greeks. We now turn to the Greeks again, for a look at a speculative science we have yet to consider and one in which their works are truly fundamental: the realm

---

* As noted earlier, by *explanations* we do not mean to imply that a rational explanation was necessarily the motive for these myths, even if such a motive might be implicit.

of natural philosophy. We place philosophy at the end of our exploration of the speculative sciences since early natural philosophy fits our definition of a speculative science (describing or offering an "explanation" of Nature). It also leads directly into the hard sciences. It is, in fact, the least speculative of the speculative sciences. We might even call it a *pre-science*.

Since natural philosophy, at least at first, drew heavily on mythological traditions, a brief review of some aspects of mythology is appropriate. This will provide a backdrop against which to view the intermediate position of philosophy, the bridge between mythology and science. In the meantime, we'll continue our search for cycles in the realm of natural philosophy.

Greek legends are laden with a mixture of practical observations of Nature and what appears to be religious speculation on its workings. The Demeter and Persephone myth offered an "explanation" for the seasons: spring/summer is the time when Persephone is with her mother Demeter, and fall/winter, especially winter, is when she is with Hades in the underworld. A cycle is established and these changes within Nature are, seemingly, "explained." Thus, the farmers—and ultimately, all of us, who depend upon the seasonal products of the soil—can rely on the regularity of the seasons. Spring will follow winter and summer will follow spring. Then, while Demeter grieves for the underground Persephone, crops will not grow, land must lie fallow; this is part of the winter months. But Persephone will return, for that is the pattern ordained by Zeus.

So much of the appeal of mythology lies in its ability to take a clear observation of Nature—in this case, the cycle of seasons—and present it in emotionally tangible, human stories. Some of our observations of the natural world haven't changed since the time of the Greeks. We each still see the workings of our world. We stop to notice that there are seasonal rotations, and then we want to "explain" them. By now, however, we have had enough observations communicated to us to know that the seasons aren't the same all over the world, that the northern and southern hemispheres operate on a different timetable, that some places have only two seasons, others no seasons. (It would be hard for us now to accept the Demeter/Persephone "explanation" of the seasons.) Yet, the general cyclical pattern in the myth still remains for much of the earth, even if it is out of phase in the northern and southern hemispheres.

Some of the gaps in our current knowledge are mirrored in this ancient myth. There are several versions of this tale and they all differ on the same point. There is no specified seasonal duration; they specify only that each season will recur. To this day, we don't know the precise durations of individual seasons. In fact, a current topic of heated scientific debate is whether we are currently in a warming or a cooling trend. Are our winters actually longer, or, like the whimsical gods, are they merely sometimes more or less severe?

The tale also contains some of the same element of mystery that we still face: how these seasonal rotations actually began. What is this pomegranate seed that has such power to form a bond between Persephone and the world of Hades? The Greek legend provides no information to enlighten us in this respect. We are merely to accept that part of the tale on faith. As with mythology and religion, certain givens must be accepted. A leap of faith then offers a "logic" that transcends the uncertainties of the senses or the mind. It would be fascinating to speculate on just how far science will actually be able to go toward completely understanding the origins of these natural phenomena and at what point we will have to be satisfied with our knowledge. Even today, there are rival theories of the origin of the earth. But, in *principle*, are the speculations of science "better" than those of mythology? Before we try to answer that question, we need to turn first to natural philosophy and then to modern science.

Our progression from mythology to philosophy to science isn't meant to be taken as strictly chronological, although there are some who would say that this is indeed the evolutionary pattern of human thought about Nature and man's place in Nature. The methods of analysis change; in other words, how modern man *seeks out* evidence in support of his theories differs in each "culture." Man has seen cycles as a structure of Nature in his artistic expressions. He continues to find in cycles a focal point for philosophic discussions on Nature. In philosophy, his observations of these natural structures are refined, even though the rigorous standards of evidence required in hard science are still not applied. We choose subjects and examples from ancient natural philosophers in order to put some perspective on the findings of modern science about the structure of Nature and man's place in it.

HESIOD

An apt place to begin would be with a philosopher whose works hover between mythology and natural philosophy. Hesiod was such a man. As a frame of reference, Hesiod's work dates from approximately the same time period as that of Homer, the eighth century B.C. This is interesting to note, since both Hesiod and Homer dealt with a world of gods and heroes and both men attempted to record the deeds of each. However, the work of Hesiod differs from that of Homer in one important way. As Mircea Eliade, an authority on mythology, points out in *Myth and Reality*, Hesiod did more than merely record these myths; he made an effort to systematize them and, by so doing, added a dimension of rational order not previously included.

Hesiod's major work is his *Theogony*, a poem that has not had the appeal of the more popular works of Homer (or of Ovid's *Metamorphoses*) but that does provide an organization of much of the same material. It also offers some of its own speculations on human life. Hesiod's *Theogony* deals with three important areas: the nature of the divine cosmos, the nature of the physical cosmos, and the nature of the human cosmos. He begins by offering a lengthy creation myth, or rather, an organization of the fragmented creation myths already scattered throughout Greek mythology. From that organization spring various genealogies of the gods, tales of the confrontations between gods and goddesses, structures of the natural elements established because of these confrontations (and at the whims of the gods), and Hesiod's own speculations on man's ideal behavior. The *Theogony* is a compendium of mythological stories blended with Hesiod's own philosophical musings.

We have already noted, in relation to the speculative sciences, the recurrent theme of man's dependence on Nature. Hesiod, too, propounds this view. He deals with primal Nature-personifications, like those we saw in the myths we looked at from a variety of cultures. Not only does he continue to deify the natural world, clearly showing its importance in relation to man, but he also uses Nature personifications. He refers to Earth as "Mother" and Sky as "Father."

Hesiod provides us with a means toward understanding man's interaction with the cycles of Nature. As we contended earlier, man's interactions with Nature are often dependent on his system of values. Hesiod introduces the principle of opposites, as in light/dark or sorrow/desire, using different gods for each set of opposites. From his framework, built on opposites, we can extrapolate man's dealings with Nature. We see that man has frequently reacted to Nature in one of two diametrically opposed ways: either with fear or with reverence. The reverberations of this polarity were amplified in the previous chapter when we showed how man's values, fear or reverence, largely influence the way he sees his place in Nature and profoundly affect the future structure of cycles in Nature.

PYTHAGORAS

Pythagoras placed belief in the cyclical aspect of Nature within a framework of natural philosophy in which his influence was widespread. Although Pythagoras was a Greek, Ovid's *Metamorphoses*, a Roman work, bears the influence of this Pythagorean school and itself contains a chapter on Pythagoras. Even though these passages from the *Metamorphoses* are not pure philosophy but actually a combination of mythology and philosophy, they still contain much of relevance to our consideration of the natural world. In the words of Pythagoras, as related by Ovid,

> Not even the so-called elements are constant,
> Listen, and I will tell you of their changes.
> There are four of them and two, the earth and water,
> Are heavy, and their own weight bears them downward,
> And two, the air and fire (and fire is purer
> Even than air) are light, rise upward
> If nothing holds them down. These elements
> Are separate in space, yet all things come
> From them and into them, and they can change
> Into each other. Earth can be dissolved
> To flowing water, water can thin to air,

And air can thin to fire and fire can thicken
To air again, and air condense to water,
And water be compressed to solid earth.
Nothing remains the same: the great renewer,
Nature, makes form from form, and, oh, believe me
That nothing ever dies. What we call birth
Is the beginning of a difference,
No more than that, and death is only ceasing
Of what had been before. The parts may vary,
Shifting from here to there, hither and yon,
And back again, but the great sun is constant.[1]

Pythagoras' structure of cyclical Nature begins with his presentation of a system of observation and analysis of the natural world. He breaks the natural world into four Elements: Earth, Water, Air, and Fire. (Actually, we know now that "Earth" to the Greeks really encompassed solids; "Water," liquids; and "Air," gases. These, as we indicate in Chapter 7, are not chemical *elements*, as they are called today.) These four Elements are well known to us; they have remained the foundations of man's early observations of his natural world. The Pythagoreans, the philosophic school that followed his principles, conveyed the thoughts of their time, along with their own considerations and speculations.

The use of the four Elements is extremely important, for it indicates a new mode of thought, a reduction of Nature into component parts. It is a philosophic proposition based— even if only implicitly—on *observation* of the natural world. While the mythmakers created tales that implicitly gave an explanation of why the world evolved or appeared as it did, Pythagoras' system of the four Elements was offered as a rational explanation of Nature. The motives of the mythmakers are unclear, or open to interpretation; the motives of the natural philosophers are more explicit: they were searching for rational understanding of the natural world.

Pythagoras, then, accepts the four Elements as fundamental to the structure of Nature. He goes on to show that these Elements are not constant but in a continuous state of flux. No one with eyes open to the functioning of Nature can dispute the general thrust of his evidence. Solid earth can become mud; water does evaporate into mist and air; and so on. A similar idea can be found in the works of Hesiod and other early philosophers. They observed that there are opposites in the world. Hesiod went so far as to say that life itself is in a perpetual state of flux. Not only are life and Nature fluid, but they are also regenerative or cyclical, an idea that Ovid attributes to Pythagoras in the passage quoted above. According to Pythagoras, the forms of Nature are, in some instances, interchangeable. Therefore, they can be seen as forming a cycle, with dependent parts. One life form leads to another and to yet another. As we have seen in mythology, religion, and literature, this cycle holds true. Life continues in a variety of forms. Nature is regenerative or cyclical. What is new in the structure that Pythagoras established is that he shows Nature to be cyclical because it is composed of four interactive Elements. An examination of these Elements reveals that Nature is regenerative. Science, as we shall see later, will actually be able to strengthen dramatically this early philosophic postulate, although it will drastically alter the detailed accounts of these early natural philosophers.

HERACLITUS

The four Elements appear in various incarnations in the works of other Greek natural philosophers. In fact it will be easier for us to pursue our philosophic investigations of cycles in Nature and of the man/Nature relationship by following the interpretive path of these four Elements. Such a route leads to the work of Heraclitus, one of the Ionian philosophers, a group that focused its attention primarily on the world rather than on cosmic orders. His interpretations of the four elements fit into the cyclical themes we've already seen so often in the arts.

Heraclitus believed that four Elements do exist and that they can partake of each other. Their partaking indicates a circularity. John Mansley Robinson, in *An Introduction to Early Greek Philosophy*, puts it this way:

> Heraclitus describes change as a way up and down, and the world-order as coming into being in accordance with it. For fire, when it is contracted, becomes moist; when it is contracted still further it becomes water; and water, when it is contracted, turns to earth. This is the downward way. And earth liquifies again; and from it water arises; and from water the rest. For he refers nearly everything to the evaporation of the sea. And this is the upward way.[2]

Here we can see that Heraclitus' views are quite similar to those expressed by Pythagoras in the earlier-quoted passage. Pythagoras shows how similar the Elements are to each other, how they each can become the other. Heraclitus follows the changes of one particular Element—Fire—rather than discussing them all. However, although their approaches are different, their conclusions are similar. Both natural philosophers note that the Elements do share cyclical qualities, that they are highly interrelated.

What the Elements have in common is their transmutability in a state of flux. As already seen in our brief quote in Chapter 4 from the Chinese *I Ching*, this concept is not one unique to the Greeks. In fact, Heraclitus' famous aphorism, "The way up and the way down are the same," is almost the same message as that found in the Chinese philosophy of Confucius. Both believed in the state of flux, motion, and commonality of factors among the Elements. Even the occult sciences, as we saw in Chapter 3 in the tarot's wheel of fortune, have the same message. In classical natural philosophy, as in the other speculative sciences, similar conclusions were drawn in a variety of cultures at different times. These cross-cultural philosophical observations and "explanations" of Nature as composed of cycles bear further testimony to the universality of this concept.

Heraclitus, like other philosophers of his time, saw the cyclical quality of Nature in the four Elements. He differed from other philosophers, though, by focusing on Fire as the main Element. It is not surprising that someone who had no observational tools other than his own senses and who also believed in flux as a fundamental quality of Nature would choose as a dominant Element the one whose main visual characteristic is motion.

Digress for a moment and look at Fire alone. What are some of the main qualities of Fire that have become part of our literary and artistic tradition? A major characteristic expressed often in the arts is the same one Heraclitus espoused: flux, or the ability to change. Within the Western traditions, we see fire both as something to be revered and as something to be feared. This is to say that the duality of values postulated earlier applies to fire. For example, fire has cleansing qualities. In Hindu belief, fire can be used to purge the soul from the body. In much of Christian tradition, on the other hand, there is the fire of eternal damnation in the flames of hell. Evil spirits have been said to disappear in a burst of flames, or at least, that was the belief professed by those who burned witches at Salem, Massachusetts, and elsewhere. Similarly, a combination of Fire and Air has mystical, spiritual connotations, as with the Holy Spirit. Fire must be feared as well, for fire has the power to destroy the body and, in some traditions, the soul. The combination of Fire and Earth has connotations of eroticism, passion, of physical energy. While the expression "burn with desire" isn't meant to be taken literally, it does show the association of fire with passion. Within some Eastern traditions, cremation is a spiritual regeneration, a release of the eternal soul from the body upon its death. Various primitive African and Indian cultures also believed that fire was a means of testing man's endurance—hence, another of our expressions, already mentioned, "trial by fire."

In the works of Heraclitus, then, we find a treatment of the four Elements, and especially of Fire, that makes the cyclical nature of our world evident. Heraclitus goes on to philosophize that man is of lesser importance than the Elements in this great natural scheme. He states that man should follow in the ways of Nature, using Nature as his guiding light when acting. This reflects the affinity/preservation set of values: man should appreciate the ways of Nature and should not only work to preserve them but follow its examples. "Moderation is the greatest virtue, and wisdom is to speak the truth and to act according to nature, giving heed to it."[3]

Heraclitus' "speculative" tendencies are strongest when he discusses Fire as the primary Element. On the whole, though, his work certainly belongs in this sketch of the classical philosophic propositions that "explain" our natural world. His general speculations on Nature and man's place in it have much in common with what we have noted earlier in other speculative arts. However, as Giorgio de Santillana[4] points out, he may also have unconsciously taken one of the primary steps in the progression from metaphysical to physical sciences. Heraclitus was among the first of the great thinkers to consider the mystery inherent in our natural world. To him, this mystery was flux, change, progression. Others pondered the mystery of the spiritual world, but not primarily of the natural world. It is the enigmas of the natural world—and the universe beyond—that have stoked the imagination of those who were to become our scientists.

EMPEDOCLES

Empedocles, another Ionian philosopher, also propounded the four Elements as the primary aspects of our natural world. But Empedocles added to these four Elements certain properties and certain emotions intrinsic to man himself rather than to Nature. He also included the very principle of opposition—and of attraction—in his scheme of the natural world. Empedocles' work did much to strengthen belief in the cyclical nature of the physical world and to show the emotional reactions man has in response to Nature.

Empedocles begins his philosophical statements with an affirmation of belief in the four Elements. He then goes on to draw a parallel between man and these Elements. Just as these Elements come together in different ways, so man comes and goes in different ways, always preserving a pattern. A natural cycle is suggested.

> When these [the Elements] have been mingled in the form of a man, or some kind of wild animal or plant or bird, men call this "coming into being"; and when they separate men call it "evil destiny" (passing away). This is established usage, and I myself assent to the custom.
>
> Fools! They have no far-reaching thoughts who imagine that what was not before can come into being, or that anything can perish and be utterly destroyed.
>
> For to come to be out of what is utterly nonexistent is inconceivable, and it is impossible and unheard of that what is should pass away. For it will always be, wherever you put it.[5]

As new combinations of the Elements form and reform, so man re-forms. Nature establishes a life cycle, according to Empedocles. Man's life cycle is part of Nature's. Therefore, man is dependent upon Nature, for Nature sets the patterns. Here Empedocles agrees with the other philosophers we've discussed thus far, all of whom acknowledge Nature's supremacy over man.

Where the work of Empedocles is particularly important, though, is in his addition of emotions to the realm of the four Elements. To Empedocles, the emotions of Love and Strife have the same importance and kind of reality as the Elements themselves. He sets some of the Elements off in opposition and adds the emotions at their appropriate polar ends. For example, water and fire are placed at opposite sides, for water has the ability to blot out fire. Similarly, he adds Love and Strife, two emotions that rule the world of man and that have the power to cancel. We may note here that Love is analogous to the appreciation of the natural world, which we postulated earlier in our discussion of Hesiod, as one of man's main reactions to Nature. Its contrasting emotional reaction is Strife, according to Empedocles, or fear, by analogy to our value dichotomy. Fear indicates uneasiness about our dependence upon Nature and often leads to attempts to control it. Empedocles does not go on to suggest (as did Heraclitus) how to act in accordance with these emotional reactions. However, although he avoids the political problem of making specific value choices, he does lay the groundwork for such actions, at least by implication.

We should note that Empedocles added certain observed natural properties to his general scheme. These fundamental properties are hot, cold, wetness, and dryness. As with the Elements, he established these in their opposite/similar relationships. He even went so far as to try to interpret the workings of the seasons in terms of these properties. It was not enough to ascribe the seasons to cyclical aspects of Nature. Empedocles, though, was interested not merely in the *existence* of the regularity but in understanding how it works, in a rational framework. Here he went further than the previous thinkers we have discussed. Empedocles observed in Nature, and attempted to discover, underlying principles of how it all worked. As Frisinger points out in *The History of Meteorology: To 1800,*[6] Empedocles believed that summer arose when the hot, dry air was dominant, and, conversely, that winter arose when the cold, wet air had control. It isn't important at this point to challenge the accuracy—or at least the generality—of such statements with the observations of modern science; it is enough just to note that they were made. For Empedocles' attempt to explain Nature rationally, through a chain of interconnected physical processes, was a point of departure from the unrestrained imagination of the mythographers or the uncritical pronouncements of the early natural philosophers. His approach leads into the next realm of our investigation, the physical sciences, or the hard sciences.

But before turning to modern science, we should first look at the works of two major philosophers, whose thinking sets the stage for a transition from ancient natural philosophy to modern science. These two important men are Aristotle and Thales.

ARISTOTLE

Aristotle is important for two reasons. First, he recorded the philosophies of many great thinkers of his time. To him we owe a large part of our knowledge of early Greek philosophy. The second major reason is that he constantly forced the thinkers of his time to reevaluate their ideas and the ideas of their contemporaries. He served as both chronicler and critic, trying to keep philosophy aware of the problems it was encountering from the inconsistencies it showed both with relation to the empirical world and in its internal logic. Aristotle substantially helped the process of transition from the metaphysical to the physical sciences, although he himself often wildly speculated on the how's and why's of Nature.

Aristotle's main approach was the use of the technique of questioning. He disputed the works of Empedocles and criticized the philosophical validity of the works of Hesiod. He kept his contemporaries from blindly accepting any of the sundry theories of the day. He, like other philosophers he criticized, formulated theories by observing the workings of Nature. However, rather than building his theories from what he could directly observe (i.e., inductive reasoning), he often used deductive reasoning; that is, he extended his theories beyond available observations and used those "laws" to explain various natural phenomena. These preconceived hypotheses, although based initially on observations of Nature, were often little more than speculative extrapolations—as are many of the preliminary theories of our modern scientists. Nevertheless, he knew—or more accurately, believed—that there were laws governing Nature. His theories, speculative as they were, set the tone for a search of natural laws that was to consume natural philosophers and scientists for two millennia.

Our description of the works of Aristotle, though, makes him seem like more of a revolutionary than he most likely was. In spite of his critical analyses and refutations of other philosophers and his search for more general laws of Nature, Aristotle remained deeply committed to the theories of his time. In natural philosophy, in fact, his work was instrumental in strengthening the beliefs about Nature expressed in the artistic examples at which we've been looking. In particular, Aristotle dwelt on the cyclical aspect of Nature.

One of his major works on natural philosophy is the *Meteorologica*. Here and in other works, he held to the well-established theory of the four Elements yet offered his own interpretation of their organization. He "refuted" the concept of polarized Elements, proposed by Empedocles, and the concept of dominant Elements, proposed by Heraclitus and Thales. Instead, Aristotle returned to the basic concepts of circularity and interdependence to form his structure. The result was a new interpretation: his Elements were concentrically layered around the Earth, each reacting with the others.[7] Thus, he introduced the idea of strata (part of which modern science now believes accurate and part inaccurate). To Aristotle, the four Elements were equal in importance, all partaking of the continuity of Nature.

We would be mistaken if we interpreted Aristotle's strata of Elements as being a negation of his belief in the circularity of Nature. In fact, Aristotle did believe in the interdependence of the Elements and even went so far as to say that Nature is harmonious because of this interdependence, or cyclical quality: circular motion is actually necessary for each stratum to function:

> Coming-to-be and passing-away will, as we have said, always be continuous, and will never fail owing to the cause we stated. And this continuity has a sufficient reason on our theory. For in all things, as we affirm, Nature always strikes after "the better . . ." The cause of this perpetuity of coming-to-be, as we have often said, is circular motion: for that is the only motion that is continuous . . . . For when Water is transformed into Air, Air into Fire, and Fire back into Water, we say the coming-to-be "has completed the circle," because it reverts again to the beginning. Hence it is by imitating circular motion that rectilinear motion too is continuous.[8]

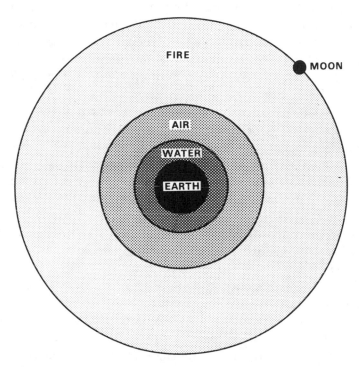

FIGURE 5-1. Aristotle introduced a circular scheme—concentric layers of elements around the earth. These strata are not isolated, however, and can interact, transform, and reform, all participating in the cycles of Nature. Of course, Aristotle did not have the observational tools needed actually to measure the space above the earth in which he hypothesized his strata. The fact that he could not verify or test his hypotheses is what kept him a step out of the body of methods we now call *science (From H. H. Frisinger, The History of Meteorology: To 1800, Science History Publications, New York, 1977, p. 16).*

This passage from Aristotle seems to be defending belief in the cyclical aspect of Nature and, what's more, to be holding it up as an ideal. Man, by imitating, or, as we have said earlier, by appreciating Nature, may find similar harmony. Man also imitates Nature by striving after a "better," which, to some, defines the goal of "progress." We can infer that man should be—if he isn't already—dependent on Nature for examples of moral behavior.

Aristotle's *Meteorologica* provides more than merely general observations of Nature. It is a compendium of philosophical thought on a wide range of natural subjects, from winds, rain, clouds, and thunder to climatic changes overall. By building on an already-established framework of the four Elements, and by introducing a critical quality into the philosophical thinking of the time, Aristotle must surely have helped the philosophers to question their own methods of natural observation. And a questioning of their methods could not help but lead to the development of better methods. Aristotle's failing from the point of view of modern science, as we will see later, was an almost arrogant acceptance of his own hypotheses, which his limited observational tools could hardly verify, or deny. Furthermore, he believed in four causes of things: formal, material, efficient, and final, while we, in terms of science, pursue only one, the efficient.* This

---

* Aristotle believed in the mutual coexistence of both form and matter. The "cause" of any changes in these he subdivided into four parts. The first, the "formal cause," is the role played by the form within the matter, or, in other words, the essence or pattern in the matter that persists as the matter undergoes change. The second, or "material" cause, is the substratum, the matter in which the form or essence is contained. The third is the "efficient cause," which describes the proximate agents of change. This is the "cause" by which modern scientists seek to explain the changes they observe. Lastly, the fourth, or "final," cause is the *purpose* for which the change was initiated. To Aristotle, then, there was a purpose behind all changes, whether the initiator of that change was man or Nature.

different perspective, combined with a strong belief in un-
verified hypotheses, kept him a step out of the realm of what
we regard as *science*.

THALES

It is fitting—at least for the one of us who is a professional
climatologist—that we close our examination of the metaphysical sciences with a brief look at the works of a man who
was a prime kindred spirit. Aristotle said of him that he was
the first natural philosopher, and he has been tagged by some
as our first climatologist. Thales of Miletus was a rare blend
of speculative thinker and pre-scientist.

There seems to be very little actually known about
Thales. Evidence suggests a man with a probing mind and
also one full of contradictions. The contradictions stem primarily from the tenacious grip that the contemporary mythology had on him. Like the other natural philosophers we
have already discussed, Thales believed in the four elements
as the foundations or primary components of the natural
world. Some philosophers were seeking the key to the understanding of the natural phenomena in the positing of one
Element as dominant, just as one god was supreme. Thales
falls among this group. To Heraclitus, this dominant Element
was Fire. To Thales, it was Water. He came to this conclusion
from natural observation and perhaps also from the associations Water called to his mind. There are many images of
Water as primary Element that easily spring to mind. To
Thales, Water lay at the foundations of all things. The Earth
rests on it; life springs from it. We emerge from water, in
amniotic fluid. Conversely, water has the power of death,
too, as in floods or in the lack of water, drought. Water is

even the boundary between life and death, symbolized by the mythical river Styx, with its guardian, Charon. Water falls from the sky, making the crops grow and the land generally fertile. Moisture is essential to life, so water must be the primary Element. Whether or not Thales was influenced by these varied qualities of water is entirely open to speculation, of course. We can note, though, that moisture is essential to life and that water is not an obscure choice for a primary Element.

Aristotle explained Thales' philosophy and emphasis on water as follows:

> However, they do not all give the same account of the number and form of such a first principle. Thales, the originator of this sort of philosophy, says that it is water (for which reason he declared that the earth rests on water). Possibly he based this assumption on the observation that the nourishment of all things is moist, and that heat itself comes into being from this and lives by it (that from which they come to be being the first principle of all things). He bases his assumption, then, on this and on the fact that the seeds of all things have a moist nature, water being the natural first principle of moist things.
>
> There are some who think that the very ancient theologians made this sort of assumption about nature; for they made Charon and Tethys the ancestors of coming into being, and the oath of the gods water, which they called Styx (for the most ancient is the most honored, and an oath is the most honored thing). Whether there was any such ancient and venerable belief concerning nature is unclear. At any rate, Thales is said to have made this declaration about the first cause.[9]

But Thales was not satisfied with mere speculations on the Elements and on water. Although he may have drawn on some mythical associations of Water, his observations of Nature tended to be more careful than those of his fellow philosophers. Thales noted that Water falls from the sky and then evaporates into the clouds and the air. In other words, he saw a physical process at work. A cycle was established. Since we already know that Nature is believed to be cyclical, what better choice for a primary Element than one whose motions are likewise cyclical. Thales adopted the mythic theme of the circularity of Nature into actual observations and statements based on these observations. Thus, he blended both speculative and nonspeculative sciences into the proposition that Nature is cyclical.

Thales seems to have generally been interested in meteorological phenomena. We've already seen that he studied the clouds. He also studied the movements of the heavenly bodies and the very movements of the earth itself, felt in such occurrences as earthquakes. He is credited with having predicted the solar eclipse of 585 B.C.,[10] the date from which the field of astronomy marks its beginnings. It is curious to note that Thales, who elevated Water to the primary element, was directly involved in minimizing human dependence on it. A man of various contributions, he is reputed to have been a builder of bridges.

Although we cannot be sure to what extent Thales actually understood the process of condensation (in fact, it is not fully understood today), or how greatly he was influenced by the myths and legends of his time, he remains notable for several reasons. His are among the earliest studies in astrology. His are among the earliest studies of weather phenomena. We might even go so far as to call him the father of meteorology. Whatever he used as a basis of his philosophy, some mix of myth, his own observations, and logic, he did record certain observations of the natural world, search for unifying concepts, and then *seek out* evidence to substantiate the statements. Thales was a transitional natural philosopher.

"It would be very wrong to imagine only medicine men behind him, or sad mythographers like Hesiod,"[11] Giorgio de Santillana has said. However, Thales may be seen as a principal link between the speculative and the hard sciences for the one important step he did take. He began the search for proof.

DR. WATSON: *"What do you imagine it means?"*
SHERLOCK HOLMES: *"I have no data yet. It is a capital mistake to theorise before one has data. Insensibly one begins to twist facts to suit theories, instead of theories to suit facts."*
—ARTHUR CONAN DOYLE

Chapter 6 / WHAT IS SCIENCE?

LET'S BE SCIENTIFIC ABOUT IT

Sci·ence (sī ens) *n.* 1. Any department of knowledge in which the results of investigation have been logically arranged and systematized in the form of hypotheses and general laws subject to verification. 2. Knowledge of facts, phenomena, laws and proximate causes, gained and verified by exact observation, organized experiment, and ordered thinking. 3. An orderly presentation of facts, reasonings, doctrines, and beliefs concerning some subject or group of subjects: the "science" of theology. 4. Systematic knowledge in general. 5. Expertness, skill, or proficiency resulting from knowledge. abbr. sc., sci. (< OF < L *scientia* < *sciens, -entis,* ppr. of *scire* to know)[1]

Thales bridged the gap between natural philosophy and science because he began the search for proof. But Thales didn't always find proof—and neither does science. Indeed, science is in large part the very *search* for proof. Albert Einstein, certainly one of our greatest contemporary scientists, was a man who had a wealth of scientific knowledge. When asked how long it would take to confirm his theory of relativity, he is reputed to have said that while no number of experiments could prove him right, one could prove him wrong. If science isn't strictly the "knowledge of facts" or the "exact observation" of Nature that the dictionary makes it out to be, what is it?

We may come closer to a more accurate definition by comparing and contrasting the speculative* and nonspeculative sciences. Bearing in mind what we now know about the speculative sciences, we can see that they share two characteristics with the hard sciences. First is a set of observations of the natural world. Second (at least within the realm of philosophy) is the need to analyze, and theorize on, those observations, hoping to find patterns that connect seemingly chaotic events. Both find unity in variety.

The speculative sciences begin at the same starting point as science, that is, with observations of Nature and man. The limitations of their observational tools—the human senses— and the analyses of these observations, though, are markedly different from those of science. More fundamentally, their respective motivations may also differ. Most important of all, the speculative sciences do not demand the rigorously high standards of evidence and verification required of science. It

---

* Recall that we defined the "speculative sciences" broadly to include mythology, art, religion (including some from the occult), literature, and natural philosophy, when they offer "explanations" or descriptions of nature.

Science + Nature

In the science, humanities branches world of

From the findings of those scientists who dare to discover.

is the very search for proof that most distinguishes modern scientists from their prescientific predecessors.

IS SCIENCE VALUE-FREE?

The speculative sciences also differ from hard sciences by the way in which human values are treated. More correctly, speculative sciences allow, and often encourage, their treatment. In the hard sciences, it is believed that values follow from findings. Therefore, scientific hypotheses cannot be defended on scientific grounds merely to support particular values.* To a further degree, the speculative sciences can frequently omit, emphasize or alter the reporting or interpretation of actual observations of Nature for value purposes. This concept is dramatized in Bertold Brecht's play *Galileo*. Galileo's new telescope yielded celestial observations that contradicted the "scientific" dogma preached by the 15th-century Church. These observations led Galileo to doubt the Church's teachings that the earth was the center of the universe and that the planets were fixed onto celestial spheres. In the play, Galileo discovers that Jupiter has four moons that are visible through his telescope. He observes that they move. Unlike past "heretics" who had postulated theories, Galileo could prove his findings. Even so, his explanation was different from the Church's teachings, and he was therefore summoned to Rome.

> GALILEO: Because he [the pope] wants the See of St.
> Peter to be in the center of the world! That's the crux
> of the matter. You're right; the question is not the

---

* Like a good detective, the honest scientist must follow his clues wherever they lead, no matter whom they may implicate and regardless of what doctrine or dogma they may challenge.

> planets, but the peasants of the Campagna. . . . You
> want me to lie to your people?
> MONK (*in great agitation*): The very highest motives bid
> us keep silent: the peace of mind of the wretched and
> lowly![2]

Since Galileo's observations could challenge its doctrine, the Church feared a reduction in its credibility. Revealing errors in these astronomical issues could spread doubt on other areas of Church doctrine. By showing the pain-fearing scientist their torture instruments, the Vatican silenced Galileo from spreading his "truths." In essence, the Church believed that their ends justified their means. That is, people's faith in the Church's infallibility was more important than these scientific truths.

As we mentioned, such value-laden actions as the Church's suppression of Galileo, should not, theoretically, be allowed in science, where theories based on human values are not permitted. As values are present, however, in choices, they implicitly creep into scientific activities. In fact, the very search for proof, or truth seeking, is itself a commitment to truth as a value. This shows a way in which science is more like the speculative sciences than many of its practitioners often care to admit.

Even if we acknowledge that truth seeking is held to be important by many, we must also recognize that it can conflict with other human values. The Galileo/Vatican dispute is one example. A more modern one is the debate over "genetic engineering." As scientists learn more about how to read the genetic codes of our inheritance, the more likely it becomes that people will *apply* that knowledge to manipulate genes. This activity would conflict with the belief that our biological inheritance should not be tampered with by man. In other words, knowledge is not likely to remain long in a vacuum.

Technology is the application of knowledge to the construction of practical products or services designed to achieve human purposes. Truth seeking can lead to products that cause value conflicts.

Nuclear energy is another example. Are we better or worse off because scientists seeking to understand Nature learned some of the secrets of atomic energy? Some people point to nuclear medicine or nuclear power plants as welcome consequences of our basic knowledge of the atom. Others note that nuclear power plants and—especially—nuclear weapons are a threat. Some of these people would prefer to have had scientific investigations of atomic physics suppressed, even at the sacrifice of the value of truth seeking. Most scientists, however, strongly oppose societal intervention in the process of truth seeking, just as most journalists oppose government attempts at "prior restraint" of publication (as in the case of the Pentagon Papers). We are again confronted by a conflict of "ends versus means."

Jacob Bronowski pointed out another dimension to the issue of values and science. Since science is based on the *value* of truth seeking, the society in which scientists work, he argues, must also provide an environment in which free inquiry can proceed. Bronowski is impassioned in his defense of what he calls scientific values, "free inquiry, free thought, free speech, tolerance." Integral to the scientific method are "independence and originality, dissent and freedom and tolerance: such are the first needs of science, and these are the values which, of itself, it demands and forms."[3]

Bronowski did recognize that implicit in these values are conflicts, "a constant tension between dissent and respect; between independence from the views of others and tolerance for them. The crux of the ethical problem is to fuse these, the private and the public needs."[4] Unfortunately, he does not tell us how. Rather, he counsels the scientist, like the proverbial shoemaker, to stick to his last: "but it is not the scientist who can govern society; his duty is to teach it the implications and the values of his work."[5]

In his attempt to keep values apart from truth seeking, Bronowski neglects to mention the scientists' rights as citizens to express their individual opinions on the issues of the day. These opinions are not expert judgments. In medicine, expertise is limited to diagnosis and prognosis. The patient must then decide whether the cure is worse than the disease.

Bronowski depicts scientists almost as if they were a separate thread in the fabric of society:

> Science at last respects the scientist more than his theories: for by its nature it must prize the search above the discovery, and the thinking (and with it the thinker) above the thought. In a society of scientists each man, by the process of exploring for the truth, has earned a dignity more profound than his doctrine.[6]

This statement is itself doctrine. It places a high value on truth seeking that is not shared by the leadership of countries— many of which are Communist—containing literally billions of people.

We are not debating here in any depth the conflict of values between certain Western capitalist and Communist views of society. A brief mention is needed, though, to show how science is part of such conflicts. In the capitalist democracies, individuals' rights to search for "truth" (or for personal gain) are, within the limits of the law, valued as paramount. Marxist or Maoist ideologies, on the other hand, affirm the primary goal of collective gains, even at the expense of individuals' abilities to seek truth or profit. The question of which is "better" involves values.

The emergence of a China relatively free of famine in the three decades after the Long March could be cited as evidence for the need, at some times and places, for strong discipline and a repression of the individual liberties. Bronowski refers to such liberties as "scientific values." During the Chinese "cultural revolution," for example, there are many stories of scientists' taking their turn in rotation with other workers in fields and factories. Indeed, it is widely believed in the West that the inability of Chinese scientists to remain full time in the laboratories in the pursuit of scientific knowledge accounted for a great decline in the scientific progress in China in the 1960s. Interestingly, China has recently backed away from this practice and is moving toward what it calls "modernization." Implicit in this new direction is the elevation of science, technology, and the scientific values that permit individual efforts to seek knowledge. In particular, cultural and scientific exchanges between China and Western countries have expanded dramatically. It will be instructive to observe the extent to which the Chinese social system may be modified along the way.

The example of China allows the criticism that Bronowski's plea for society to uphold scientific values is "politically naive." That is, at some times and in some places, a majority of people may choose collective gains over the maintenance of scientific values—even to the detriment of scientific progress. On the other hand, the support of basic individual rights to "free inquiry, free thought, free speech and tolerance" can be defended on the grounds of values beyond that of scientific progress. In fact, Bronowski, like other scientists writing during the Cold War era, used scientific progress as an argument to bolster support for the value of individual liberties. However, in their zeal to uphold scientific values, writers like Bronowski often overlooked the serious conflicts over values that can emerge from pure adherence to the seeking of truth.

It is difficult in *practice* to separate the uses of knowledge from the decision to pursue scientific inquiry. Modern science, like the speculative sciences, involves issues of human values. However, unlike the speculative sciences, the scientific method prescribes that values cannot be allowed to interfere in either the gathering or the interpretation of data— once a *value decision* has been made to seek knowledge in the first place.

SCIENCE AND SPECULATIVE SCIENCE: HOW DIFFERENT ARE THEIR METHODS?

Let's return to our basic theme from the speculative sciences: that there are cycles in Nature. In a mythological example we've cited, Nature is cyclical because of the common observation that the seasons repeat their overall pattern. Specific observation in this case has led to a more general statement. In the story of Persephone, mythology creates an "explanation" for the seasons. In other words, a quite specific observation of one pattern leads to a general theory offering a specific "explanation." Mythology invents an "explanation" of Nature, often from a specific observation that has been generalized.

Science looks at Nature and also sees that it can be cyclical. It selects one particular, smaller aspect of the natural world to consider and begins tracing that aspect. Like mythology, it then tries to generalize. Later, unlike mythology, science insists on testing that generalization. Water, one of the classical four Elements, is one such traceable aspect. Is water cyclical in Nature? We'll see that it is—with exceptions, though. We'll also see that the other natural elements can be cyclical, again with exceptions. However, only after reexamination of the specific does science offer its "explanations." Even if no experiment has yet been found to prove it wrong, science holds that explanation as *forever* tentative.

We can say that science, as speculative science, conjures up a "rule" for the general from observation of the specific, but science must constantly retest its "rule" on new, refined observations of additional specifics. These two kinds of reasoning are known as *deductive* and *inductive*, deductive reasoning being the prediction of specifics from a general rule, and inductive reasoning being the generalization of specific observations into laws. Which is the approach of the hard sciences? Or the speculative sciences? Actually, both. We will see that in this aspect, the two areas need not differ significantly nor do they need to contradict each other. Rather, it is the insistence on *verification* of these generalizations that most separates hard from speculative sciences.

Indeed, it would be difficult, if not foolish, for us to say that the two fields fundamentally contradict each other, when so much has been said here to show how one grew out of the other, and how they are still interrelated. There are many who would argue that science, as it has developed in our 20th century, has a mythology of its own. Technology, some feel, has created new gods and a new cosmogony. Paul Simon and Art Garfunkel, for instance, popularized this concept in the modern ballad "The Sounds of Silence" with such lines as "And the people bowed and prayed, to the neon gods they made."

One of the great thinkers who has traced the progression from the metaphysical sciences to the hard sciences is Sir James Frazer. His ground-breaking classical study of primitive cultures, *The Golden Bough*, states:

> If we then consider, on the one hand, the essential similarity of man's chief wants everywhere, and at all times, and on the other hand, the wide difference between the means he has adopted to satisfy them in different ages, we shall perhaps be disposed to conclude that the movement of the higher thought, so far as we can trace it, has on the whole been from magic to religion to science. In magic man depends on his own strength to meet the difficulties and dangers that beset him on every side. He believes in a certain established order of nature on which he can surely count. . . . When he discovers his mistake . . . he ceases to rely on his own intelligence and his own unaided efforts, and throws himself humbly on the mercy of certain great invisible beings behind the veil of nature. . . . the more we scrutinize the succession, the more we are struck by the rigid uniformity, the punctual precision. . . . Thus the keener minds, still pressing forward to a deeper solution of the mysteries of the universe, come to reject the religious theory of nature as inadequate, and to revert in a measure to the older standpoint of magic by postulating explicitly, what in magic had only been implicitly assumed, to wit, an inflexible regularity in the order of natural events, which, if carefully observed, enables us to foresee their course with certainty and to act accordingly. In short, religion, regarded as an explanation of nature, is displaced by science.[7]

In other words, myth and science can share a common element: the desire and indeed the need to explain. Where they differ is in their means of explaining, in their methods of analyzing (or, in the case of myth, of not analyzing) the observations; and, of course, they can differ in their results!

Science must test its generalizations deductively, as we have already postulated, and thus, it breaks its analyses down into parts for verification. The Socratic method, which is a questioning technique, may have been an early version of deductive reasoning. The search for refinements, as in the Socratic method, has now been extended into what in modern times is called *reductionism*. The microscope is one of its chief symbols. With a microscope we can examine the head of a pin and discover, surprisingly, that it isn't sharp, but jagged and blunt! Similarly, a newspaper photograph looked at closely reduces to patterns of black and white dots. These patterns are called the resolution of the grain or the maximum level of detail. Science can be seen as the introduction of what Ernest Nagel, a philosopher of science, has called "refinements" into what seem to be ordinary conceptions.[8]

When we return to the comparison between myth and science, the distinction can be explained in yet another way. H. J. Rose, a scholar of mythology, states, "We may then define a myth proper as 'The result of the working of naive imagination upon the facts of experience.' As a large proportion of these facts are natural phenomena, it follows that the nature-myth is a common kind."[9] (To Rose, "imagination" is meant to suggest the mental processes as a whole, rather than merely the powers of invention.) While also offering an explanation for the predominance of nature myths, Rose is here establishing a perceptual difference between mythology and science on the basis of their chosen means of analyzing observations. For example, both mythology and science offer explanations of the natural phenomenon of thunderstorms. One myth tells us that thunderstorms occur because Zeus so wills it. This explanation seems naive to us in light of the "factual" evidence (i.e., refined observations) that science has by now revealed to us. Science, on the other hand, may be thought of as the "skeptical imagination" because it not only observes and generalizes but also tests.

Just as we tend to emphasize the naiveté of mythology,

we tend to deny the imaginative element of science. Science has its creative component also: the interpretation of the evidence amassed in the formulation of a unifying hypothesis is itself a creative act. The evidence available is frequently far less than we need for well-founded theories—as in our inability to explain uncontroversially the causes of cancer. We are certainly familiar with the common dilemma of scientists unable to agree on an interpretation of "facts." Does saccharine cause human cancer, for instance, if large doses lead to tumors in rats? The conclusions of science aren't precise and definite. They are as good as the available observations of Nature and their interpretation by imaginative people. The only constant of science is that most of its theories will fall and its "facts" change.

We are now coming to the actual nature of science. Science is not "exact observation." Exactitude of observation is impossible in Nature. Only increasing precision is attainable. Science can hardly be characterized as merely "knowledge of facts" either. It is the interpretation of reasonably tested theories by frequently repeated observations of increasing precision, always short of exactitude. One could state that a "fact" can begin only after all further investigation ends. Ironically, the judgment that "enough" investigation has been conducted involves values. Science is the *state-of-the-art* of the knowledge of facts, not ultimate truth. (The truth of the previous sentence is certain and, unfortunately, not widely understood.) Ernest Nagel puts it this way:

> It is the desire for explanations which are at once systematic and controllable by factual evidence that generates science; and it is the organization and classification on the basis of explanatory principles that is the distinctive goal of the sciences.[10]

Science—and perhaps much of mythology—is motivated

by the desire for explanations. But the explanations themselves are their chief differences. As we have already stated, science progresses by a continual series of critiques. One more observation can lead to a new series of tests, and an entirely new statement of findings often follows. Unfortunately, we have come to equate the term *science* with *absolute* precision and accuracy. When we try to be "scientific," we often mean "certain" in our knowledge, but we fail to realize that the scientific attitude of skepticism applies to science itself. Consider a contemporary example. We are out for a drive and are not quite sure where we are. A small debate breaks out. Finally, someone in the car says, "Stop guessing and let's be scientific. Get out the map."

"Let's be scientific" equals "Let's be exact." Even though our dictionary definition encourages this equation, we've seen now that this is not actually what *scientific* means. Our carload of travelers have not been wholly "scientific" in their approach if they believe the accuracy of the map to be incontrovertible. Furthermore, if the place they are looking for is a small town, it might not even be on the first map they consult. In that case, they would need a more detailed map. To put it in scientific terms, they need a more precise empirical basis (i.e., a very detailed map drawn from refined observations) to test their respective theories of where they are. Having found the town on this second, more detailed map, can they be sure that the map is drawn to scale? The distance and location can be assumed as only approximate. Yet, is approximate good enough?

What we are doing by consulting the map is extending our own powers of observation by checking the prior refined observations of the mapmakers. Precision itself is relative. The maps don't prove anything with certainty; they merely narrow the uncertainty as to the location of the town. The map itself is questionable. It is contingent upon how much we trust the observations of the cartographers or the reproductions of the draftsmen, both of whom were involved in the production of the maps. Similarly, science is a continuing series of refinements. It is actually a never-ending series of observations designed to test *current* hypotheses and refine current theories from the existing data pool of information.

We questioned the precision of the map by asking, "Is it good enough?" We didn't refine our question to its important, deeper issue: "good enough" for what? A purpose, a value, is implicit when asking if something is "good enough." For us, merely traveling as tourists in no particular hurry, even a sloppy map would probably do. But for the real estate developer whose eyes are on two specific acres of land, nothing less than the precision of an official survey would suffice. In each case, the *purpose* defines what degree of precision is necessary.

Let's take another example. Probably, most of us have thought it certain that a piece of steel is solid. We could make a "scientific" test, for example, and show it to be watertight. Steel also feels and looks solid. If you poke it with a pin, the point blunts. Water cannot flow through it. These observations seem to prove "scientifically" that steel is solid. However, as science developed more "extended eyes," it learned that a piece of steel is 99.999...% empty space! Steel is made up of trillions upon trillions of tiny atoms in a widely spaced lattice. Its seeming impenetrability comes from the electromagnetic forces exerted among the atoms. Of course, it is not all impenetrable to certain things, such as strong X rays. Thus, the knowledge "necessary" to describe steel is relative, as with the travelers' map. The atomic microdescription may be necessary for molecular physicists who are trying to understand the structure of matter or for the X-ray machine designers of medical instrument companies. However, it is wholly unnecessary for the civil engineer building a bridge, for whom observations of the macrostructure of steel (e.g., an empirical knowledge of the steel's bulk strength) is more than sufficient. The level of microcomplexity understood—or needed—depends, in part, on the required degree of accuracy and the resolution of our observing instruments. We have said "required" accuracy, for this assumes a purpose, which again assumes a value. In the case of the civil engineer, the purpose may be the ability of the steel-constructed bridge to withstand winds of up to, say, 200 miles per hour. Having ascertained that a certain steel product will fit this bill, the designer need not be concerned with the microlevels or the molecular structure of the steel. Here, too, the "level of description" of what is being studied is relative to our needs. There may always be a level of knowledge more refined than the one that we are seeking. That level could be at either a micro or a macro stratum. For example, before earth satellites could look down on the earth as a whole, we didn't know very well how brightly our planet shines in space—an important factor to our climate, but not very relevant to the forecast of frost tonight. Of course, our need may simply be to understand all we can about our phenomenon, in which case we would study it at many levels of description.

In *The Structure of Science*, Ernest Nagel notes that the difference between common knowledge and scientific knowledge is also a question of degree. He makes a comparison between scientific knowledge and the handling of firearms:

> Most men would qualify as expert shots if the standard of expertness were the ability to hit the side of a barn from a distance of a hundred feet. But only a much smaller number of individuals could meet the more rigorous requirement of consistently centering their shots

upon a three-inch target at twice that distance. Similarly,
a prediction that the sun will be eclipsed during the autumn months is more likely to be fulfilled than a prediction that the eclipse will occur at a specific moment
on a given day in the fall of the year.[11]

An aspect of scientific striving for refinement that Nagel
doesn't mention here is that although our specialist (scientist-
by-analogy) marksman can repeatedly hit a small target on
the side of the barn, he doesn't often notice, or can't tell
through his telescopic sight, that the target is even on the
side of the barn! This stereotypical, narrow perspective of
scientific reductionists has led to some disenchantment with
science. It is often expressed by humanists or interdiscipli-
narians who value "holistic" approaches to explain Nature.[12]

The "best" level of description explains most aspects of
Nature, possibly changing as new observations or theoretical
interpretations become available. Many examples are evident
in which different levels of description compete to explain or
predict something, as, for example, the climate. It can be
viewed as the long-term average of individual weather
events. One could say that the whole (the climate) is the sum
of its parts (individual weather events). Alternatively, one
could view the local details of the weather as a consequence
of large-scale, long-term climatic conditions. In other words,
the parts must fit into an overall large-scale pattern. Some
have worded these two approaches as "top down" or "bottom up." In fact, meteorologists and climatologists argue
heatedly about the relative merits of these alternative views
of the structure of the climate. As new information changes
the details of these debates, both sides are searching for what
is often called a *unifying theory*. The ultimate satisfaction in
scientific research is the formulation of a unifying concept

that reconciles the contradictions or open questions apparent when some phenomena are viewed at different levels. (Similar satisfaction can be found in a good detective story, when a new theory emerges that not only explains the mystery but also puts contradictory or partial theories in perspective.)

Science is not the only field that argues over the relative merits of alternative descriptions of some issue. Even poetry is divided into similar rival schools of thought. One is called *structuralism*. Structuralists attempt to discover the system of conventions that enables a poem to exist as a poem.[13] Within this school is a group that examines poems quantitatively. For example, they might count the number or kinds of images used or even the number of trisyllabic words within a poem or throughout a body of poetry. Other schools believe that such a purely structuralist approach misses the purpose of poetry, which can be found only by viewing and *interpreting* as a whole. Like their scientific counterparts, those studying poetry are in a constant search for evidence to refine existing concepts.

Although recently we seem to have been harping on the limits of science, we have also been evolving a more realistic definition of science than is popularly conceived. When now asked, "What is science?" we should be able to answer: Science is the process of investigation built on the scientific method. It builds on increasingly careful observation of the natural world, the formation of hypotheses, and the testing of these theories. It is the continuing search for unifying concepts to explain the variety of experience. It is not absolute; it is not exact. Mathematics, with its rigorous logical structure, can appropriately talk of exactitude. So can religion, at least in the sense that a leap of faith does not call for proof. These fields transcend the always-inexact empirical world for a logical or postulated realm where certainty is possible. Yet science, even given its limitations, certainly does lead to a deeper knowledge of the mysteries of the universe.

Thus, science spurs a way of thinking. This way of thinking is actually the way in which scientists analyze their observations. We know it as the *scientific method*. Many of us, perhaps unwittingly, use this approach. Sometimes more of us should.

THE SCIENTIFIC METHOD (DID THE FIRST "SCIENTISTS" USE IT?)

Our dictionary definition of *science*, despite its misplaced emphasis on exactitude, begins to suggest the scientific method of obtaining knowledge, which is "gained and verified by exact observation, organized experiment, and ordered thinking." (However, we recall, as repeatedly stated earlier, that *no* experiment in our empirical world can be "exact," and that only relatively increasing precision can be attained.)

The scientific method has already been described in the preceding section, even though we are only now referring to it in more precise terms. In essence, the scientific method consists of these continuously recycling steps:

1. The observation of nature (once a decision is made about what to look at).
2. The formulation of hypotheses or theories (often called *natural laws*) that attempt to "explain" or unify a variety of observed behavior in nature.
3. The testing of current theories on repeated, different, or refined sets of observational data.

The step from process 1 to process 2 is primarily an act of "inductive reasoning." That is, as defined earlier, we induce *general* laws from observation of two or more *specific* phenomena. Then comes the testing of *current* hypotheses against expanded evidence, which is step 3. This process is the reverse of the first, for we use "deductive reasoning" to predict, usually from an inductively derived law, the behavior of an unobserved specific phenomena. Part of this process entails designing an experiment to observe that "unobserved" phenomenon to see if our theory has correctly predicted its behavior. If our experiment "fails" (doesn't prove the theory to be valid), then we must formulate a new theory, which we subsequently test in the same way. If, on the other hand, our experiment is "successful"—that is, our theory has correctly predicted the behavior of some phenomenon—we *do not* claim the theory as certain but only as more likely to be true. The process is not finished yet, for we now must devise more stringent tests to increase further our confidence in our theory.

Let's take a case in point. We begin with an observation: the sun rises and the day gets warmer. Now we can be creative and formulate hypotheses to connect (or unify) these diverse phenomena: (1) the sun has caused the warming, or (2) the warming has caused the sun to rise, or (3) they are unrelated or coincidental events. We need more observations or tests of all these theories to determine which, if any, is valid. We have noticed, for example, that snow melts when exposed to the sun and not in the shade, even though the general air temperature is the same. We can therefore conclude that the sun does provide warmth. What we've done here is make a prediction (that the sun is warm) and look for supporting evidence (that the exposed snow melts). We'd follow the same procedure for the testing of each hypothesis.

Let's look at an example of how all of us might use the scientific method, consciously or not, in our daily lives. Suppose we meet a friendly fellow on an airplane trip and discover that he is from New York. This "discovery" is, of course, merely an empirical observation. We could, for example, have read his address from the tag on his hand luggage, or we could have heard it from his conversation. For the sake of this example, we'll assume that our observations are correct. This need not be the case, though: we could have heard him incorrectly, or he could be from Cleveland and traveling with luggage borrowed from a friend in New York. In well-conceived scientific experiments, great care is taken to be sure that observations (and thus the subsequent hypotheses) are not faulty at the outset. But back to our friend on the plane. After further observations—in this case, conversations—we find that he is a cab driver. Knowing no other New Yorkers, we can use inductive reasoning to arrive at a tentative, but more general, theory: All New Yorkers are cab drivers! Of course we "know" that all the people in one town can't be cab drivers, so we suspect (yet another deduction) that we'd best refine our observations to test this theory. We begin a new experiment. This is our deductive step. We ask another New Yorker sitting beside our cab driver what he does, and again we assume that the answer is accurate. (Does he really tell the truth, though, and do we hear the answer correctly?) As it turns out, he is not a cab driver, and we reject our first inductive theory on the basis of this new evidence. Since our theory predicted that the second New Yorker would be a cab driver, and refined observations show that he is not, then our theory must be in error. Our second New Yorker, it turns out, is a bus driver—information that can be added to earlier observations in the forming of a new hypothesis. Through the use of inductive reasoning, the following new hypothesis is formed: All New Yorkers are professional drivers. On the basis of evidence gathered so far, we could also conclude—quite logically—that all New Yorkers are men or that all New Yorkers ride on airplanes, and so on.

The scientific method, like the arts, searches for unifying principles. Unlike mythology and most other speculative sciences, though, science demands deductive tests of our current hypotheses. We next ask our stewardess about herself, and she too turns out to be a New Yorker. So much for our inductive theories that all New Yorkers are professional drivers or men. However, they still might all ride on airplanes.

Our main point should be evident by now. The "laws of Nature," as we perceive them, are merely our current best hypotheses to explain or unify diverse observed phenomena: Any such theory is "accepted" as likely to be true, not by a definitive experiment, but, rather, by a *value judgment* that "enough" evidence has been marshaled for us to be "reasonably certain" that our "laws" are, in fact, laws. (Our example also shows how easily, and dangerously, false conclusions or prejudice can develop from limited personal experience.) Every time we harbor a pet theory, we should remember the warning of a great scientist: only one experiment is necessary to prove that theory wrong. It is easy to see why scientists have been referred to as "professional skeptics."[14]

Our lengthy definitions of science and the scientific method have taken us away from our earlier discussion of the four elements. Now we will be able to look at the extent to which these first "scientists," while examining structures of Nature, really used the scientific method in their inquiries.

For 2000 years, the theory of the four elements—air, earth, water and fire—was widely accepted by the best minds of the day. A Sicilian, Empedocles of Arigentum (ca. 492–430

B.C.), believed these elements to be the basic building blocks of the universe, and a host of variants of his theory were offered in subsequent years, as we've already seen. A good discussion of the rival climatic theories of these early philosophers is given by H. Frisinger in *The History of Meteorology: To 1800*:

> Applying his four-element concept of the universe, Empedocles attempted to employ the opposition of fire and water to explain the cause of the different climates—summer and winter. The basic elements of fire and water continually opposed each other in the atmosphere. When the hot, dry fire gained the upper hand, summer resulted; when the wet, cold water gained mastery, winter resulted. That these two basic elements moved about in a random manner did not explain why the seasons of summer and winter were so regular in their occurrence.[15]

Among the important philosophers who "explained" Nature with variants of the four-element theory, Aristotle (384–322 B.C.) stands out as the most important. His treatise *Meteorologica* stood for millennia as the authoritative work on the subject. We will examine a few examples of his philosophy of Nature (we won't call it *science* for reasons that you will soon see) and look to see the extent to which Aristotle used the scientific method in this "scientific" work.

His arguments in *Meteorologica* rest on two principal assumptions:

1. All the heavenly bodies—moon, planets, stars—move about in concentric spheres with the earth at the center.
2. The inner or terrestrial region of these spheres (which, incidentally, includes the moon) consists, as Frisinger

relates:

> . . . of four elements—earth, water, air, and fire—arranged in concentric spherical strata with the earth at the center. This stratification, however, was not rigid. Dry land arose above water, and fire often burned on the earth. Also, all elements were thought to be in constant processes of interchange, one into the other. When the heat of the sun reached the earth's surface, it mixed with the cold and moist water to form a new substance, warm and moist, essentially like air. The sun's heat similarly acted upon the cold and dry earth to produce another substance, warm and dry, essentially like fire.[16]

Thus, it seems that Aristotle stressed the two elements air and fire, making them strata in the atmosphere. But the differences between fire and air led him to theorize that there was another stratum, the stratum in which clouds formed. Aristotle rightly observed that the atmosphere contained clouds. However, clouds could not form very high up in the atmosphere, he believed, because that air contained fire and celestial motion. On the other hand, they could not form very close to the earth either, because of reflected heat from the surface. Therefore, he decided, there must be a stratum between the height of the mountain ranges and the earth's surface in which the formation of such clouds was possible.

One wonders how Aristotle could possibly have *verified* his very imaginative theories, given his inability to measure Nature directly or indirectly in those remote cloud-forming regions. How, then, could he appropriately use the deductive step of hypothesis testing that is at the core of the scientific method?

In order to examine his approach, we need to quote a primary source, Aristotle himself. Look at the following pas-

sage on his theory of compound bodies and then try to reconcile how consistently it appears to hold to the scientific
method. We, not Aristotle, are responsible for the italicized
words:

> *All* the compound bodies—all of which exist in the
> region belonging to the central body—are composed of
> *all* the "simple" bodies. For they *all* contain Earth be-
> cause *every* "simple" body *is* to be found specially and
> most abundantly in its own place. And they *all* contain
> Water because (a) The compound *must* possess a definite
> outline and Water, *alone* of the "simple" bodies, *is* readily
> adaptable in shape: moreover (b) Earth has *no* power of
> cohesion without the moist. On the contrary, the moist
> *is* what holds it together; for it *would* fall to pieces if the
> moist were eliminated from it completely.[17]

This passage is a highly imaginative collection of available
observations transposed into theories of Nature. However,
we now know (better to say "believe") that much, if not most,
of his scientific theories is speculation, but that is not our
primary concern. It is easy, with the hindsight of modern
technology, to accuse Aristotle of "speculation of the most
absurd sort." He cannot be much blamed for failing to provide
verification of his theories since such verification was beyond
the capability of his times. But largely absent in this passage
is a fundamental component of the scientific method: doubt—
at least, for his own theories. Our italicized words are *all*,
every, *is*, *must*, etc. Where are the qualifiers that must—and
we do mean *must*—attend the untested theories of limited
observations? Where are the words *some*, *could be*, *might*, and
so forth? Where are the suggestions for new experiments to
verify these theories? At least, where are the apologies for
those untested elements of theory, or—in those days—un-
testable elements? How could Aristotle, then, so decisively

attack his fellow philosophers' theories when the lack of verification left all of them in much the same vessel, the ship of speculation. For example, in *Meteorologica*, Aristotle discussed the formation of precipitation, particularly hail, and "dissected" a rival (who, *by accident*, turned out to be more accurate than Aristotle):

> Now we know that hot and cold have a mutual reaction on one another (which is the reason why subterranean places are cold in hot weather and warm in frosty weather). This reaction we must suppose takes place in the upper region, so that in warmer seasons the cold is concentrated within the surrounding heat. This sometimes causes a rapid formation of water from cloud. And for this reason you get larger raindrops on warm days than in winter and more violent rainfall—rainfall is said to be more violent when it is heavier, and a heavier rainfall is caused by rapidity of condensation. (The process is just the opposite of what Anaxagoras says it is: He says it takes place when clouds rise into the cold air: we say it takes place when clouds descend into the warm air and is most violent when the cloud descends farthest.) Sometimes, on the other hand, the cold is even more concentrated within by the heat outside it, and freezes the water which it has produced, so forming hail. This happens when the water freezes before it has time to fall. For if it takes a given time to fall, but the cold being freezes it in a lesser time, there is nothing to prevent it freezing in the air, if the time taken to freeze it is shorter than the time of its fall. The nearer the earth and the more intense the freezing, the more violent the rainfall and the larger the drops or the hailstones because of the shortness of their fall. For the same reason large raindrops do not fall thickly. Hail is rarer in the summer than in spring or autumn, though commoner than in winter, because in summer the air is drier: but in spring it is still moist, in autumn it is beginning to become so.

For the same reason hailstones do sometimes occur in late summer, as we have said. If the water has been previously heated, this contributes to the rapidity with which it freezes: for it cools more quickly. (Thus so many people when they want to cool water quickly first stand it in the sun: and the inhabitants of Pontus when they encamp on the ice to fish—they catch fish through a hole which they make in the ice—pour hot water on their rods because it freezes quickest, using the ice like solder to fix their rods.) And water that condenses in the air in warm districts and seasons gets hot quickly.[18]

Frisinger notes that this passage is indicative of Aristotle's common manner of discussion. He usually begins by presenting, and then refuting, the theories of others, all by way of introducing his own theories. Here he criticized the concepts of Anaxagoras without admitting that they were based largely on observation (that is, they were inductive). Aristotle, on the other hand, was frequently influenced by societal preconceptions (if not misconceptions) and sometimes "found" his "evidence" to support these theories. It is questionable to what extent these ideas were based on observations of weather.

Aristotle, we can say, was a deductive thinker. That is, his theories predicted specific phenomena. For example, he says, "a heavier rainfall is caused by rapidity of condensation." However, his discussion lacks a hypothesis-testing step to verify this prediction from his theory. Aristotle would not have easily been able to know that heavy rainfall depends upon a complex mixture of factors. These range from the obvious need for the presence of much moisture, to the less obvious modern finding that the right kind and number of dust particles must also be present. Lastly, a vertical temperature structure of the atmosphere conducive to tall cloud formation—the kinds of clouds that typically have the heaviest rainfalls—needs also to be present. Even today, our theories of the nature of precipitation are uncomfortably tentative, for the potential role of factors such as atmospheric electricity or man-made pollutants remains controversial (primarily because of a lack of sufficient observational or experimental evidence).

Later, we will see what modern science has added to the hypotheses of the speculative sciences about cyclical structures in Nature, but first, we have an immediate observation to make: Aristotle could not possibly have gone very far toward verification of his theories because he lacked the means to make the appropriate measurements. A hard, if somewhat frustrating, fact of life for most scientists is the realization that acceptance or rejection of their theories of Nature may well be forestalled for years, often beyond even their lifetime. This frustration reserved for scientists takes on the societal proportions of a crisis when the knowledge sought is vital to human affairs, yet it cannot be obtained when or before it is needed. At the present time, we are grappling with the issue of whether air pollution causes lung cancer—just such a societal question. The verification of such a theory may well come only after many have suffered. Yet, should we offer no theories of Nature if we cannot provide "reasonable" assurance that they are correct? Was Aristotle guilty of offering a theory prematurely? These are, of course, value issues. Nevertheless, we believe that verification cannot easily precede a theory. The mere offering of the theories themselves is not necessarily dangerous. They become dangerous only if they are prematurely accepted. Rather, we must be careful to qualify their likelihood of truth and what we can or can't do to refine them. Aristotle was as entitled to his theories of

Nature as any modern physician is to his/her theories of cancer. Neither, however, is allowed by the scientific method to state them as absolutely as Aristotle did in *Meteorologica*.

We must learn to live with uncertainty, even on life-and-death matters. We can best accomplish this through a realistic appraisal of what is reasonably well known, unknown, and, within a particular time frame, unknowable. How, then to act on this information is a personal value choice based on the relative weights of risks and benefits of various actions based on available knowledge. Later on, we'll see how dire such issues can be. Returning to our major theme, that Nature is structured in cycles, we must ask next whether the thousands of years of transcultural expressions of cycles in the speculative sciences have been overthrown by modern science, now that we have some idea, at least, of what science really is.

"We may find ourselves and all other living things to be parts and partners of a vast being who in her entirety has the power to maintain our planet as a fit and comfortable habitat for life."
—JAMES E. LOVELOCK

Chapter 7 / THE GLOBAL CYCLES OF LIFE

In our discussion of the humanities, we were not only looking for expressions of man's relationship with Nature but also seeking unity in variety. Cycles have provided unifying links, within the humanities, between the various art forms, and across seemingly disparate cultures. Our search for unity in variety continues within the realm of hard science. Cycles here link the elements themselves.

THE CLASSICAL FOUR ELEMENTS

The Four Elements—Earth, Air, Water, and Fire—have their own cycles; modern science calls them the *sedimentary*

177

cycle and the *hydrological cycle*. All these cycles can be viewed as part of a set of larger cycles, which we call the *global cycles of life*. Within this more important context, we'll be looking at the cycles of carbon, nitrogen, phosphorus, and sulfur. In all these areas, we'll be comparing what the humanists felt to be true with what science is proving to be true.

Can the cyclical theme so evident in the humanities survive the penetrating analyses of modern science? Once again, we'll look backward to move forward, drawing first on a principal philosophic belief that stood for more than two millennia after the Greeks: the theory of the Four Elements. What modern science has revealed about these Elements will plunge us into new depths of man's relationship with Nature. Now our primary question is: What is the current scientific understanding of Earth, Air, Water, and Fire? Does this understanding sustain or contradict the almost timeless belief that Nature is structured in cycles?

EARTH

Science starts with specifics. We began our discussion of science with its definition. Now, once again, we have to be sure of the meanings of the other terms we use.

We have already learned that while science cannot provide exactitude, it attempts to find a continuous series of reductions. Early Greek philosophers divided the world into four Elements, thinking that these Elements were the foundations of all Nature. This was certainly a reduction into component parts. However, the scientific method allows for a constant search for the rarification of already existing reductions. We, with modern science, will now further reduce the Greek reductions.

When we refer to the planet Earth, we are including

everything on our celestial sphere.* This includes air, ice, oceans, life, and the minerals of the earth's crust. The early Greeks, though, did not use the element Earth to embody this all-encompassing form. (We remember, for example, the disparate personifications of all these components that Hesiod offered in his *Theogony*.) The solid component of the planet's upper part, the earth's crust, is probably closer to what the Greek philosophers really meant by the element *Earth*. Given that there are at least two possible meanings for the term *Earth*, why not examine them both to see what modern science has shown us about Earth, either as a whole planet or as simply its crust.

The Greeks were on the right track. Perhaps that is why science has adapted some of the Greek terminology. When modern scientists examined what the ancient Greeks called *Earth* they revealed that it is not really one "Element." Rather, the earth is itself made up of various combinations or chemical compounds of what we have also called *elements* (without the capital *E*). Whereas the Greeks reduced Nature to 4 Elements, modern science has shown that there are 92 (known) natural elements and (at the moment) about 10 man-made chemical elements. Among these elements are such familiar elements as hydrogen, carbon, oxygen, nitrogen, iron, and sulfur, and such less familiar ones as selenium, phosphorus, uranium, and americium. Whereas the Greek mythographers may have deified each element, giving it a personality of its own, modern science has confined its symbolic representations to mere letters, that is (following our list above), H, C, O, N, Fe, S, Se, P, U, and Am. But even this is not the end of the reduction. Each of these elements is then comprised of a different

---

*Actually, the earth is a slightly flattened sphere called an *oblate spheroid*, which bulges in the middle (i.e., equator).

number of "fundamental" atomic particles. These are called *protons, electrons,* and *neutrons.* Each element is also assigned a number—its *atomic number*—depending on how many protons each of its atoms contains. Hydrogen, the lightest element, has 1 proton, and uranium, the heaviest known *natural* element, has 92 protons per atom. And atomic particles seem to contain such "subatomic" particles as *muons, neutrinos,* and *quarks.* Although modern science has only penetrated to this level of microreduction, we do have massive observational confirmation of the relative proportions of each chemical element that comprises the earth.

Returning to what scientists would call the *macro* level, or complete Earth, we see that scientific progress has been made here as well. We can apply the modern elemental theory to the ancient Element Earth, both as a planet and as its crust. The planet Earth is comprised of the following amounts[1] of natural chemical elements (in percentage by weight): iron, 34.6%; oxygen, 29.5%; silicon, 15.2%; magnesium, 12.7%; nickel, 2.4%; sulfur, 1.9%; calcium, 1.1%; aluminum, 1.1%; sodium, 0.57%; chromium, 0.26%; and others of less than a few tenths of a percent each. Earth's crust, the solids of which are what the ancient Greeks apparently took to be the Element Earth, has the following average composition: oxygen, 45.2%; silicon, 27.2%; aluminum, 8.0%; iron, 5.8%; calcium, 5.1%; magnesium, 2.8%; sodium, 2.3%; potassium, 1.7%; titanium, 0.9%; hydrogen, 0.14%; and others of trace abundance. Of course, the Greeks didn't understand all this. Nor did they realize that their "Element Earth" was itself made up of a percentage of each of the 92 natural elements. However, they did hypothesize that each of their four Elements could combine to form mixtures. Similarly, our elements can combine. For example, pure water is a chemical compound whose molecules are made up of two atoms of hydrogen and one of oxygen. The chemical symbol for water is H_2O, such a commonplace term that many people use it conversationally instead of the name *water*.

We can see now that Earth is a much more complex "Element" than the ancient Greeks realized. But how does this new (actually 19th-century) knowledge relate to our cyclical theme? The answer involves a complicated analysis, and we'll restrict ourselves now to the cyclical characteristics of the earth's crust. Our individual human senses and experience would seem to say that the earth's crust doesn't function cyclically. After all, the seas, continents, and mountains have remained, for the most part, as they are today throughout all human experience. If they are as immutable as they seem to our senses, then Earth cannot be seen to be an Element fully able to recycle. We have already said, though, that modern science has been able to extend our senses, to allow us to see and explore the natural world beyond the superficial level. And modern science—in contradiction to what a sensory impression will tell us—does provide abundant evidence that Earth is cyclical. Some specific examples will show why modern scientific findings support this long-lived, transcultural concept.

THE CONTINENTAL DRIFT THEORY. Geology, a science of the earth, has dug deep into our planet to discover that its layers have a variety of different characteristics. The outermost, the earth's crust, ranges in thickness from a few miles below the ocean floor (itself a few miles deep on the average) to as much as 50 miles below the largest mountain ranges. Below the crust is a denser layer known as the *upper mantle*. In essence, the crust floats on the mantle, and the continents and the sea floor can actually rock up and down. This can happen as ice forms or melts from one ice age to the next, as a consequence of the immense weight of the massive ice sheets. When they melt, the land masses "spring" upward as they are freed from the heavy ice. However, such movement is usually* an extremely slow process, operating on a time scale of hundreds to thousands of years—too long for any generation of humans to see with their own eyes. Below the mantle is the earth's core. At its molten center of liquid iron and nickel, it has a temperature of several thousand degrees, quite a contrast to the upper crust, where ice can exist.[2]

The upper crust, including the continents and the ocean basin, is today believed to consist of some half dozen "plates." These are huge continent-sized blocks floating on the earth's mantle and moving horizontally at a slower-than-a-snail's pace of a few centimeters per year. (An inch is equivalent to 2.5 centimeters.) Once again, such movements are beyond our unaided sensory perception—but not beyond our precision instruments. Even at this rate, these motions, over hundreds of millions of years, inexorably result in continental drifts of tens of thousands of miles.

(Recall that Aristotle had recounted Thales' belief in Water as the primary Element: "he [Thales] declared that the Earth rests on water." Interestingly, although neither Thales nor Aristotle could possibly have known about the great continental plates that float [albeit, not exactly on water] on the earth's mantle, it is true that Thales' speculation that "the Earth rests on water" is not entirely rejected by modern scientific findings.)

---

*In some places it is very rapid. In Hudson Bay, a mark near sea level made on a rock by the Henry Hudson expedition several hundred years ago is now tens of feet above today's sea level. This is because the land there is still rebounding from the breakup of a mile-high ice sheet from the last ice age 10,000 years ago.

Those geologists who accept this "theory of continental drift"—and they comprise the vast bulk of today's scientists—have deduced that the boundaries of the great plates should be regions of intense stress, since the plates either pull apart or bump together at their boundaries. Indeed they are. The stress manifests itself in the form of earthquake activity, which is abundant at the interfaces of the plates. One renowned example is the meeting place of the American and Pacific plates. It stretches from Alaska down the California coast through Mexico to Central America and, ultimately, to the west coast of South America. Just east of San Francisco on the American plate lies Mount Diablo. Precision instruments have shown that it is moving several centimeters a year relative to Mount Tamalpais, its neighbor a few miles to the west on the edge of the Pacific plate. The resulting stress occurring along fault lines like the San Andreas is believed to be responsible for earthquakes like the one that destroyed San Francisco in 1906. The stress is rebuilding once again.

THE SEDIMENTARY CYCLE. Clearly, then, the earth does move, even though its noticeable displacements largely follow time scales many times greater than the life spans of humans. However, any motion is not necessarily cyclical motion. We have now gone beyond the limited knowledge possible through the sole use of our unaided senses, the kind of knowledge presented in early Greek philosophy.

Modern science has shown that two processes dominate the evolution of physical changes on earth: (1) the physical transport of materials and (2) the chemical transformation of elements and compounds. Evaporation and precipitation are two major natural processes that transport materials of earth. Other forces involved in this movement are flows of rivers,

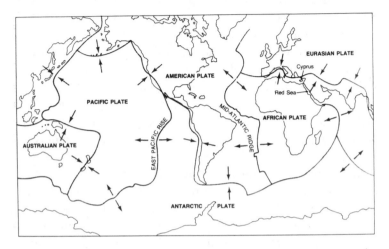

FIGURE 7-1. This map shows the six principal "plates" comprising most of the earth's surface. These move slowly, at a few centimeters per year, at least according to the continental drift theory. The arrows show the relative motions of these plates at their boundaries. Note that at the West Coast of the United States, the American and Pacific plates are moving in opposition to each other. Many scientists believe that this friction leads to the high frequency of earthquakes along plate boundaries, where plates collide.

Where plates contact, one edge of a plate can be "driven" under another, thereby burying crustal materials into lower layers of the earth's interior. At this juncture, the plate is recycled into the material below the crust. On the other hand, note the mid-Atlantic ridge, along which the American and African plates are pulling apart. At this boundary, crustal material is being formed as magma (lava) rises from lower layers of the earth's interior. Thus, crustal material is recycling slowly, being buried in the earth's interior at some plate boundaries and upwelling from the interior to form new crust at the gaps created where plates pull apart from each other. This scientific finding confirms the existence of cycles in the life history of the earth's crust *(From P. R. Ehrlich, A. H. Ehrlich, and J. P. Holdren, Ecoscience: Population, Resources, Environment, W. H. Freeman, San Francisco, 1977, p. 18).*

groundwater, and ice; winds; ocean currents; volcanic activity; continental plate movements; and even the travels of organisms.

We often see these processes at work, although we may be unaware of them. An example from common experience is rainwater, which plays a major role in a cycle of Earth. Rainwater falls through the atmosphere. While falling, it picks up some of the carbon dioxide (CO_2) in the air and mixes it with its own chemical compounds, thereby forming weak carbonic acid. This acidity is enough to slowly dissolve a number of chemical compounds in exposed rocks, a process commonly known as *weathering*. Limestone is a rock that falls victim to this weathering process because it contains a carbon compound called *carbonate*, which is one of the major minerals dissolved by weathering. Weathering is one of the most important examples of transport and transformation. The dissolved minerals then flow through streams, rivers, or groundwaters to the sea. (Groundwaters are trapped in underground reservoirs or flow in underground streams. For a well to work, it must be dug to the level of the groundwater.)

Weathering is just one form of erosion. When a river's flow is driven by rain that washes soil and other particles of "Earth" into the streams, the river carries these particles and dissolved minerals toward the sea. In the process, rivers carrying large quantities of such minerals usually look muddy. The mighty Mississippi, which could be interpreted as one of T. S. Eliot's "strong brown gods," is brown only because the river is transporting particles of Earth that obscure the clarity of the water. Likewise, trout fishermen know that after heavy rainstorms, the fishing deteriorates because the stream muddies and the fish can't see the lure as easily. Of course, the streams feed the rivers, and ultimately, the rivers carry some of their cargo to the oceans. There, the trapped soil particles or weathered minerals enter the next phase of their sedimentary cycle. Here the weathering process is reversed. These particles or minerals no longer dissolve but fall to the bottom to form sea sediments (i.e., seafloor mud).* The cycle is now half complete (i.e., land minerals have been transformed and transported to sea sediments). But before we complete the cycle by bringing the sea sediments back to the land again, we need to point out an important thing that happens along the way.

A number of chemical elements and compounds of Earth essential to life, called *nutrients*, are captured from the water by living organisms. These nutrients are necessary for the organisms' life processes. It is remarkable that the Element Earth not only interacts with other Elements (e.g., Water) but is also part of the life process!

Meanwhile, the weathering of continents and sedimentation in the oceans ends up in a cycle. Geologic evidence has proved that cycles exist. Figure 7-2 shows part of the sedimentary geologic cycles. Rocks weather into soils and sediments. The slow process of chemical transformation and physical movement, typically taking over tens of hundreds of millions of years, wears them down and carries the materials to the sea, as we have shown. Contrary to what we might assume, the weathered elements or particles of earth that fall to the bottom of the sea as sediments are *not* lost forever. Rather, the sea floor spreads outward and eventually may resurface as mountain ranges, as seen in Figure 7-3. The ocean floor is part of the continental plate system and moves like other plates across the earth's surface. The sea floor in the middle of the Atlantic Ocean, for example, is spreading apart along a great crack called a *rift*.

---

*The sediments also contain the remains of a continuous "rain" of dead organisms that settle to the bottom after their deaths.

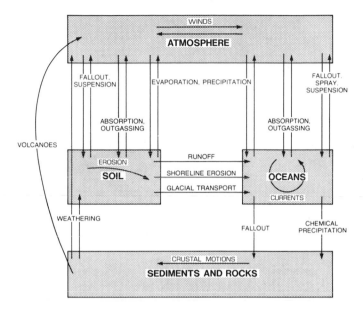

FIGURE 7-2. The arrows show how materials are transported among the major "compartments" of the physical world. The weather creates winds, precipitation, and runoff, which carry materials from the land to the sea. These "weathered" substances can be chemically transformed or may just fall to the ocean floor to form oceanic sediments. Under intense pressures, these sediments can be transformed to rocks. As the continental plates move, sediments buried at least tens of millions of years ago can rise to create new land forms. These, in turn, become subjected to weathering and erosion, eventually forming the next cycle of oceanic sediments. The combination of chemical transformation and transport, along with the crustal motions of drifting continents, forms the sedimentary cycles. Although the speed of this process seems imperceptible compared with the life span of a human, the recycling of the earth's surface materials through the sedimentary cycle is a further demonstration of the universality of the concept that Nature is structured in cycles (Ehrlich, Ehrlich, and Holdren, p. 69).

FIGURE 7-3. (A) The view is of the Pacific Ocean at the California coast, some hundred miles north of San Francisco. The circular-shaped patch of light-colored water in the center of the picture is actually the muddy runoff from the rain-swollen Russian River as it empties into the relatively clear Pacific Ocean waters. The heavy rains, combined with agricultural practices that expose large areas of land to water erosion, lead to a flow of "Earth" out to sea. Eventually, these eroded materials fall to the bottom to make ocean sediments. Tens to hundreds of millions of years later, as the continents move, oceanic sediments can rise to form new land. When the land is uplifted and tilted, mountains can form from what was, previously, ocean bottom. And this, in turn, may once have been eroded land a "generation" older. (B) A view of the Flatirons, which are found where the Great Plains meet the Rocky Mountains at Boulder, Colorado. These foothills are formations made from uplifted ocean sediments laid down hundreds of millions of years ago when shallow seas covered what is now the more-than-mile-high eastern slopes of the Rocky Mountains *(Photos by Stephen H. Schneider).*

There is, then, considerable scientific evidence that Earth recycles. To cite yet another case from common experience, highways have been built that cut through sedimentary rocks. These rocks are often the petrified remains of sea sediments hundreds of millions of years old. Their layers are often visible evidence of the sedimentary cycle. These rocks are being eroded today, and some of their materials are being transformed and transported to the sea. To complete the cycle, some of the new sea sediments formed from their debris are spreading outward and will rise as new land forms in hundreds of millions of years. The modern science of geology strongly suggests that these cyclical processes have gone on for most of what we can gather to be the 4.6 billion years of the earth's existence. It would seem that for the Element Earth, the "speculative science" concept of cycles is still valid based on the findings of modern science. What about the other Greek Elements?

AIR

Like Earth, Air can be decomposed into a list of chemical elements. For clean and dry air, the relative percentages by volume of the principal components are: nitrogen, 78.09%; oxygen, 20.95%; argon, 0.93%; and carbon dioxide, 0.03%. Many other trace constituents comprise the remainder of the 100%. The celebrated gas ozone, whose presence in the stratosphere (that part of the atmosphere between about 10 and 40 miles up) has been threatened by propellants in some aerosol spray cans, comprises only about 0.000001% of the volume of the air. Even in this small percentage, it is crucial to the evolution of life on Earth, which illustrates how delicate is the intricate balance Nature has devised for the existence of life on Earth.

Real air, we all know, is never fully clean or dry. It contains dust, pollen, pollution, "dirt" (the Element Earth), and water vapor and water liquid (the Element Water). It can also contain Fire, the fourth of the Greek Elements, as anyone who has ever seen lightning or its effects can testify. We know that Air is not itself a separate and distinct Element unless we qualify it as clean and dry, and even then, it is a mixture of chemical compounds and elements in the gaseous state. Of course, the ancient Greeks were as unaware of these details as they were of certain details of Earth. Yet, they postulated its ability to combine with other Elements, which we know it can do. What they failed to realize was that these four Elements are not independent fundamental entities but are comprised of various combinations of chemical elements, all of which obey the physical laws of Nature.

Back to the cyclical quality of Air. When Columbus demonstrated that the earth was round, he also, unwittingly, demonstrated that Air is cyclical. Air blowing over one place on a round earth will ultimately blow over every other place. With no edges to blow off, air thus must recycle continuously—or be transformed or transported out of the atmosphere.

The modern science of meteorology[3] provides us with more concrete evidence of the cyclical quality of Air. It tells us that the vast bulk of the air is recycled within the atmosphere. However, some fraction of it—some of the carbon dioxide, nitrogen oxides, sulfur oxides, ozone, water vapor, and other trace gases—gets dissolved in water or is otherwise chemically transformed and transported out of and into the atmosphere continuously. A small part of this small fraction is not necessarily recycled. But when the amount taken out of the atmosphere is equal to the amount added, an equilibrium results. As long as this balance is maintained, the relative concentration of those gases remains fixed in the air. These processes are extremely complex, both in themselves and also as a result of the disturbances by human activities, such as farming and energy use. Later on, we'll examine more fully these trace gases, some of which are vital to the survival of life on earth. For now, it is enough to know that Air is also, by and large, cycled.

WATER

It is already clear that Water is an Element that intermixes with two other Elements, Air and Earth. We know that soil (Earth) contains moisture (Water), without which most plants could not survive. The processes of evaporation and transpiration show us that Water also mixes with Air. Moisture evaporates directly into the air or is evaporated through living plants. The latter process is known as *transpiration*. *Evapotranspiration* is a combination of the process of transpiration by living things and the direct evaporation of water from the land or sea. Once in the air, water exists in several forms: as droplets and ice particles in clouds and precipitation, or as water vapor, or in combinations with other substances.

Again, as before, the question of whether Water is cyclical is complex. Water, like Earth and Air, is mostly cyclical. Most materials in the Earth's crust, we believe today, are recycled over millions of years. We know now that some water may be incorporated into living matter or minerals (Earth) and may become part of the sedimentary cycle. However, not all the material is recycled. Water is only a part of the sedimentary cycle's composition. Thus, some small fraction may be lost or may remain in one form.

Likewise, some water in the air may be lost from the *hydrologic cycle*, which is the process of evapotranspiration, precipitation, and reevaporation. Water may be lost from the air in a rather complicated way. Very high up in the atmosphere, ultraviolet radiation from the sun decomposes water vapor, H_2O, into its two chemical elements: hydrogen and oxygen. (This ultraviolet radiation doesn't reach the lower atmosphere, where it would be extremely harmful,* for most of it is filtered out in the ozone layer before it reaches below.) Once the very light hydrogen atoms are freed from their heavier water-mates, the oxygen atoms, they are able to travel at high speeds in the upper reaches of the atmosphere. At such great speeds and heights, some of the hydrogen atoms escape from the gravitational pull of the earth and are set loose forever into space. Many of us are familiar with this principle, for it has been used by scientists in our space program. Rockets are built so that they are powerful enough to accelerate their payload to escape velocity. They then launch space probes to Mars, Venus, and beyond, at speeds fast enough to overcome the pull of our planet's gravity.

For the most part, Water is not lost to space, nor is it trapped into the slow sedimentary cycle. It is generally recycled on Earth through the process known as the *hydrologic cycle*. This remarkable cycle is what most distinguishes Earth from the other planets in our solar system. Earth is the water planet. Water, and the hydrologic cycle in particular, sustains life. Without transpiration, most organisms as we know them on Earth could not exist. The hydrologic cycle is a physical process to be sure, but it is also more. It is part of a global cycle of life. But before we can understand the important expression *global cycle of life*, we need to examine the hy-

---

*Ultraviolet radiation is absorbed by certain organic molecules in living things. This absorption can cause damage that leads to mutations, and sometimes cancer. A strong link between exposure to ultraviolet light and skin cancer is well documented.

drologic cycle in more depth so that we see what it tells us about the cyclical concept as it applies to the Element Water.

THE HYDROLOGIC CYCLE. Although the oceans and ice caps contain over 99% of all the water on Earth, the remaining 1%—located in the atmosphere, lakes, streams, soil, and sub-surface layers—plays a predominant role in shaping the face of the land. Weathering, for example, as described earlier, is highly dependent on rainfall. Perhaps most unique, though, is the essential role that the hydrologic cycle plays in determining where various organisms may live. A desert is clearly different from a tropical forest, and the main reason is water.

People, animals, and plants depend on fresh water, supplied by Nature's gigantic solar-energy-driven distillation system. Evaporated water from the ocean (and, to a lesser extent, from wet soil and plants) recycles locally—through precipitation—and is also carried to faraway lands and oceans. Water is distributed to the continents by the general wind systems. After falling as rain or snow, it evaporates or drains from these land areas, primarily through the rivers, but also through groundwater runoff. It is then returned to the oceans, thereby closing the cycle. The vigor of this cycling depends on the amount of solar energy put into the system. Figure 7-4 gives estimates of the vigor of this cycle.

The sun heats the tropical regions much more than it does the colder polar areas. The atmosphere and the oceans tend to make up these heating imbalances by transporting heat from the warm tropics to the colder poles, thus generating the wind/ocean current circulation patterns that determine the climate. One such "circulation cell" has a rising arm in the tropics and a descending branch in the subtropics. In the rising arm, water vapor is transported vertically. As the water vapor rises, it moves into air of lower pressure, thereby

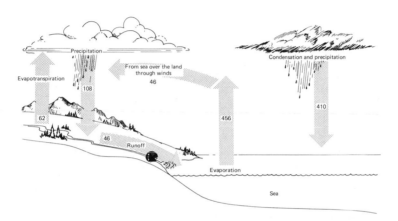

FIGURE 7-4. The arrows show the flow of water from the oceans to air to land and back to the sea. (The numbers are in units of 1000 cubic kilometers of water per year.) Evaporation and transpiration (evaporation through plants)—together known as *evapotranspiration*—on land and runoff in surface and underground rivers return to the sea the water originally evaporated. The input of solar radiation provides the primary energy source to drive the hydrologic cycle. Since water is an essential nutrient for life, and since transpiration contributes to the hydrologic cycle, we can see that this process provides a link between natural cycles and life. Indeed, the hydrologic cycle is part of a global cycle of life *(Ehrlich, Ehrlich, and Holdren, p. 30).*

expanding—a process by which it cools, condenses, and finally falls as precipitation. In the descending arm of the circulation cell, the opposite effect is produced. The dried air sinks, is compressed, and tends to produce a region of hot and dry air—a desert. This sinking motion then inhibits the formation of precipitation, even if there is a water surface below. Some ocean regions are even "deserts," since it rarely rains there!

The principal driving force behind the world's weather patterns is, then, the differences in heating between the tropics and the poles. The climate is basically the result of a gigantic "weather machine," driven by the sun and controlled by the unequal heating of the earth. The processes that contribute to this heating are known as the components of the earth's *energy budget*. Significantly, a change in the climate in one region is likely to be related to a change in the conditions thousands of miles away. The hydrologic cycle is a major component of the weather machine. In addition, it is an important regulator of the very energy flows that drive the climate, a point we will explore shortly.

The artists or philosophers who have so deeply believed that Nature is cyclical and have expressed these feelings in countless images have not been fundamentally contradicted in their beliefs by the findings of modern science.

FIRE

For now we'll consider the Element Fire under the category of "energy." As we all know, energy is needed to power the activities of both man and Nature. We will consider energy in more detail later.

NUTRIENT CYCLES: THE GLOBAL CYCLES OF LIFE

We have said that as the Elements Earth, Air, and Water intermingle and recycle, certain chemical elements and compounds are incorporated into or flow through the life cycles of living things. The chemical elements essential to life are called *nutrients*. The suitability of any environment—be it land, sea, ice, or air—to support life depends upon the availability of sufficient quantities of the appropriate nutrients. We call the totality of processes that control this availability the *nutrient cycle*, because the basic materials that support life often move through the environment in a cyclical manner (in a way similar to the earlier-described hydrologic cycle). Scientists can see now that the distribution—indeed, the very possibility—of life in any given environment depends upon the biogeochemical cycles of Nature. These cycles are crucial in two ways: not only must the appropriate nutrients for life be supplied by these nutrient cycles, but those factors that damage life must also be limited.

Some ancient Greek speculative thinkers postulated a group of gods called the Eumenides, the protectors of the natural order. Here we can see that Nature does actually have regulators of life, and that they are indeed intrinsic to life itself. They are, in fact, so much a part of the natural order that it is easy to overlook their seemingly obvious functions. For example, a nutrient essential to the life of one organism can be lethal in the same quantity to others. Although several basic elements are needed for most kinds of life, the form and amounts appropriate for distinct life forms vary greatly. We know that both air and water are essential for most life, but we also know that fish cannot live long in the air, just as mammals cannot survive for long under water. Fish take their oxygen in dissolved form from water and mammals get theirs from the air. And oxygen can even kill some kinds of bacteria essential to plant life. The variability of natural environments—their wetness, dryness, chemical composition, temperature, lightness, darkness, and nutrient availability—affects primarily where each kind of life form can exist, its so-called "ecological niche."

LIFE (AS A CHEMICAL FORMULA)

Although we are just now introducing the term *nutrient cycles*, we have already learned (see Figure 7-2) that these biogeochemical cycles involve the two basic processes of natural recycling: the physical transport of materials and the chemical transformation of various nutrients. Two of our previous examples, the hydrologic and the sedimentary cycles, are actually nutrient cycles. Other important nutrients include nitrogen, carbon, sulfur, and phosphorus. Not surprisingly, these, too, follow cyclical structures, and we will look at aspects of these crucial global cycles of life shortly. But in the interests of being "scientific," we need to step back temporarily and clarify a definition. In order to look at the cycles of life properly, we should attempt some further refinements of what "life" actually is. Most of us are already familiar with the various legal, religious, and philosophical definitions of life. Here, though, we'll look at a lesser-known definition, a chemical one.

Ecologist Edward S. Deevey, Jr., once summarized "life" by the chemical formula[5]

$$H_{2960}O_{1480}C_{1480}N_{16}P_{1.8}S_1$$

This formula merely tells us the relative proportions of the six most abundant chemical elements in the general compound: living beings. That is, there are 2960 atoms of hydrogen; 1480 atoms of oxygen; 1480 atoms of carbon; 16 atoms of nitrogen; 1.8 atoms of phosphorus; and 1 atom of sulfur. Of course, each *individual* species and organism has a different amount and proportion of these (and other) elements in its individual physical being. However, the general formula holds as a chemical stereotype of life, for these are the rough proportions of the basic chemical elements of living materials.

Remarkable experiments have been performed whereby the four basic chemical elements of life—C, H, O, and N— were combined in a container and "zapped" by an electric spark. An organic ooze was synthesized. The process has been described by ecologist Barry Commoner:

> The geochemical origin of organic compounds has been imitated in the laboratory; a mixture of water, ammonia, and methane, exposed to ultraviolet light, an electric spark, or just heat, produces detectable amounts of such organic compounds as amino acids—which linked together become proteins. Ultraviolet light was readily available from solar radiation on the primitive earth's surface. There is now good reason to believe that under this influence the simple compounds of the earth's early atmosphere were gradually converted into a mixture of organic compounds. Thus, to use an image favored by the originator of this theory, Professor A. I. Oparin, there appeared on the earth a kind of "organic soup."
>
> It was within this soup that the first living things developed, two to three billion years ago. How that happened is a fascinating but poorly understood problem; fortunately we do know enough about the characteristics of the first forms of life to establish their dependence— and their effects—on the environment.[6]

Incredibly, scientists have been able to synthesize the organic materials of organisms. But no one has yet synthesized life itself. What Barry Commoner politely calls "a poorly understood problem" is, in fact, not understood at all! Those who favor a religious explanation can take comfort in the fact that human "gods" cannot, today, create life. At best, they can synthesize organic matter from basic elements or transform the material of one living being into a different form. That latter ability is the cause of the "genetic engineering" controversy, for our ability to alter the genetic structure of organisms is growing so that succeeding generations will have a different form from that of their parents. Despite this awesome power, those who manipulate the genetic structure of life to create different life forms must still start with *an already living organism or its parts.* We can *modify* genetic material, but a living being will result only if we start with parts of a living, albeit different, being. We cannot yet—and may never know how to—*create* life itself. Whether we should, if we could, is an issue that splits scientists from religionists, religionists from politicians, politicians from scientists, and even scientists from scientists. The debate rages on, while Nature continues to keep the secret.[7] Perhaps the Greeks neglected to mention one important factor in their myth of Pandora's box, for it seems that the secrets of the spark of life have also remained locked in the box.

THE CARBON CYCLE

Let's return now to some areas that we described earlier: the basic processes of the nutrient cycles. Photosynthesis is the process that green plants use to build their tissues. It links the hydrologic, carbon, and oxygen cycles and is essential to life as we know it on earth. (Who knows if life on other planets would be dependent upon water?) The energy that drives the process of photosynthesis comes from the sun. This

FIGURE 7-5. *Michelangelo Buonarroti, The Creation of Adam, 1508–1512, The Vault of the Sistine Chapel, the Vatican, Rome.* Among the famous paintings by Michelangelo in the Sistine Chapel is this panel. It is often interpreted as God about to impart the spark of life to man at the point where the fingers almost touch. Cosmologists (scientists who study the foundations of the universe—and the origins of life) have tried to synthesize life in the laboratory with a spark of their own. Putting nonorganic chemicals containing the elements carbon, hydrogen, nitrogen, and oxygen together into a container, they have sparked the mixture with electric discharges (a man-made lightning of sorts) in the hopes of creating life. Indeed, organic compounds have thus been made! But whatever "spark" will be needed to make this creation *live* is still a mystery.

radiant solar energy, what we're calling "Fire," is captured and used by the plants. The simplest chemical formula for photosynthesis is:

$$6CO_2 + 6H_2O + \text{Solar energy} \rightarrow C_6H_{12}O_6 + 6O_2$$

The opposite reaction, respiration and decay, also takes place in plants, as it does in animals and humans. It, too, has a simple formula:

$$6O_2 + C_6H_{12}O_6 \rightarrow 6CO_2 + 6H_2O + \text{heat}$$

These formulas[8] show that the cycle is completed. That is, six molecules of the compound carbon dioxide (CO_2) and six molecules of water (H_2O) are taken up in the photosynthetic process and transformed by green plants, using the sun's energy, into one molecule of the carbohydrate compound glucose ($C_6H_{12}O_6$), and six molecules of oxygen gas (O_2). Then the respiration process returns the CO_2, H_2O, and heat back to the environment.

Each spring, when grasses turn green and leaves reappear, the process of photosynthesis speeds up. Both increasing sunlight and warmer temperatures contribute. At this time, carbon dioxide gas is taken out of the air (see the first formula above) faster than it is returned to the air through respiration or decay (see the second formula above). The radiant energy of the sun is used by the plants to convert that CO_2 into the carbohydrates (of which $C_6H_{12}O_6$ is one) that build living plant materials. Yearly, in the northern hemisphere, the concentration of carbon dioxide in the air drops by roughly 3% from spring to fall as a result of the seasonal growth of the plant world through photosynthesis. (This process involves some 70 *billion* net tons of CO_2 in and out of the atmosphere each year. For comparison, in 1978, humans produced only about 1.3 *billion* tons of food grains, and less than 20% of this quantity fills up all the grain elevators on earth.) In the southern hemisphere, the exchange of CO_2 between the air and life is only approximately one third as great as in the northern hemisphere, for the southern hemisphere has fewer green plants. (The northern hemisphere surface is about 40% continents and 60% oceans, while the southern hemisphere is dominated by water—80% oceans and 20% continents.) Then, in the fall, when temperatures drop to retard photosynthetic rates and less solar energy is available to convert CO_2 to carbohydrates, the reverse process of respiration and decay (also called *oxidation*) dominates the cycle. More oxygen is consumed and carbon dioxide released to the air during the winter months than during the summer. Photosynthesis, respiration, and decay occur all the time. The important difference between seasons, though, is one of *rates.* Photosynthesis and respiration slow down or speed up at different rates, and photosynthesis almost stops during the winter. In the spring, the available sunlight increases, the climate warms, and photosynthesis dominates over respiration once again. The carbon cycle of life is established.[9] It is shown graphically in Figure 7-6.

However, there are many factors other than CO_2 in the air controlling the speed of the carbon cycle. The vigor and extent of the carbon cycle correlates strongly with the location and quantity of plant life on earth. We have already noted that adequate water and sunlight must be available for photosynthesis to proceed. It is essential that other nutrients be present as well. Furthermore, the temperatures of the air and soil are also important to photosynthetic processes. In this way, not only does the chemical element carbon recycle and take its part as a cycle of life, but it also—like the Greek Ele-

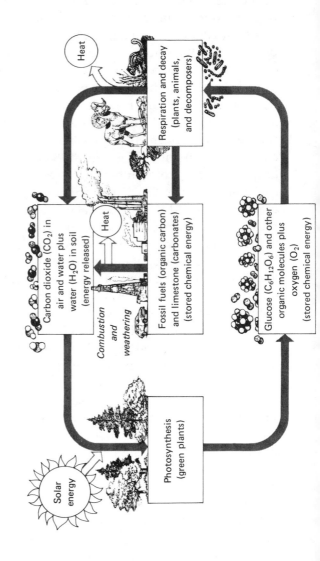

FIGURE 7-6. The chemical element most associated with life is carbon. Indeed, a whole scientific discipline dedicated to studying carbon in organisms is known as *organic* chemistry. We can see here why the carbon cycle is so important to life. At the top of the figure is represented the carbon dioxide molecules stored in the air, water, or soil. When the energy from sunlight strikes green plants (left box), photosynthesis takes place, where the inorganic carbon in the form of CO_2 is transformed into carbohydrates like glucose. Oxygen is produced as well (bottom box). These organic molecules store in their chemical bonds some of the sun's energy used during photosynthesis. They are the building blocks of plant tissues. Plants later die, or are eaten, after which bacteria and other decomposers transform some of the carbohydrates back to CO_2 and water vapor, using oxygen and liberating heat in the process. (Similarly, respiration takes place in both plants and animals.) This is why burning a log produces heat and carbon dioxide and uses up oxygen. The log is "giving back" heat and the materials used by the green plants to make the organic molecules in the first place (right box). However, as the figure shows, fossil fuels (coal, oil, or gas, for example) are being burned by humans. These remains of the organic molecules of ancient life also yield heat when burned—which is why they are used by us as fuels. But their burning also gives off CO_2, thereby altering the amount of this gas in the atmosphere. Such a disruption of the natural course of the carbon cycle of life can have serious implications for both Nature and man (*From G. Tyler Miller, Jr., Living in the Environment, 2nd ed., Wadsworth, Belmont, Calif., 1979, p. 73*).

ments Earth, Water, and Air—is strongly interactive with other cycles of life.

NITROGEN CYCLE

Another chemical essential to life is nitrogen, which is present in all proteins. Nitrogen also functions cyclically. The nitrogen cycle is chemically one of the most complex and biologically one of the most important of the nutrient cycles. For our purposes, the nitrogen cycle is particularly complex because nitrogen goes through its cycle in many forms. Its principal "incarnation," nitrogen gas, N_2, comprises 78% of the atmosphere. However, some of this gas is transformed into other forms of nitrogen compounds, all of which move through the nitrogen cycle. A part of it is converted by bacteria in the soils and waters to ammonia (NH_3), nitrite compounds (NO_2), or nitrate compounds (NO_3). This conversion process is known as *nitrogen fixation*. The name is more than jargon. It is a literal description of what actually happens. Nitrogen is "fixed" or attached to other chemical elements, and a strong chemical bond is formed between the nitrogen and other atoms. The species that can accomplish this "metamorphosis" are called *nitrogen-fixing organisms.*

A look at the process of nitrogen fixing will lead us *into* the nitrogen cycle itself. A little detail here is essential to develop some perspective on the question of how humans are modifying this natural cycle. Nitrogen fixation is especially important in our discussion, for not only is it a biological function, but it can also occur "abiologically," that is, without organisms directly in the process. Nitrogen can be fixed abiologically by fires. These fires can be caused by natural processes, such as lightning or forest fires, or they can result from human activities, such as using automobile engines, power plants, steel mills, and even atomic bombs! Keep in mind that humans do influence the nitrogen-fixing process, for this is a major component of the question: What is man's place in nature? For part of the answer, we must explore the route of the fixed nitrogen atoms in the nitrogen cycle.

NITROGEN FIXATION. Fixed nitrogen resides in the air, in the soil, and in water. It can also be produced abiologically in Air, Water, and Earth. It resides principally in the air as nitrogen oxides (NO, NO_2, N_2O), ammonia (NH_3), nitrate (NO_3), or nitrite (NO_2) compounds. These fixed nitrogen molecules can enter the soil or the water in rain or snow.

Until the advent of man, most nitrogen fixation is believed to have been effected in the soil or the water by special bacteria. These microbes often take energy from the plants to do their work, to fix nitrogen. The best-known example of nitrogen-fixing species for land plants are the bacteria called *Rhizobium.* They often live in special nodules on the roots of legumes—nitrogen-fixing plants that bear their seeds in pods. Such members of the pea family as alfalfa, beans, peas, and clover can fix nitrogen. Because these plants are able to fix nitrogen, they are widely used by farmers in crop rotation schemes. When other non-nitrogen-fixing crops, such as wheat, corn, or tomatoes, deplete the soil of its fixed nitrogen, one of these nitrogen-fixing crops is planted to replenish the soil. Thus, of course, we are brought to another question: Why is fixed nitrogen so important to have in the soil?

Nitrogen is important for the life process of all living things. Most plants cannot fix nitrogen themselves, and it is for these that a reserve of fixed nitrogen in the soil is essential. Compounds of fixed nitrogen such as ammonia or a variety of nitrates are the fertilizers that allow plants to incorporate nitrogen into their tissues. These fixed nitrogen compounds are taken up by the plants' roots and internally converted to proteins after an initial chemical transformation to amino acids.

The bacteria that live off some plants repay their hosts by providing them with fixed nitrogen. Animals, including man, cannot synthesize all their needed amino acids through their own internal chemical processes. Nor can they host any known form of bacteria to do it for them. They must obtain the ones they can't manufacture themselves from other sources, primarily their food. Those that are obtained from the diet are called *essential amino acids*, while those that are synthesized internally are called *nonessential*. (The latter term may be misleading, because both are actually essential to life.) Plants are at the bottom of the food chain, taking their needs from sunlight, atmosphere, soil, and water. They, in turn, serve the needs of "consumers," starting with tiny insects and ending with large mammals. At the top of this complex food web sits man.

We can now retrace our steps and put all of this into the perspective of a cycle. We have followed the nutrient nitrogen through its initial phase as nitrogen gas to the intermediate steps of nitrogen fixation—biologically or abiologically—to its biological role as protein in living beings. Fixed nitrogen, which is fertilizer, already exists in, is washed into, or is "fixed" in the soil. This soil then supports the growth of plants, which, in turn, support a chain of animal and human needs. We have proceeded through several steps to get to protein nitrogen from the original nitrogen element. In order to complete the cycle, we need next to discover how the nitrogen fixed in the bodies of living things gets back to its original form: nitrogen gas in the air.

LIFE AND DEATH: AN INTERNAL LOOP IN THE CYCLE. All living things go through a life cycle of formation, existence, and death. While we are living, we consume food and leave waste products behind. In these very waste products lies the key to the completion of the nitrogen cycle. We know that excretion from animals (including humans) contains a significant amount of proteins and other fixed nitrogen compounds. The manure from livestock is well known as a fertilizer because it contains, among other things, fixed nitrogen compounds. The fixed nitrogen is taken up by plants from the soil, as we have said. These are then eaten by the livestock and returned to the soil to complete an internal loop within the nitrogen cycle. Alternatively, plants are eaten by insects that are eaten by "higher" animals on the food chain (e.g., fish or birds), which are then eaten by higher beings—including humans.

Not all of the fixed nitrogen is returned as excretion by animals along the food chain. Most of it remains in plants, which, at least before humans got into the picture, merely had to die in place to return to the land or water the nitrogen molecules they had "borrowed." The bodies of animals and insects recycle nitrogen only after they die and their carcasses decompose. However, if we remove an animal from its grazing land and eat it, the nitrogen that would have been recycled through its eventual decomposition is lost to the land. Some of this fixed nitrogen and the proteins from the animals get incorporated into our bodies and excreted as wastes—or recycled in graveyards—and still reenter the nitrogen cycle, although at a different place and via a different route. While functioning in a cycle, these compounds do not return to their initial point of origin as fixed nitrogen; so a deficit can be created in the place of origin—usually the grazing lands of the animals. Similarly, an excess can develop at a point of dumping—like a lake or stream polluted with large quantities of raw sewage.

Agriculture works in a similar manner. Plants are grown—wheat or corn, for example—that take fixed nitrogen from the soil but never return all of it, since these crops are taken from the farmland and consumed elsewhere by animals or by us. This is one reason that the soil's supply of fixed nitrogen can be so easily depleted, necessitating crop rotations using nitrogen-fixing legumes and/or artificial nitrogen fertilization to make up for what is lost to agriculture.

The manufacture of artificial fertilizer by man now accounts for a significant fraction of all fixed nitrogen in Nature and represents a serious intervention by man in this global cycle of life. The potential consequences of this interference in the nitrogen cycle will be covered in the next chapter.

DENITRIFICATION: THE CLOSE OF THE CYCLE. The final step in the nitrogen cycle is to trace how the fixed nitrogen tied up in soil, or in the bodies and excreta of plants and animals, gets back to its start as nitrogen gas. Up to this point, the process of transforming nitrogen from gas to fertilizers or to living tissues is known as *nitrification.* The energy needed to carry out the process biologically comes through sunlight from the plants that host the nitrogen-fixing bacteria. Alternatively, energy to fix nitrogen abiologically comes from the fires that converted nitrogen gas to nitrates. The man-made industrial plants that manufacture nitrogen fertilizer are themselves no exception to this rule, since they use energy from the burning of fossil fuels to create the chemical bonds for fixed nitrogen fertilizers. (Even when man intervenes in the natural processes, he must do so in accordance with the general strictures of Nature.)

The fixed nitrogen in organisms returns to the soil in one of several forms: as animal wastes, as dead animals, or as plants (e.g., decaying leaves or tree trunks). These compounds then encounter other bacteria that can undo the process set in motion by the nitrogen-fixing bacteria or fires. That is, the proteins are converted back to amino acids, then to fixed nitrogen compounds like ammonia or a variety of nitrates. (A backyard compost pile works this way, converting organic waste materials back to soil rich in fixed nitrates and other nutrients.)

Thus, nitrification; internal cycling of fixed nitrogen compounds among soil, water, plants, animals, and the air; and denitrification all go on simultaneously. The temperature; rainfall; soil acidity, composition, and structure; and other environmental factors determine the relative rates of each of these subprocesses of the nitrogen cycle. However, there is an important asymmetrical aspect to the denitrification subprocess. When nitrification takes place, nitrogen gas (N_2) is changed into fixed nitrogen. But when fixed nitrogen is denitrified, not all of it is returned to the atmosphere in its original form, as N_2. A small percentage is given back as the gas nitrous oxide (N_2O), also known as the anesthetic *laughing gas*. Only about 0.03% of the atmosphere is made up of this gas, but even this trace is enough to influence the climate. Like carbon dioxide, nitrous oxide contributes to the greenhouse effect.* And beyond that, scientists are now finding that it is involved in the complex set of processes that determine the ozone balance.

The nitrous oxide is first transported vertically by the winds more than 30 kilometers up in the higher atmosphere known as the *stratosphere*. This process can take years to accomplish. There, it is destroyed by intense ultraviolet light from the sun that doesn't penetrate down to the lower at-

---

*Like the glass in a greenhouse, these gases trap heat "inside" the earth's atmosphere, that is, near the earth's surface.

mosphere. It doesn't penetrate because it is filtered out by the ozone layer that resides in the atmosphere primarily between 20 and 40 kilometers (12.5–25 miles) in altitude. Even this long-reaching step, though, isn't the most remarkable part of the N_2O story, for one of the products of the destruction of nitrous oxide by solar ultraviolet radiation above the ozone layers is other nitrogen oxide gases (NO_2 and NO). These nitrogen oxides are believed to be involved in the complicated chain of chemical reactions that control the amount of ozone in the stratosphere.[10] Ozone screens out most of the biologically harmful ultraviolet radiation before it reaches the earth's surface. Thus, even though the bulk of it is 20–40 kilometers overhead, ozone is tied to life on earth. Yet life and the global nitrogen cycle of life produce and transport nitrous oxide. This gas, in turn, can influence the amount of ozone in the stratosphere. The cycle contains a circular process, or *feedback mechanism*. Nitrous oxide is decomposed by ultraviolet radiation into products that can change the amount of ozone. Ozone then screens out ultraviolet radiation that can damage the life forms that lead to the original production of the nitrous oxide! The subtleties and complexities of the biogeochemical cycles of life are as intricate as they are important to our survival. We are barely beginning to understand how they work. Even though our actual understanding of the details of these mechanisms is limited, human activities are well along in disrupting the natural processes of the nitrogen cycle. A glimpse of the cycle can be seen in Figure 7-7.

PHOSPHORUS CYCLE

The major global nutrient cycles of life are the hydrologic, carbon, and nitrogen cycles, all of which we've looked at so far. However, there are other cyclically functioning elements that exist in smaller quantities and are also essential to life. It is likely that you are fairly well convinced already that the findings of modern science include cycles. Yet, we should look at a few more findings, not merely to give further credibility to cycles in Nature, but to emphasize how human activities are modifying the natural processes. One such cycle is that of phosphorus, which, although it is required in quantities only one-tenth as much as nitrogen, is also essential to life.

Phosphorus is often referred to as a *limiting nutrient* because in its absence, plants can't proliferate, even if they have ample supplies of other essential nutrients, and also because of its scarcity in forms accessible to plants. Although there is a great deal of phosphorus dispersed in sedimentary rocks, phosphorus compounds lack two important properties possessed by nitrogen and carbon compounds: (1) they do not possess a common gaseous form; and (2) their principal salts, called *phosphates*, do not dissolve easily in water. These characteristics severely limit the two primary pathways of travel for nutrients like carbon or nitrogen: movement through air and water. Only a small portion of phosphorus in plants and animals is transported each year by water, birds, and other animals from the land to the sea or from phosphate-rich rocks to farm fields. Thus, tracing the phosphorus cycle over the long run involves the agonizingly slow process of making and destroying rocks through the sedimentary cycle: weathering, sedimentation, and uplift. There are, though, as in the case of nitrogen, important intermediate steps in the cycle, as seen in Figure 7-8.

The reserves of phosphate salts in the soils and oceans are taken up by plants and incorporated into the process of protein formation. Phosphorus is also a constituent of DNA (deoxyribonucleic acid), the genetic material that codes the

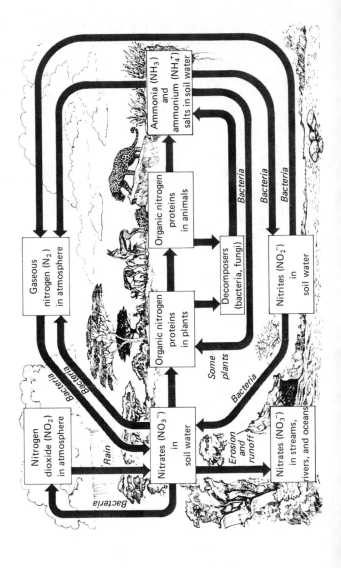

FIGURE 7-7. Nitrogen is another principal nutrient essential to life whose various chemical forms travel by means of a global cycle. A simplified version of this cycle is shown. Even a glance at the figure shows that this is a very complex cycle, since nitrogen moves through the air, soil, water, and living things in many loops and in many forms. Bacteria are the principal agents of change, transforming nitrogen gas in the atmosphere to "fixed" forms usable by plants and animals. Bacteria also transform fixed nitrogen from dead organisms, for example, back to nitrogen gas. Humans intervene in the system by taking organisms from the land for their food. They replace the lost nitrogen with fertilizers manufactured with fossil fuel energy. This alteration to the supplies of fixed nitrogen compounds affects the entire nitrogen cycle. One additional complication, not shown on the figure, is the fact that a small fraction of the fixed nitrogen compounds are transformed to N_2O, nitrous oxide (laughing gas), before its final recycling into pure nitrogen gas. This is important, since N_2O is believed to be related both to the maintenance of the earth's ozone layer and to the climate. Not only does the nitrogen cycle depend on the climate and life, but these, in turn, depend on this global cycle of life (Miller, p. 74).

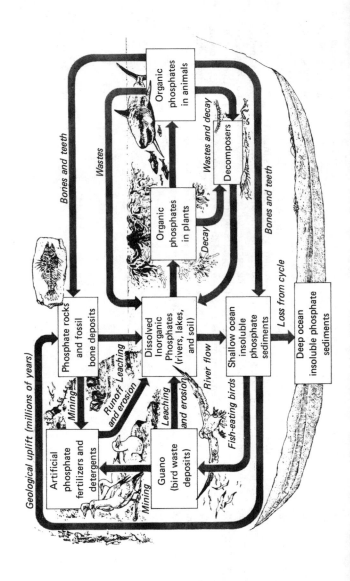

Geological uplift (millions of years)

FIGURE 7-8. This greatly simplified representation of the phosphorus cycle shows that it, like that of nitrogen, is both essential to life and highly complex. There is a major difference, however, between the phosphorus and nitrogen cycles. The latter is comprised of numerous forms of nitrogen, most of which are easily dissolved in water. Thus, they are readily transported by winds, rain, ocean currents, or rivers. Phosphorus compounds, on the other hand, are relatively insoluble in water and cycle much more slowly. Thus, it is a very long natural process to replace the phosphorus lost from a farm field when plants or animals containing phosphorus are removed. As a result, humans have replaced this phosphorus by mining phosphate-rich rocks and converting this natural reservoir of phosphorus to fertilizers. By tapping the stocks of phosphorus that normally cycle slowly through sedimentary processes, humans are speeding up the flows of phosphorus in order to satisfy their purpose: feeding a growing human population. But there are repercussions to both man and Nature for this disruption to the phosphorus cycle. One of the most serious is water pollution (Miller, p. 75).

information of inheritance. In animals, the phosphate form of phosphorus is an important component of shells and other bony structures. In short, phosphorus is an essential nutrient for the life process.

The phosphorus cycle works analogously to the nitrogen cycle. When organisms die or excrete, they return phosphorus to the environment, but in the chemical form characteristic of living tissues (called *organic phosphorus*). This then needs to be reconverted to phosphate salts (called *inorganic phosphates*) before it can be taken up once again by living things. Bacteria intervene to maintain this cycle of life. These *phosphatizing bacteria* work with other decomposers to reconvert the organic phosphorus in the decaying materials back to inorganic phosphates usable (by the plants), so this internal loop of the phosphorus cycle can repeat itself. And, as with nitrogen, we humans break the internal cycle by exporting crops without completely returning the wastes to the land. Thus, depletion of phosphorus, as of nitrogen, has necessitated man's substitution of phosphorus fertilizers. These fertilizers are obtained by mining rocks rich in phosphate—which are in diminishing supply. In essence, we are speeding up the effects of the naturally slow processes of weathering, sedimentation, and uplift by artificially transporting phosphate-rich rocks to our farm fields. By pushing this cycle to keep up with perceived needs, man has become an important factor in this particular global cycle of life.

SULFUR CYCLE

Although there are others, the last nutrient cycle we'll study is that of sulfur. Sulfur is important because it plays a role in the structure of proteins, thus influencing all life. In addition, certain quantities and forms of sulfur can be toxic to plants or mammals, while others are instrumental in determining the acidity of rainwater, surface water, and soil. Acidity governs the rates of many processes, including denitrification. Sulfur is also a major pollutant of industrial activities. These roles qualify its cycle as an important global cycle.[11]

Like nitrogen, sulfur can exist in many compounds. It can take the gaseous form of sulfur dioxide (SO_2) or hydrogen sulfide (H_2S), the latter being a gas that helps give rotten eggs the odor for which they are infamous. The dissolving of sulfur dioxide in the water droplets of haze or clouds in the air forms sulfurous acid (H_2SO_3), which, in the presence of sunlight, can be converted to the highly caustic compound sulfuric acid (H_2SO_4). Sulfuric acid particles floating in the air are major contributors to the eye-irritating, unhealthy smog that enshrouds so many industrial cities.

The effects of sulfur, particularly in the form of sulfuric acid, are potentially quite dangerous, and safe levels—for us—of this nutrient must be maintained. When sulfuric acid falls to the earth in rainwater, the acidity of soils, lakes, and streams is increased. This can be a serious threat to many life forms and plays an important role in the growth rate of plants and the ability of fish to survive.

As with the carbon, nitrogen, and phosphorus biogeochemical cycles, scientists are only now beginning to account quantitatively for the sources, sinks, and flows of sulfur. Active research efforts continue, not only for the intrinsic intellectual interest in understanding more about these vast global cycles of life, but, more practically, to assess the relative importance of the growing human interventions in these natural processes.

We do know that the sulfur cycle is extremely complex because sulfur atoms can move through the sulfur cycle in many different chemical combinations. Let's start by tracing the part of the sulfur cycle important to life. We can do this by following the gas SO_2 or the particles of sulfate (SO_4) compounds in the air. These sulfur compounds leave the atmosphere after a week or so, on the average, by fallout or rain. In soil or water, sulfur compounds (SO_2 or SO_4) can be taken up by plants and incorporated into their tissues. Then, as with nitrogen and phosphorus, these organic sulfur compounds are returned to land or water after the plants die or the animals that eat the plants die or leave excreta. Once again, bacteria enter the process and transform the organic sulfur, as well as some sulfate, in decaying biota to hydrogen sulfide gas (H_2S). In a matter of minutes, much of the H_2S is converted (again by helpful bacteria) back to sulfur and sulfate compounds, which reenter the atmosphere, water, and soils to continue the cycle. Winds, river flows, and ocean currents transport these sulfur compounds rapidly, creating exchanges of sulfur between land and oceans.

Superimposed on this fast series of internal loops of sulfur cycling is the very slow process of weathering, sedimentation, and uplift of rocks containing sulfur. Finally, there is the intermittent process of direct injection of sulfur compounds into the atmosphere from volcanoes. These slow processes, like those for phosphorus, continue all the while SO_2, H_2S, S, and SO_4 compounds are rapidly cycling among plants, animals, air, water, and soils. Thus, these nutrient cycles are really a series of cycles structured within cycles. Modern science has shown that the structures of these cycles of life aren't precisely "ashes-to-ashes and dust-to-dust." They are better described as "particles-to-gases, gases-to-gases, gases-to-particles, gases-to-oozes, oozes-to-oozes," and so forth. The nutrients undergo continuous chemical metamorphoses as they cycle through the environment, regulating the endless chain of life, death, and life.

Once again, man is playing a contributory role in increasing the levels of sulfuric acid in the environment. Most of the sulfur that gets into the environment from human activities comes from the burning of fossil fuels (coal, oil, and, to a lesser extent, natural gas), all of which are high in sulfur content. This is why "low-sulfur" fuels are both desirable and expensive, and diminishing in supply.

We'll next examine the significance of human intervention in this and other life cycles, but first, one final—and probably most important—point must be made. The rate of flow of materials through each of these cycles also depends partly on the climate. We've seen that transport by the winds, rainfall, river flow, and ocean currents all contribute to and regulate the speed of material flows in each cycle. We've also seen that the chemical transformations such as photosynthesis or nitrogen fixation depend on factors like temperature, solar radiation, carbon dioxide concentration, ground wetness, and soil acidity. All these factors are directly part of, or dependent on, the climatic conditions. And modern science has shown us a remarkable catch: the climate itself is dependent on the global nutrient cycles!

CLIMATE AND THE GLOBAL CYCLES

The weather comprises, among other things, the *immediate* temperature, rainfall, winds, pressure, humidity, air quality, snow and ice extent, and oceanic conditions all over the globe. The *average* of these weather elements over some period of time is what we refer to as the *climate*. The climate is not a static quantity, for not only does each region possess a set of mean statistics for its climate, but there is also considerable variability in the climate over time. Ice ages come and go over tens of thousands of years, and many lesser, but still important, climatic changes occur on much shorter time scales. The variability in climate both geographically (from place to place) and in time (at each place) determines to a considerable extent where and how we can live: what we can grow, what grows naturally, what we must wear, and how much food, water, or energy we must store away to "get us through" the bad-weather cycles. However, it is not our immediate purpose to detail the myriad ways that man depends on climate, even though it is a major aspect of the question we raised earlier about man's place in Nature. Here, we'll explain briefly how our climate works, stressing the role of the cycles of life.[12]

The sun is the prime mover. Its radiant energy occurs in invisible waveforms that radiate in all directions from the source: the thermonuclear reactions of the sun. A thermonuclear reaction is the process by which some light chemical elements (hydrogen, for example) join or "fuse" under intense heat and pressure to make heavier elements (e.g., helium). In the process, enormous quantities of heat are released. This heat, which leaves the sun mostly in the form of radiant energy, is what we commonly call sunlight. (As a sidelight, the hydrogen bomb works on a similar thermonuclear principle. Fortunately for us, the continuous nuclear reactors on the sun remain a safe* 93 million miles away!) The radiation from the sun occurs at relatively short wavelengths. That is, each wave of energy has a "crest" only about one half a millionth of a meter (e.g., the size of a typical dust particle in the air) from the crest of the waves in front and in back of it. The very short wavelengths, called *solar ultra-*

---

*At least for the next few billion years, this will be true. Since the sun is, according to latest astrophysical theory, slowly heating up, life on earth will eventually be heated to extinction. But considerable time remains!

violet rays, have wavelengths measuring approximately one-tenth to one-third of a millionth of a meter. These rays can be harmful to life and are duly screened out, mostly by the ozone shield in the upper atmosphere. In addition to the ultraviolet and visible wavelengths, the sun emits energy with longer wavelengths called *infrared radiation.* Even though we can't see them, these infrared rays carry heat.

Most of the sun's energy comes to us as radiation with wavelengths between one-third and about three millionths of a meter (the latter comparable to the size of a very small raindrop). These rays are partially reflected back to space when they encounter the earth. About 30% of the incoming radiation is reflected by the combination of air molecules, clouds, dust, and the earth's surface. The fraction of reflected energy is called the earth's *albedo.* About one-third of the sun's energy is absorbed directly by the earth's atmosphere. Another third reaches the surface, and the remaining third, as said earlier, is reflected back into space. Many things, ranging from photosynthesis to the earth's climate, depend upon the amount of the sun's energy reaching the surface.

When the remaining sunlight reaches the surface, it is absorbed or reflected by the materials that are exposed. The absorbed part is then transformed into a variety of energy forms. If the surface is dry, the absorbed energy is transformed directly to heat in the form of a temperature increase. If the surface is wet, only a tenth or so of the absorbed energy is transformed to heat at the surface, and the remainder is used to evaporate water.

A great deal of energy is needed to break the chemical bonds that keep water in a liquid state and to transform it to water vapor. Just a brief digression on the evaporation of water is in order here, for we can now see how the hydrologic cycle is driven by energy from the "fire" of the sun. The evap-

oration of water keeps wet surfaces cooler than dry ones because the heat absorbed isn't primarily converted into an immediate temperature increase as it is at a dry surface; part of
it is used to transform the liquid water to water vapor. Later
on, when the water vapor rises into the atmosphere, cools,
and condenses into cloud droplets and then to rainfall, the
condensation process releases to the air the enormous quantities of heat initially used to evaporate (or transpire) the liquid
water at the earth's surface. This transformation and transport of heat by evapotranspiration and condensation from the
earth's surface to the air is important in determining our climate.

Recall that Aristotle criticized Anaxagoras on his theory
of condensation:

> . . . the process is just the opposite of what Anaxagoras
> says it is: He says it takes place when clouds rise into
> the cold air; we say it takes place when clouds descend
> into the warm air and is most violent when the clouds
> descend farthest.

Now we have vastly more quantities of data than were available to either Greek philosopher and can see that Anaxagoras
was, indeed, correct. Condensation generally takes place
when moist air parcels "rise into the cold air." Since the deserts of the earth exist where air predominantly sinks, Aristotle was clearly wrong in his speculations. However, given
that neither philosopher had sufficient data, nor relied on the
rigorous steps of verification demanded by the modern scientific method, the fact that the speculations of Anaxagoras
in this case were superior to those of Aristotle is just an accident.

Let's return to the use of the sun's energy on the earth's
surface. If the surface is covered with green plants, then some
of the energy will be used to evaporate water. This is the

process that, as we have seen, is called *transpiration*. Some of the energy is also used to break the chemical bonds of carbon dioxide molecules and transform them, through photosynthesis, to carbohydrates or other organic materials that store even greater amounts of energy than do CO_2 molecules. This particular use of the energy is cyclical, for when plants die (or are burned or eaten), the energy from the sun used to make carbohydrates is given back to the environment, along with the carbon dioxide. All our "fossil" fuels are actually buried fossil remains of carbohydrate-rich life. We call them *fuels* because they contain, in the chemical bonds of their hydrocarbon molecules, the solar energy that made them hundreds of millions of years ago. When we burn a lump of coal, we are really giving back to the environment the solar energy that, long before, had been captured and transformed to carbohydrates by photosynthesis. Unfortunately, the burning of these fossil fuels has a negative aspect as well. Not only do we get the energy we want, but we also get carbon dioxide and a host of other less welcome air pollutants, such as the sulfates and nitrates that are principal components of smog.

Let's return to the solar energy absorbed by the surface, air, dust, and clouds, since the amount of absorbed energy is a major factor in determining the earth's temperature. A look at a picture from space shows light and dark regions. (See Figure 7-9.) The light regions have a high albedo, indicating a large reflection of solar energy back to space. By and large, the bright spots on the earth are clouds and snow and ice fields. All these are forms of water and, thus, parts of the hydrologic cycle. This global cycle of life controls the properties of the earth that account for the bulk of the reflection of solar energy to space. It is the absorption of solar energy that both drives the hydrologic cycle *and* regulates the earth's

FIGURE 7-9. Nearly everyone has seen satellite photos of the earth, a beautiful blue-water planet with swirling white clouds and bright ice caps. Beyond their aesthetic—and even political—virtues, these views reveal the fantastic interconnectedness of life, the global cycles, and the earth's climate. We know that the hydrologic cycle is regulated by winds, temperatures, and other climatic factors, and that the distribution of rainfall regulates where things can live. At the same time, plants transpire water vapor into the air, a process that contributes to the amount of moisture in the hydrologic cycle. One result of the hydrologic cycle can be seen on the satellite photo: clouds and ice caps. But these bright spots reflect more sunlight away from the earth than do darker spots. Thus, the brighter the earth, the *cooler* the earth will be, since the clouds and snow absorb less of the sun's heat than the darker-colored plants, land, or water. Not only is the hydrologic cycle determined by the climate, it also regulates the heating of the earth, which, in turn, drives the climate—and life depends on both. Beyond the imagination of most who have offered images of cycles in the speculative sciences, modern scientific findings not only confirm the presence of cycles in Nature but also establish a strong link between life, the cycles of life, and the climate! *(Photo courtesy U.S. National Aeronautics and Space Administration).*

temperature. The interrelationship between the climate and the hydrologic cycle may be the most basic of all those we've considered so far. The climate regulates the hydrologic cycle, and the hydrologic cycle regulates the amount of solar energy absorbed by the earth, which, in turn, regulates the climate, and so on. Nature, indeed, consists of a fantastic web of interlocking systems, and we have just looked at one strand of that web. Let's look at a few more.

The clouds and water vapor in the air also absorb sunlight and contribute to the heating of the earth. However, at this point, we've told only half of the story of determining the earth's temperature. If the sun's energy absorbed by the earth were not *exactly* balanced by an equal amount of energy leaving the earth for space, then the earth would continue to heat up. Any object that is heated gets continuously hotter unless an equal amount of heat is withdrawn. We know this from our own everyday experience. For example, water boiling in a pot at sea level stays at 212°F (100°C) only because the amount of heat going into the water is used to convert the liquid water to water vapor. Before the water reaches boiling point, it gets continuously hotter because additional heat is being applied. The earth would work in the same way. Its temperature would grow until the oceans would begin to boil—unless exactly as much heat were to somehow leave the earth as is absorbed from incoming sunlight. Luckily for us, this is, in fact, what happens.

Every object that has a temperature greater than what is called *absolute zero* (− 273°C, − 459°F) gives off heat in the form of radiant energy. Hotter objects give off more radiant heat and radiation with shorter wavelengths than do colder objects. For instance, if we were to put an iron in a hot fire, it would first glow dull red, an indication that it is giving off infrared-wavelength radiation, often called *long-wave radia-*

tion. The red glow would then change to yellow, visible-wavelength radiation, then to blue, called *short-wavelength radiation*, as the rod gets hotter, and so on. Even though at room temperature, the rod is not hot enough to give off light that our human eyes can see, energy is always being radiated from its surface. Similarly, objects colder than many hundreds of degrees (F or C) in temperature won't give off enough radiation at the short wavelengths for us to see it, even in a dark room. What we do see is the reflected short-wavelength visible light bouncing off its surface. Once again, energy is radiated, even if our eyes can't see it. In the case of the earth, we can "see" the effects of its long-wave radiation in our climatic structure. We can also see it with instruments on space vehicles.

On the average, the earth radiates energy into space at a level equivalent to that of a "black body" that has a temperature of $-18°C$. Not all bodies of the same temperature give off the same amount of radiation. A black body is one that gives off the maximum amount possible at its temperature. While the earth is not a black body, it radiates like one at $-18°C$. Actually, the earth's *surface* has a temperature much warmer ($+15°C$ or $57°F$) on the average than the very cold ($-18°C$) temperature at which the earth radiates energy to space. The difference between the warm earth's surface ($+15°C$) and the colder black-body radiation temperature of the earth ($-18°C$) is due to the presence of certain gases and particles in the atmosphere that together create the celebrated greenhouse effect.

This greenhouse effect is an important climatic component. The glass of a greenhouse lets most of the sun's energy in and traps most of this heat inside. Similarly, some chemical compounds in the atmosphere let in the sun's radiant energy more efficiently than they let out the earth's radiation. The earth loses heat to space as long-wavelength infrared radiation (with wavelengths between 5 and 100 millionths of a meter—something like the thickness of a human hair). The rate at which the earth loses heat is equivalent to that of a black body of the temperature of $-18°C$, as we've said. This rate of heat loss is enough to balance exactly the absorbed energy from the sun, and the earth's average temperature is fixed by this balance. However, there are other intervening factors. Gases such as water vapor, carbon dioxide, nitrous oxide, and ozone, as well as particles of dust, liquid water, ice, and sulfuric acid, all contribute to both the albedo and the greenhouse properties of the earth. Together they tend to let a larger fraction of the sun's energy through the atmosphere to the earth's surface than they allow to escape to space in the form of long-wave infrared radiation from the earth's surface. The temperature—and the climate—of the earth's *surface* is controlled by a precise balance among the solar energy absorbed, the amount of long-wave infrared radiation emitted, the properties of the surface itself, and the distribution of gases and particles in the atmosphere.

We can see that the earth's surface temperature and the climate are balanced and regulated by the character of sea, land, and air. Now let's look at the regulators of radiation passing up and down in the atmosphere. The most significant ones include cloud droplets, water vapor, carbon dioxide, nitrous oxide, and sulfuric acid. These are the very compounds whose travels are a part of the global biogeochemical cycles of life. We've seen that each functions through a series of interconnected cycles. Now we can see that their combined effects guide nothing less than our ability to live on earth! The climate regulates the speed of the flow of materials within these cycles of life. The constituents of the cycles, in turn, regulate the radiation flows between earth and space, which determine the climate, as well as life itself (e.g., through photosynthesis). It's almost as if life were some great collective intelligence, regulating itself in part through biogeochemical cycles that depend on the climate they control.

The physical, chemical, and climatic environments determine the ecological niche that each species can occupy. But the climate itself both determines and is determined by the nutrient cycles. Two scientists, James Lovelock from the University of Reading in England and Lynn Margulis from Boston University, struck by the almost theological essence of this web of climate and life cycles, called the self-regulating interactions among life, the cycles of life, and the climate, the "Gaia hypothesis."[13] Even contemporary scientists use the wealth of legends found in Greek mythology to make more abstract concepts understandable. The name was chosen because of the watchfulness of the ancient Greek Mother Earth goddess, Gaia.

In addition to the natural quantities of water vapor, carbon dioxide, dust, ozone, nitrous oxide, or sulfuric acid in the atmosphere are those added by human activities. How resilient are the seemingly self-regulating natural processes of life—the cycles of life and climate—to our insults in the form of pollutants? Not only are we modifying the amounts of nutrients flowing in the cycles of life when we burn fossil fuels or spread nitrogen fertilizers, but we are also changing the earth's albedo and greenhouse properties. Modern science has made this possible. However, it also is telling us that we may be altering the climate upon which all life, including our own, depends. Up to the 20th century, our climate influence has probably been relatively small, except in isolated regions of high-density population or industry.[14] However, we are the first generation in history to be interfering with the cycles of life *on a global scale.* The consequences

FIGURE 7-10. This tropical plant is an epiphyte. It is able to attach itself to many structures—in this case (inset) a power line—and carry out its life processes; yet it is not a parasite. Epiphytes use sunlight to convert atmospheric carbon dioxide to plant tissue through photosynthesis. They capture rain as it falls. And they take nutrients like nitrogen and sulfur from chemicals dissolved in the rain. Indeed, the nutrients in the rain are their main fertilizer. Earlier, we noted that Earth is associated with the mother in mythological imagery. In Greek legend, Zeus fertilizes women, and in his role as the rain god, he also fertilizes Earth—much as these epiphytes are fertilized. The realization that life, the global cycles, and the climate all have evolved together struck two scientists, Lynn Margulis and James Lovelock. Remembering the significance of Mother Earth, Gaia, they named the theory of the co-evolution of climate and life the "Gaia hypothesis," borrowing the terminology from artistic expression in literature *(Photos by Stephen H. Schneider)*.

could be as far-reaching as a change in the climate. The seriousness of the long-term threat and the immediate need for corrective actions are issues we'll look at in the next chapter.

FIRE: DOES IT RECYCLE?

So far, we've seen that the Greek "Elements" of Earth, Water, and Air aren't really elements as we use the term today to describe hydrogen or oxygen. They are more like what we call today the states of matter: solids, liquids, and gases. However, the Greeks correctly recognized that these Elements could transform into one another, and some put Fire in this category. Up to now, we've hardly discussed Fire, other than to mention that the energy from the "fire" on the sun, which fuses hydrogen to helium, provides the energy for life processes and climate on earth. We've also pointed out that energy is taken up or given off in processes that are central to the cycles of life (e.g., solar heating and long-wave infrared radiation cooling; evapotranspiration and condensation; photosynthesis and respiration; nitrification and denitrification). Energy is also necessary to human society, as the current "energy crisis" reveals daily. What we want to talk about here, though, is the "Element" Fire. Does Fire reflect the cyclical theme it has described in the speculative sciences?

Based on our present knowledge, Fire does not seem to be an element at all. It is a process, and a process that liberates energy. The process we call fire is the "burning up" of a material. Of course, the matter isn't really destroyed by the fire; it is merely transformed into other matter. For example, burning a log means the liberation of the energy stored in the hydrocarbon molecules of the wood. Carbon atoms in the wood combine with oxygen atoms from the air to produce carbon dioxide. Hydrogen atoms in the wood combine with oxygen atoms in the air to form water vapor. The end result of the burning of the log is the transformation of a given weight of solid wood (i.e., hydrocarbon molecules) to a nearly equal* weight of hydrogen and carbon atoms. These are combined with the additional weights of some oxygen atoms to make carbon dioxide and water vapor gases. In addition, there is the liberation of energy in the form of heat and light. Other processes, including the use by our body cells of hydrocarbons in our food, work similarly to keep us warm. So, fire is a process that produces energy and transforms matter. The laws of nature that we now believe govern processes involving energy are called the *laws of thermodynamics*. Because they have important implications for life, we'll briefly review them here in the context of energy.

THE FIRST LAW OF THERMODYNAMICS

Many processes, as we've seen, transform energy from one form to another. An important aspect to consider is whether anything is lost along the way. The first law of thermodynamics tells us that nothing is. This is a bookkeeping law that says that energy is always conserved, that it cannot be created or destroyed: it is recycled. If energy disappears in one form, it must then reappear in the exact amount in other forms. As stated by Ehrlich, Ehrlich, and Holdren:

> When we burn gasoline, the amounts of energy that appear as mechanical energy, thermal energy, electromagnetic radiation, and other forms are exactly equal all together to the amount of chemical potential energy that

*Einstein pointed out, through his famous equation $E = mc^2$ that a very small fraction of the mass can be transformed to energy. This transformation is the basis of nuclear power either on earth or in a star.

disappears. The accounts must always balance; apparent exceptions have invariably turned out to stem from measurement errors or from overlooking categories. The immediate relevance of the first law for human affairs is often stated succinctly as, "You can't get something for nothing."[15]

Even so, this is a happy state of affairs, for along with the inability to create energy goes the inability to lose any. This is where the all-important, frequently poorly understood second law of thermodynamics comes into play.

THE SECOND LAW OF THERMODYNAMICS

This law deals with the *efficiency* with which energy that is stored (e.g., in a gallon of gasoline) can be converted to useful, applied work (e.g., moving a car). Different kinds of stored energy are converted differently into useful work. Even though no energy is destroyed, some of the energy from our gallon of gasoline is unavailable to move the car because it leaves the car as heat out the exhaust pipe, friction at the tires, or wind resistance on the car body. (The latter two also end up as heat given off to the environment.) No process has yet been discovered in our world that can convert all stored energy in one form to useful work without losses. The search for such a "perpetual-motion machine" has an amusing history, but its actors leave a legacy of frustration.

We have finally come to an Element—Fire—whose process involves energy, a quantity that in practical applications *does not fully recycle!* Our cyclical theme is finally not supported by the findings of modern science. Energy in the universe is slowly running out on us. Not only are we unable to win, as the first law of thermodynamics has told us, but the second law teaches that we cannot break even. What's more, we can't get out of the game! There is an urgent message in the discovery of these laws. Again Ehrlich, Ehrlich, and Holdren express this well:

> More generally, the laws of thermodynamics explain why we need a continual input of energy to maintain ourselves, why we must eat much more than a pound of food in order to gain a pound of weight, and why the total energy flow through plants will always be much greater than that through plant-eaters, which in turn will always be much greater than that through flesh-eaters. They also make it clear that *all* the energy used on the face of the Earth, whether of solar or nuclear origin, will ultimately be degraded to heat. Here the laws catch us both coming and going, for they put limits on the efficiency with which we can manipulate this heat. Hence, they pose the danger that human society may make this planet uncomfortably warm with degraded energy long before it runs out of high-grade energy to consume.[16]

THE CYCLICAL THEME IN THE PERSPECTIVE OF MODERN SCIENCE

What, then, have we learned of the cyclical theme since the Greeks? We now have had a glimpse of the fantastic web of interconnected global cycles of life through which both life and life support systems are mutually regulating. Most materials do recycle, as was believed by speculative science. We also know that we are far from a complete understanding of their workings. We have seen that Fire—more properly, energy—drives that system, with the primary power coming from the thermonuclear fire of the sun. Other important energy sources—at least, for our society—come from the use of stored energy in the chemical and nuclear fuels on earth.

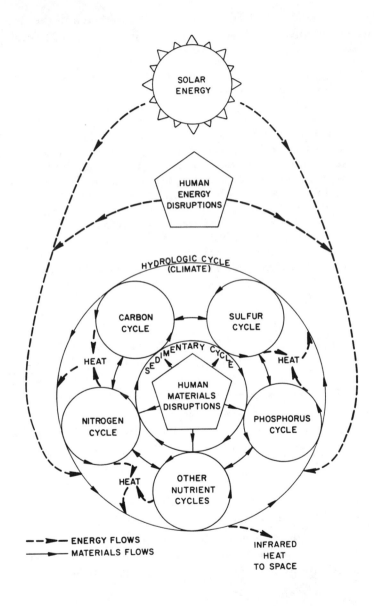

SOLAR ENERGY

HUMAN ENERGY DISRUPTIONS

HYDROLOGIC CYCLE (CLIMATE)

CARBON CYCLE

SULFUR CYCLE

HEAT

SEDIMENTARY CYCLE

HUMAN MATERIALS DISRUPTIONS

HEAT

NITROGEN CYCLE

PHOSPHORUS CYCLE

HEAT

OTHER NUTRIENT CYCLES

- - ► ENERGY FLOWS
——► MATERIALS FLOWS

INFRARED HEAT TO SPACE

FIGURE 7-11. Life on earth depends on the cycling of nutrients through air, water, soil, and living things. This mandalalike figure represents the interconnectedness of life, the biogeochemical cycles, and the climate. The climate regulates the flow rates of materials (represented by solid lines on the figure) through these global cycles. The one-way flow of energy—the only Greek Element that does not generally recycle—is shown by the dashed lines. Solar energy degrades to heat at each stage of the cycling process and is eventually returned to space as so-called infrared or heat radiation. The earth's temperature results from the balance between the solar energy absorbed and the infrared energy emitted into space by the earth. The composition of the earth's atmosphere regulates the radiative balance, which, in turn, controls the climate. Modern scientific findings show that life and climate are linked by a complex web of interconnected cycles. Man has intervened primarily through agriculture and energy use. The next question to examine is *how* our alterations can affect both man and Nature. Finally, we will ask whether we need to change the way humans alter the global cycles of life *(Drawing by Stephen H. Schneider).*

Also, we know that nothing can be done on earth that uses energy—and everything we do uses energy—without generating some wastes that interfere with the natural global cycles of life. The question that then emerges is: What is the meaning of mankind's interference in the global cycles of life? The answer will have a profound impact on the future of humanity.

The environmental systems of the Earth would collapse if the attempt were made to supply all human beings alive today with a European style of living. To suggest that such an increase in living standards is possible for a world population twice the present size by the early part of the next century is preposterous.

—PAUL AND ANNE EHRLICH

Chapter 8 / HUMAN DISRUPTIONS OF THE GLOBAL CYCLES OF LIFE

One side of the earth (the side man has thought of as "night") is no longer in the dark. Thanks to Edison's inventions, satellite photos (e.g., Figure 8-1) show that the back side of our planet literally "glows" in the dark!

Electricity has become a central prop of modern lifestyles. We have tapped the great natural reservoirs of nutrients for raw materials and then transformed them by gigantic engineering schemes into "useful" products like electricity, fertilizer, and gasoline. They are transported and distributed to us through the mechanism of complex social organizations like corporations, labor unions, and governmental regulatory agencies. Thus, through technology and organization, hu-

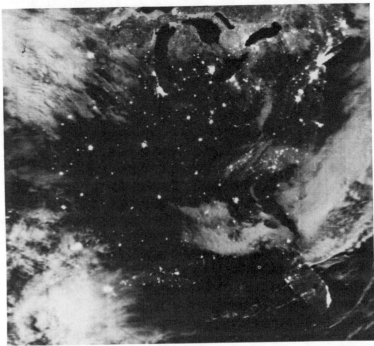

FIGURE 8-1. The climate is a result of the balance among energy flows in the natural world. Man can alter the climate to the extent that human activities disrupt these flows. A night-time photo from space shows that the back side of the earth literally glows in the dark. The lights of major urban concentrations of the eastern United States are clearly seen. Energy use in these areas is very high. The release of heat in industrial areas is in some cases as powerful as the energy input from the sun. Man is becoming a major influence on the local climates. The influence is called the *urban heat island effect*. It is evident in the daily weather reports, which often cite temperatures in the center of urban areas that are much higher than in rural surroundings (*Photo courtesy U.S. Air Weather Service*).

mans not only tap the flows of energy and nutrients that Nature provides through the global cycles of life, but we also contribute a substantial measure to those natural flows, often without regard to consequences, if we take any notice at all. The size of that measure is a main concern of this chapter. So is the way in which our relationships with Nature and other people have been changed by the use of technology and organization to maintain modern lifestyles. These problems, *taken together*, comprise our "ecological crisis."

A MORNING ROUTINE: MAN APART FROM NATURE?

For John Phillips, our "average American," typical work-day mornings mean waking up with an incipient headache. There is traffic to face on the way to work, board members whose concern with profit and loss must be faced, and clients' needs to be met. His first motion is to switch on the electric radio for a weather report and the latest news of the stock market. As he turns on the bathroom faucet, which stays on throughout most of his morning routine, Sally Phillips heads downstairs to the kitchen. A working mother doesn't have the time to prepare elaborate breakfasts. She relies on such convenient appliances as her frost-free refrigerator/freezer to store frozen orange juice and her percolator to heat the morning coffee. The din of radios, stereos, running water, hair dryers, and slamming drawers indicates that the three children are up and about. To save time once again, they dress in easy-to-care-for fabrics like polyester. After breakfast, Sally and John drive off in opposite directions for their respective offices, and the eldest son drives his brother and his sister to school, in the family's third car.

This routine is typical of those played out in millions of households every day, reflecting what has become a way of life for many: a lifestyle based on modern conveniences. No longer must we be subjected to a crippling dependence on Nature's extremes: heat, cold, and rain. We are striving to insulate ourselves from Nature.

The morning routine stands as a confirmation that we do not suffer from many of the harsher aspects of Nature so often endured by our ancestors—and still endured by many in poor or technologically less-developed areas. It would be wrong, though, to neglect the important ways in which we are still highly dependent upon Nature, even if these dependencies appear less obvious than in the past. They are more subtle because our technology has removed us several steps from actual natural phenomena. However, tracing the path from man to Nature through these steps makes the connections clearer.

The connections between our modern life and Nature can be seen if we look at the relationship of one natural part of our brief morning routine: climate. The amount of energy used for climate control in a building is dependent upon the outside temperature. In fact, a home's construction, its size, and its insulation requirements are, to a large extent, determined by the climatic conditions of its location, as are the heating bills and the air pollution from fuel burning.

The fresh water that flows so reliably from the faucet comes largely from the sky. This precipitation feeds lakes and rivers and is also diverted to, and stored in, man-made reservoirs, all of which provide water supplies for people in villages, towns, and cities. More importantly, the rain provides irrigation to grow most of our food.

Growing food requires certain climatic conditions. Much of the food we eat is imported from areas or countries where these appropriate conditions exist. A good example is coffee, whose price rose dramatically in the mid-1970s because of smaller harvests due to freezing temperatures. Economic juggling of pricing policies by coffee-exporting giants notwithstanding, climate in this case influenced the supply, and therefore the price, of this food item. Thus, certain fundamental dependencies on world trade arise from our demands for varieties of food, energy, and other "necessities." Our social institutions are integrated with natural phenomena like the climate, and the two combine to determine the availability of the goods we want.

Energy is a prime example of modern necessity whose availability depends on both social institutions and Nature. Most of the activities mentioned on our morning routine have a major aspect in common: they are energy-dependent. For example, food is cooked; water is pumped and heated; the house is heated; the cars need gasoline. They are all tied into our energy system. Not only are these morning activities immediately interrelated in terms of energy use, but a variety of energy services can also be found in the developmental stages of each.

We can expand on our food example. By tracing the U.S. food system, we find that much of it depends on fertilizers and pesticides, both of which are produced from energy-intensive processes. Food production is also aided by irrigation from electric or gas-driven pumps, harvested by diesel tractors, and transported by trucks. Once in the supermarkets, it is refrigerated, only to be transported, usually by car, to individual homes or apartments, where it is rerefrigerated and heated, until ground up by electrical disposal units and carried away to sewage-disposal plants. Each stage entails an energy use, and the entire process can be seen as dependent on our energy system.

It takes about 10 calories* of energy, mostly in the form of petroleum products, to deliver just 1 calorie of food energy to a U.S. table. This statistic led one ecologist[1] to quip that today, "We eat potatoes made of oil." About 15% of all energy used in the United States is involved in our food system. But most of that energy is *not* spent on the farm, despite the heavy use of fertilizers, pesticides, and farm machinery. The bulk of the energy is used not for food production but for food processing (e.g., in making TV dinners or instant breakfasts, or in packaging). The single largest transportation energy use in the food system occurs *off* the farm! It is not the use in tractors nor in trucking food from farm to processing plant to supermarket. Rather, it is the consumer's drive between supermarket and home, making us the major users of energy for transportation in the U.S. food system.[2]

Energy use per person in the United States per day is 5 times greater than the world average. It is only 2 times as great as that in Europe, but it is more than 20 times as great as that used per person in some Third World countries. Not surprisingly, then, in places like India or Nigeria, the amount of energy used to bolster food production or to aid in food delivery to vast populations is much less than that used by industrialized nations. Such a small amount helps to contrib-

---

* Several units of energy are well known. One is the calorie. In physics, this is the amount of heat needed to raise the temperature of 1 gram of water 1°C. In more familiar terms, the average adult needs about 2500 thousand calories of energy each day to run his metabolic processes. Unfortunately, in the field of nutrition, what is called a *calorie* is really 1000 of the calories defined above. We now see why dieters worry about "counting calories." Food is really energy, stored chemical energy, made up mostly of hydrocarbon molecules resulting from the photosynthesis of carbon dioxide using solar energy. If we eat more calories of stored chemical food energy than our bodies need, they store some of the excess, unhappily, as fat.

ute to the precarious balance between food supplies and demands in the many less-developed countries with burgeoning populations. The life-and-death seriousness of this balance makes headlines when droughts, floods, or political strife crimps local food production or breaks down the system that delivers food to the masses of poor (e.g., in Biafra or Cambodia).

In industrialized countries, starvation is rare, even in the worst of weather conditions. Although droughts, floods, and political problems do affect the availability of some food products and do cause prices to go up, the rich have been much less vulnerable than the poor to fluctuations in food productivity. A major reason for this difference stems from technologies that increase food production and improve its storage and distribution. Another margin of difference comes from social organizations. Highly organized and wealthier nations can distribute goods efficiently. In addition, a generally high economic level permits purchasing power sufficient to maintain high nutritional standards, even when natural catastrophes like droughts cause prices to rise. Poor people have less economic flexibility. Technology, social organizations, and the economy help the rich to minimize their vulnerability to decreases in food production. Other factors also contribute.

Cultural practices, the legacy of colonialism, international trading alignments, geography, climate, and, not least, population size—all contribute to the relative difference in vulnerability between rich and poor. In terms of population, Third World countries account for about three-fourths of the world's 4 billion plus people. About 9 out of every 10 babies are born in them. The poorer countries generally can afford less per capita use of fertilizers, modern farming techniques, medical supplies, and energy. Of course, they want to im-

FIGURE 8-2. (A) An attentive crowd watches the practice of outdoor dentistry in Katmandu, Nepal. The sanitary conditions and the appearance (B) of the "patient" certainly make our modern dentistry seem advanced by comparison. Dental equipment, drugs, dental schools, and dental insurance are examples of technologies and social organizations developed in industrialized countries in order to reduce our vulnerability to one of the nastier aspects of Nature: tooth decay. Not surprisingly, less developed, Third World countries also want to consider using technologies and organizations to help detach themselves from dependence on the harsher aspects of Nature. But there are disadvantages to this course as well as benefits. For example, few people in industrialized countries are self-sufficient. We depend on social organizations like corporations, labor unions, and government agencies to provide a continuous stream of survival goods, such as food, medicine, and energy. Thus, our reduced vulnerability to Nature has been bought in part at the price of increased dependence on other people. We now require political stability to survive.

Another problem with the use of technology to live apart from Nature is the disruption it causes to the environment. Since our societies still depend on the climate and nutrient cycles to grow our food, for example, any alterations in these natural elements influences our well-being. If the very populous poorer nations of the world managed to find the resources to consume energy and materials at the high per capita standards typical of the industrialized countries, the total disruption to the global cycles of life would be accelerated severalfold. A difficult value trade-off is emerging. We need to weigh the relative benefits of using technology and organization to raise standards of living versus risks of the loss of self-sufficiency and the threat of increased disruption to the global cycles *(Photos by Stephen H. Schneider)*.

prove their living conditions. One measure of this desire is an increase in per capita consumption of material goods and services. Many look at the industrialized nations as their example. They view these societies and assume that more technology and energy use are what they need to achieve the economic base required to reach their goals. Yet this path to a better life raises major questions for both rich and poor countries alike.[3]

Suppose that the populous Third World nations were to find the wherewithal to raise their levels of consumption to ours. Then, the *total* worldwide disruption to nutrient cycles would be many times greater than it is today. Environmental disruption is proportional to the total amount of some activity that alters Nature. Since the total amount of this activity is merely its per capita level multiplied by the total number of people involved, we can see that high consumption levels for large numbers of people mean a great amount of disruption to Nature. A serious dilemma emerges. Some have called it the "human predicament": Can we improve the living standards for several billion people in poorer nations (through social organization and the deployment of appropriate technologies) while, at the same time, arresting the dangerous increases in world population fast enough to prevent unacceptable disruptions to the global cycles?[4]

We can use scientific techniques to illuminate the prospects or consequences we face given one or another action aimed at solving the human predicament. But there is no clear scientific definition of what is "unacceptable." This is a value-laden word. Before one can make an intelligent choice, even concerning value judgments, it is necessary to be well informed on the basic facts that underlie the decision. The remainder of this chapter will address itself to the prospects for, and likely consequences of, human actions that disrupt the cycles of life. Later, we can reconsider specific actions in light of what we know about these disruptions.

HUMAN DISRUPTIONS OF THE NATURAL FLOWS OF ENERGY

The power behind both man and Nature is energy. What is power? It is a measure of the *rate* of energy flow. The most familiar unit of power is the watt. Our bodies burn energy at the rate of about 100 watts. A closed room filled with people heats up because each of us is a 100-watt heater. If there were 25 people in a room, they would give off heat at a rate of about 2500 watts—roughly equivalent to the power rating of a kitchen oven. Table 8-1 shows the relative amount of energy produced or used for each of the listed categories.[5]

The table indicates that as far as energy is concerned, Nature still reigns supreme. The last two entries tell the story. For every 8 units of energy that humans now use each day, Nature provides 150,000 units of energy in the form of sunlight to the earth. However, humans are second on a global scale, even if a distant second. On a *local* scale, though, we are, in many places, already Number One. Take New York, for instance. The heat released to the environment from human energy use in Manhattan is about twice that which falls on the island from the sun. No wonder temperatures in downtown New York City usually are considerably warmer than those in the surrounding suburbs, especially at night. This man-made climate change is common to most modern cities. It is known as the *urban heat island effect*. Recall that the sun provides most of the energy to drive the nutrient cycles and the weather elements. Where the natural balance of energy flow is significantly disrupted by human activities, one

TABLE 8-1

APPROXIMATE ENERGY IN SELECTED FUELS AND PROCESSES[a]

Energy to feed 1 person for 1 day	10
Nonfood energy use per person per day, world average	200
Nonfood energy use per person per day, U.S. average	1,000
1 tank of gasoline (15 gallons)	2,000
1 barrel of oil (42 gallons)	5,900
1 metric ton of coal	29,000
Boeing 707 flight, San Francisco–New York	1,400,000
1 kilogram uranium-235, completely fissioned	79,000,000
Summer thunderstorm	160,000,000
Fuel input to 1000-megawatt power plant, 1 day	260,000,000
Hydrogen bomb (1 megaton)	4,000,000,000
Total human nonfood energy use per day	800,000,000,000
Sunlight striking top of atmosphere, 1 day	15,000,000,000,000,000

[a] The values in this table are expressed in units called *megajoules* in physics. One megajoule is 239,000 calories, or 239 of the "calories" referred to in nutrition.

might expect alterations in these cycles or the climate. The urban heat island is tangible evidence that human disruptions of the natural flow of energy are large enough in most urban concentrations to cause noticeable environmental change.

Aside from the urban heat island (and the troublesome possibility that man-made tornadoes or thunderstorms could be generated downwind of gigantic power plants) it is not so much the heat from our energy use that threatens to alter Nature. Rather, it is human pollutants, often themselves chemical combinations of nutrients, that threaten major disruptions of the global cycles.[6]

SPECIFIC CASES OF HUMAN DISRUPTIONS OF THE GLOBAL CYCLES

Artistic expression of natural cycles has not been contradicted in principle by the modern findings of science. Perhaps beyond even the fertile imaginations of most in the speculative sciences, science has shown that nature is structured in vast interlocking cyclical processes, the great biogeochemical cycles of life. These cycles connect many pools of nutrients: carbon, nitrogen, sulfur, water, and others. The nutrients move in many forms through wind action, ocean currents, and upheavals in the earth's crust. Chemical transformations take place, and Nature evolves through the driving force of energy (the one factor in the process that does not fully recycle but forever degrades to unavailable forms). Whether biological evolution will prove to be cyclical (like most nutrients) or a chain of events (like the flow of energy) is still a matter of pure conjecture.

The climate regulates the movements of these important nutrients since it governs winds, rainfall, river flows, and temperatures. Meanwhile, some forms of the nutrients influence the brightness of the earth and the opacity of the atmosphere to radiant energy to and from space. This process, in turn, regulates the climate, which regulates the cycles. Thus, life, the global cycles of life, and the climate itself are all part of an intricate and interrelated web of phenomena, upon which human existence depends. We have also learned that everything we do has some impact on the environment and the cycles of life. Until recently, however, that impact was largely confined to local regions where high concentrations of humans and their wastes could be found. Now, through organizational "success" and our inventive "genius," we have created and deployed technologies with the ability to reshape the earth's surface, mobilize vast quantities of energy, and put materials in the land, air, and water in sufficient quantity so as to rival the magnitude of the natural flows of nutrients in the global cycles. In fact, we have even invented materials that do not occur naturally. No longer is Nature the sole important factor in determining the quality of our air and water and even our climate. Man has become part of the environmental life-support system.

LOCAL DISRUPTIONS

At a local level, we know that our impact on the environment is highly visible (and has been for centuries). Air pollution has long been suspected of having local effects harmful to our health, whether it occurs in a smoke-filled room, occurred years ago as a "killer smog" in London, or occurs today in Los Angeles, Denver, or Vienna as an eye-stinging and lung-damaging brown cloud.[7]

Scientists are studying medical records looking for differences in the health of residents of heavily polluted cities versus those of less-polluted environments.[8] Evidence suggests that more disease and deaths are associated with long-term exposure to elevated concentrations of some air pollutants, particularly carbon, sulfur, or nitrogen compounds. But the evidence is equivocal because health damage is a complicated function of combinations of air pollutants. Furthermore, many factors other than air pollution play a role in disease and death. (Cigarette smoking is an exception; the evidence associating it with a higher risk of disease or death is virtually incontrovertible.) The scientists who try to decipher these complicated statistics relating health to environmental factors are known as *epidemiologists*. As hard as it is to acquire and interpret the scientific data, the most difficult aspect of their work often is trying to decide whether a suggestive, but not yet definitive, correlation between some environmental factor and a health risk is sufficient to call for regulatory actions. This value choice is similar to many others we will confront in the process of weighing the benefits of certain human activities versus the (often hidden) costs arising from their disruption of the environment.

Another example of local disruption is water pollution. The pollutants can be directly introduced into rivers or lakes, as in the case of the runoff of nitrogen and phosphorus compounds from fertilized farm fields, or in the case of the discharge of untreated sewage or chemical wastes. Pollutants can also enter the waterways by indirect paths. Most often, they fall out in the rain or snow. Precipitation cleanses air pollutants from the atmosphere—only to dump them on the earth's surface, from which they are not as easily removed. The most notorious example is known as *acid rain*. In particular, discharge of sulfur oxides and nitrogen oxides into the air from burning fossil fuels leads to the formation of sulfuric acid and nitric acid shrouds above heavily industrialized re-

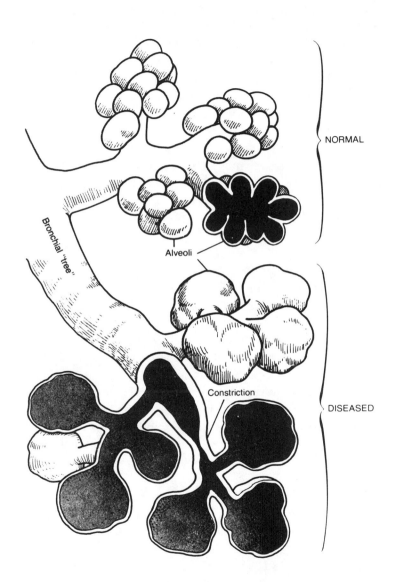

NORMAL

Bronchial "tree"

Alveoli

Constriction

DISEASED

FIGURE 8-3. The cycling of nutrients through the environment determines the "ecological niche" for each species. If the concentrations of some forms of certain nutrients are inappropriate, then stress, disease, or death can result. Bronchitis and emphysema are diseases caused or aggravated by some kinds of air pollution. "In the normal lung the bronchial tubes branch into millions of tiny chambers (alveoli), where transfer of oxygen to blood takes place. In the diseased lung the alveoli coalesce, reducing the amount of surface available for oxygen transfer. Furthermore, the 'twigs' of the bronchial tree are constricted, reducing the rate at which air is exchanged." One negative consequence of human interference in the sulfur and nitrogen cycles is the alteration of the atmospheric concentrations of some sulfur and nitrogen compounds—in the form of air pollution. Smog is more than an aesthetic eyesore; it can be a physical eyesore as well as a threat to respiratory health *(Drawing and description from P. R. Ehrlich, A. H. Ehrlich, and J. P. Holdren, Ecoscience: Population, Resources, Environment, W. H. Freeman, San Francisco, 1977, p. 546. Drawing originally from W. McDermott, "Air Pollution and Public Health," Scientific American, October, 1961).*

gions. In the atmosphere, these compounds are responsible for the kinds of health effects we just described. When it rains, they get carried into soils, streams, and lakes, spreading their impact over regions hundreds to thousands of square miles in size.

A map of the United States would show patterns in which the greatest acidity in the rainfall is around industrial centers, primarily in the heavily populated Northeast. The effects also spread hundreds of miles downwind of the area where the pollutants are released. Lakes, even in the remotest parts of New York State's Adirondack Mountains, are subjected to acid rain. Special ecological effects of acid rain, like the health damage resulting from air pollution, are difficult to isolate because the agents of ecological change are many and are highly interactive. Nevertheless, considerable evidence points to the likelihood of serious damage from acid rain. Among these are the reduction of fish populations, alterations in nitrification processes in soil (i.e., Nature's way of manufacturing fertilizer), and a change in the rates at which nutrients are washed from the soil.[9]

The mechanisms by which acidity kills fish are being actively studied. One theory stresses interference with the delicate acid-sensitive reproduction stages of fish. Acidity can reduce calcium levels. If the calcium level in female fish becomes low enough, they may not be able to produce eggs. If eggs do manage to form under these conditions, both they and the newly hatched fish can be vulnerable to comparatively low levels of acidity. Another killer of fish is believed to be active in the spring. Winter snows containing acidifying chemicals melt rapidly when the weather warms. They release a pulse of high acidity into the waters. This process has been implicated in sudden killings of fish in lakes in Scandinavia. The evidence, though, is still largely circumstantial. In *Mosaic*, the magazine of the U.S. National Science Foundation, Cornell University ecologist Gene Likens summarized the situation like this:

> The correlations are convincing, like those between cigarette smoking and lung cancer. But I can't prove conclusively that the sulfur in my rain collected in New Hampshire came from a power plant in Ohio.[10]

Public attention to the acid rain problem was first directed toward Sweden. During the Stockholm U.N. Environment Conference in 1972, many Swedish scientists and environmentalists noted a reduction of the growth rate of forests and the elimination of salmon and trout from many of their waters. They blamed this phenomenon on emissions of acidifying sulfur and nitrogen compound oxides from industrial centers in England and West Germany. Acid rain is more than a local question: it is a growing regional and international problem. Not only is the issue a trade-off between the economic benefits of technology versus their environmental costs, but it also shows that the benefits do not necessarily fall on the same people by whom the costs must be borne! *Fairness* is one of the factors that must be weighed when balancing costs and benefits. As we all know, equity is a difficult enough issue to deal with in the social context of a single nation. It becomes a staggering problem when, as in the case of acid rain, risks and benefits are spread disproportionally among different countries.

Acid rain represents a human disruption to the sulfur and nitrogen cycles. It can harm ecological systems. There are many other substances that can also damage life, even if these need not necessarily be components of the nutrient cycles. Perhaps the most serious of local environmental problems is the release of literally thousands of toxic substances. These include DDT, kepone, nerve gas, and radioactive plutonium, an ingredient created in the laboratory to power atomic weapons or nuclear plants. When it is leaked into the environment, plutonium remains radioactive for literally hundreds of thousands of years. Its release is hardly compatible with any concept of stewardship over our environment.

Many of these chemicals dumped into the environment (which then becomes nothing more than a sewer) are manmade. Others already exist in Nature, but we are increasing their concentrations well beyond the levels to which many beings, humans included, are accustomed. Ever since Rachel Carson's *Silent Spring*,[11] there has been growing public awareness of the risk in releasing large quantities of potentially dangerous chemicals into the environment before many of their adverse consequences can be understood. It is true, as TV commercials paid for by chemical companies contend, that economic, health, and social benefits can accrue from the prudent use of such chemicals. However, when the scale of their release or the magnitude of their impact becomes large "enough," the risks begin to equalize and even exceed the benefits.

A good example of such excessive danger is the unhappy affair that took place in Niagara Falls, New York, in 1978. The incident occurred, ironically, in an area known as the Love Canal. For a number of years prior to 1978, some residents of the community had complained about strange chemicals rising out of the ground. After a considerable time, investigations revealed that many homes around the Love Canal had been built on landfill that covered drums of highly toxic chemical wastes dumped there some two decades earlier by the Hooker Chemical Company. (Hooker Chemical, incidentally, denied any liability for wrongdoing, yet they made a financial contribution to the cleanup effort.) It seems that the drums were leaking and the residents had been exposed to these chemicals. Young children and pregnant mothers were advised to move out, although statistics showed that it was probably too late for many. Miscarriages and birth defects were unusually high among the residents. This discovery led the governor of New York to petition the federal government for help in relocating scores of Love Canal families. Meanwhile, all parties disclaimed direct responsibility. The federal government did eventually help fund the evacuation and relocation of some residents who had not already fled. Arguments over genetic damage to the residents and who is responsible are still raging. The incident clearly demonstrates that environmental quality is not just an aesthetic value. It is, like the global nutrient cycles, a necessity of life.

DISRUPTIONS ON A GLOBAL SCALE

So far we have mentioned examples of local disruptions of the environment. Much has been written about these "classic" environmental problems. Indeed, they are the chief substance of most "ecology books," or environmental studies. Nevertheless, as important as they are, they are still largely local or regional problems. Next, we will be concerned with a less-familiar but probably more perplexing issue: disruption of the biogeochemical cycles on a *global scale.*

It is impossible to weigh the economic benefits of activities that disrupt these cycles against the risks of such disruptions unless we have some quantitative knowledge of both the risks and the benefits. To do something about it, we also need to know *who* benefits, *who* risks what, and when. For our immediate purposes, however, we will view the risk issue, focusing on specific disruptions of some of the global cycles of life. While many cases could be cited of disruptions of a number of global nutrient cycles and their component parts, we can illustrate the scope of the problem by discussing a few aspects of disruptions of three crucial cycles of life.

DISRUPTION OF THE GLOBAL SULFUR CYCLE. Humans disrupt the sulfur cycle primarily by burning coal and oil, which contain sulfur. About 100 million tons of sulfur are added annually. As you recall, sulfur is an important nutrient for life, some of it being incorporated into the bodies of living things. Since coal and oil are fossil remains of living things, it is not surprising that they might contain some sulfur. Earlier, we pointed out that in highly populated, industrialized regions, sulfur compounds injected into the atmosphere were responsible for health-damaging smog and environmentally dangerous acid rain. The aspect of human disruption of the sulfur cycle that we will touch on here is the potential role of sulfur as a climatic regulator.

Man is not the only producer of sulfur compounds with the potential to modify the climate. Volcanoes inject vast quantities of sulfur oxides into the atmosphere following giant eruptions. The force of these explosions often hurls these compounds into the stratosphere, the part of the upper atmosphere between about 10 and 50 miles (16–80 kilometers) up. Since most of the weather occurs below 10 miles (16 kilometers), materials injected into the stratosphere can remain aloft several years. Rain and snow provide little cleansing in those regions. The sulfur compounds can blow all around the world in a few months following a major eruption. By this time, most of the sulfur that remains airborne is in the form of sulfate particles. Often, they exist as a "dust veil" of sulfuric acid (similar to the form sulfur takes in smog-filled cities). These minute particles (about 0.3 millionths of a meter in average size) can interfere with the transfer of radiant energy between the earth and space. They primarily block out a small percentage of sunlight from reaching the lower atmosphere, thereby cooling the climate.[12] Some scientists even implicate volcanoes in cold climatic episodes, like the ice ages. However, such an influence would have required an almost continuous series of big eruptions occurring for centuries, for even in the stratosphere, the dusty remains of these eruptions seem to last for only a few years.

Human injections of sulfur into the air are, over a year, much less than the amount from a big volcano. Also, most of the sulfur compounds from human activities do not reach the stratosphere. Rain and snow limit the lifetime of sulfur compounds injected into the air to a few days, perhaps a few weeks. In this time, sulfur compounds from human activities can travel thousands of miles, but not usually worldwide. Why, then, do some scientists worry about the climatic consequences of such injections, what climatologist Reid Bryson called the "Human Volcano"?[13]

Although each human source of sulfur air pollution may be able to spread its pollution only a few thousand miles, not worldwide, there is a large geographic distribution of source regions of sulfur injection: all of the industrialized world. Thus, a substantial portion of the northern hemisphere, at least, is reached by sulfur compounds from human activities. Figure 8-4 illustrates the impact of humans on the global sulfur cycle.

More importantly, the release of industrial sulfur goes on continuously—not intermittently, like volcanic eruptions. This fact has led some scientists to conclude that human disruption of the global sulfur cycle could seriously alter the global climate. Some have implicated it in a recent cooling trend, the symbols of which were very cold winters in the eastern United States during the mid-1970s. Others have even suggested that an increase in such pollution could trigger an ice age!

It is far from clear, though, if sulfur air pollution will, like volcanic dust veils, even cool the climate. Sulfate particles found in the lower atmosphere are often combined with other chemicals like carbon soot (also a pollutant—and a nutrient—

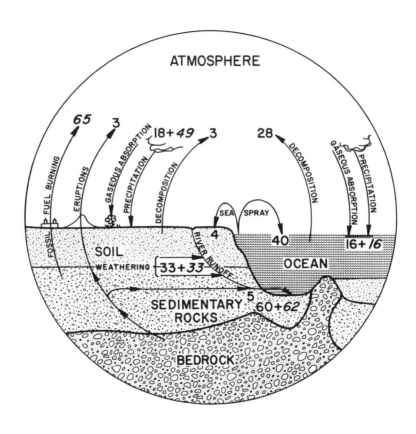

FIGURE 8-4. This schematic diagram of the global sulfur cycle shows the magnitude of the flows of sulfur compounds. It is highly simplified, omitting many local or internal loops of the total cycle in which sulfur flows at varying rates in various chemical forms. The slow geologic processes connected with weathering or continental motions through the sedimentary cycle continue inexorably, while faster internal loops exchange sulfur among living things and their immediate environment. The numbers represent present "best guesses" of the yearly flows of sulfur (in millions of tons) in each category shown. Uncertainties in these numbers range up to many tens of percent. The italicized numbers are estimates of the contributions of man to the flows of sulfur. It is interesting that before this disruption, the predominant flow of sulfur was from sea to land. Now, the situation is reversed. Even more importantly, humans are responsible for massive injections of sulfur into the air. It is a principal ingredient of urban smog. These air pollutants cause lung damage, acidify rainfall—which can disrupt natural ecosystems—and could possibly alter the global climate. Although many details are unanswered, it is already certain that humans are responsible for a major disruption of this global life cycle. The full consequences are yet to be known (*Adapted from B. Bolin and R. J. Charlson, "On the Role of the Tropospheric Sulfur Cycle in the Shortwave Radiative Climate of the Earth," Ambio 5, 1977, p. 47*).

resulting from fuel or vegetation burning). Since carbon soot is black, it can reverse the cooling effect of the sulfate particles on radiant energy flows in the atmosphere. That is, a plume of combined sulfur/carbon compounds might *warm* the climate, not cool it, as we suspect pure sulfate particles would do.

Scientists are just not yet able to determine whether the current or projected disruptions of the sulfur cycle will warm or cool the climate, or by how much. However, it cannot be said that it is implausible—or perhaps even unlikely—that we will discover that significant climatic changes could occur or already have occurred as a result of human disruption of the global cycle. The crucial question is whether we will uncover the actual effects *before* they occur.

DISRUPTION OF THE GLOBAL NITROGEN CYCLE. Although there is some nitrogen in fossil fuels, the bulk of nitrogen injected into the atmosphere from fuel burning is caused by a chemical combination of nitrogen atoms and oxygen atoms coming from the air that participates in the burning process. This combination into nitrogen oxides occurs when it is very hot, usually from combustion in fires. Whether the fires are produced by man in boilers, steel mills, automobile engines, or nuclear explosions (not reactors), or by nature in forest fires or lightning bolts, nitrogen oxides are produced. (The primary source for the *natural* production of fixed nitrogen compounds is biological—in the denitrification process of the nitrogen cycle.)

Man intervenes in the nitrogen cycle in three primary ways: (1) by combustion, (2) by land uses different from natural evolution, and (3) by the production and use of nitrogen fertilizer. It is estimated that combustion produces about 20 million tons of nitrogen annually, and fertilizer production about 50 million tons.[14] Land-use effects are more difficult to quantify. Estimates of the natural production of fixed nitrogen vary widely, but a rough figure of some tens to perhaps 100% can be set for the contribution of human activities *relative* to nature in the nitrogen cycle. Our influence is truly enormous.

On local and regional scales, this alteration of the nitrogen cycle affects the relative abundance of various plants and animals and the quality of air and water, among other things. But here we will stress, again, the global aspect of this issue.

In Chapter 7 we learned that one of the products of denitrification is nitrous oxide (laughing gas). N_2O is, as you remember, also implicated in maintaining the global ozone balance and in controlling the earth's temperature, since nitrous oxide contributes to the greenhouse effect. As in the sulfur case, considerable uncertainty still surrounds estimates of the role of N_2O in both ozone and climate regulation. Remember that human activities are responsible for something like 10% to 100% of nature's production of fixed nitrogen. Thus, it is not at all unlikely that as these fixed nitrogen compounds go through the nitrogen cycle and enter the denitrification process, considerable increases in atmospheric concentrations of N_2O will result in the future. Once again, we see clear possibilities of global consequences from the human disruption of a major nutrient cycle. And once again, the crucial question is whether we will uncover the actual effects *before* they occur.

HUMAN DISRUPTION OF THE CARBON CYCLE. The nutrient cycle most closely tied to technology and modern lifestyles is the carbon cycle. This is true because carbon-based fossil fuels are our chief energy source. It is not surprising, then, that the human impact on the global carbon cycle is the easiest to demonstrate—and probably the most far-reaching—of our disruptions of the global cycles. To make this clearer, recall three facts brought out earlier: (1) the fossil fuels are hydrocarbon molecules whose chemical energy is released (along with carbon dioxide, CO_2) when they are burned; (2) CO_2 is taken out of the air by photosynthesis in green plants during the growing season and is reinjected to the air by respiration and decay; and (3) CO_2 is a gas that contributes to the greenhouse effect, which heats the lower atmosphere as CO_2 concentrations increase.

In order to determine how much CO_2 increase is required to cause a noticeable change in the climate, we must ask how much CO_2 people add to the atmosphere relative to the amount already there. Figure 8-5 shows the carbon dioxide concentration measured at 10,000 feet on the slopes of Mauna Loa, a volcanic mountain on the island of Hawaii. The graph shows an annual oscillation—a cycle—of CO_2 increase and decrease of about 8 ppm (parts of CO_2 per million parts of air). Since the CO_2 concentration was about 335 ppm at the end of the 1970s, this annual cycle of CO_2 is about $2\frac{1}{2}$% (i.e., $8 \div 335$) of the annual average concentration. It is caused by the seasonal growth and decay of green plants. (Notice that there is a maximum of CO_2 in the late winter, the end of the decay season, and a minimum in the late summer, the end of the growth season.) According to state-of-the-art theories, a $2\frac{1}{2}$% change is not a large enough variation to cause a global temperature change of more than about one tenth of one degree Celsius—which would be undetectable. Thus, *over a year*, CO_2 change from the seasonal cycle of the biosphere cannot be a major factor in the climate. But, in the long run, over decades or more, the average concentration of CO_2 can change by enough to be of global climatic importance. In fact, Figure 8-5 shows a continuous increase of CO_2 concentrations superimposed on the annual cycle. This steady increase has been from about 315 ppm in 1958 to roughly 335 ppm for

1980, an increase of almost 7%. The question we must ask next is: What caused this increase? The answer almost certainly is: Man.

How is man able to increase the concentration of atmospheric CO_2? Several ways are possible. One, which civilization has been doing for over 5000 years, is to clear land for agriculture and settlements. Every time a tree is chopped down and burned (the way most deforestation occurs today in tropical forests), the hydrocarbon molecules that comprise the wood release their stored energy—and CO_2—into the air (just like a lump of coal, which is, as we've said, a compressed, metamorphized fossil tree). A number of scientists believe that as much as 1% of the forests in South America and Africa are being destroyed annually. This rate would release enough CO_2 to account for the increase seen in Figure 8-5. Other scientists, arguing that tropical deforestation rates are not that high, disagree.[15] They also argue that the increase of CO_2 in the air should increase photosynthesis. This process could take much of the extra CO_2 out of the air. Some agricultural scientists think that higher CO_2 concentrations could even increase food production, while others point out that it is usually not CO_2 but other nutrients (like water, nitrogen, sulfur, or phosphorus) that limit food productivity. Still others, mostly ecologists, worry that since some plants are more sensitive to CO_2 concentration than other plants, a long-term change in average CO_2 concentrations could alter the competitive balance among plants. This phenomenon would change the relative numbers of plants and animals all around the world. Understanding the complexity of this balance is still beyond human skills. We cannot predict reliably what would happen to individual members of various ecosystems should CO_2 continue to increase, let alone whether the new balance would be better or worse, and for whom.

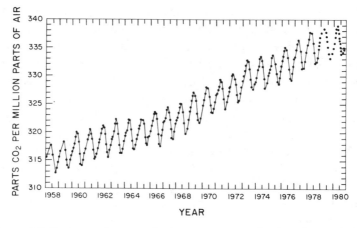

FIGURE 8-5. Each year the atmospheric concentration of carbon dioxide (CO_2) completes a cycle. About $2\frac{1}{2}\%$ of the annual concentration (in 1979) of about 335 parts of CO_2 per million parts of air (ppm) is involved in this cycle, at least at the point where this measurement was taken, Mauna Loa Observatory in Hawaii. The high point of the cycle occurs in the spring and the low point

in the early fall. Photosynthesis by green plants is responsible. When sunlight and temperatures increase in the spring, green plants efficiently use solar energy to convert atmospheric CO_2 to plant tissues by photosynthesis. During the winter, respiration and decay, which produce CO_2, proceed at a faster rate than photosynthesis, resulting in the spring maximum. But the most important feature of this record is the steady increase in CO_2 over the past 20 years superimposed on the natural cycle of the seasons. It amounts to nearly a 7% increase—and is caused by man! Clearing of trees in deforestation projects and burning of fossil fuels as an energy source are responsible, although the details are controversial. This increase is potentially very serious because CO_2 enhances the greenhouse effect, which should warm the climate. Present estimates suggest that increasing world population and thirst for energy will drive CO_2 concentrations up even faster in the future. Current projections suggest that by the end of this century, humans may become a major factor in the evolution of the earth's climate. This is not by design; it is a side effect of our disruption of the carbon cycle as we continue to grow in numbers and in the desire to consume energy, in order, among other things, to detach ourselves from Nature *(Data supplied by the Mauna Loa Observatory in Hawaii, maintained by the U.S. National Oceanic and Atmospheric Administration in collaboration with Dr. C. D. Keeling and others at the Scripps Institution of Oceanography, La Jolla, California).*

Despite our relative ignorance of the relationship between the biosphere and the observed CO_2 increase, the available evidence has led most scientists familiar with the problem to believe that deforestation is not the primary cause of the almost 7% CO_2 increase in the 1960s and 1970s. Rather, it seems more likely that another human activity is the principal culprit, an activity that, as we have seen, is a fundamental prop of modern industrial lifestyles: the use of energy.

Most of the energy we use comes from fossil fuels, and the burning of fossil fuels produces CO_2 as a by-product pollutant. We've said this several times. Now is the time to look at some actual numbers. How much CO_2 do we produce from the fuel burning each year to run global society? The answer is a staggering amount: about 18 times 10^{15} grams of CO_2 are produced this way each year. That is, about 40 trillion pounds or 20 billion tons of CO_2 are injected annually into "thin air." (Comparing this number to the weight of a familiar man-made leviathan will make it more easily understood. The CO_2 produced annually is the equivalent weight of about 450,000 large battleships, each like the U.S.S. *Missouri* of World War II, which weighed about 45,000 tons!) Remember, this annual injection of CO_2 is only 0.5% of the total amount of CO_2 already in the air. And this is only about 0.03% of the volume of all gases in the atmosphere. "Thin air" is indeed very heavy when weighed on a global basis.

Our purposes, however, are to explain the observed 7% CO_2 increase in the 20 years since continuous measurements were begun at Mauna Loa in 1958. If all the CO_2 injected into the air from the burning of fossil fuel since 1958 were to have remained in the air, then the CO_2 increase should have been about 13%, roughly twice that observed. What has happened to the missing half?

The most likely place to look is the oceans. It is known that the oceans contain vast amounts of dissolved CO_2. Most chemical oceanographers believe that the oceans are the "sink" for the missing CO_2.[16] As usual, there is controversy. No one has sufficiently precise measurements of the net rates at which the upper layers of the oceans take CO_2 from the air. Nor do we know well enough the net rates with which the deep oceans accept CO_2 from the seas' upper layers.

Meanwhile, as scientists debate uncertainties about the sources, sinks, and flow rates of CO_2 in the carbon cycle, each year the observations show a slightly larger increase in the CO_2 concentration than in the year before. That is, the *increment* of CO_2 increase is rising each year. That means that although there has been a 7% increase in CO_2 in the 20 years since 1958, the following 20 years will see much more than a 7% increase, and so on. The reason is human lifestyles. More energy is being used to increase standards of living. At the same time, more people are alive each day to demand even more energy. Thus, the combined effects of increased affluence and increased population size are causing a rapidly rising use of energy—and, as a result, an escalating disruption of the global carbon cycle.

The 7% CO_2 increase since 1958, the latest greenhouse-effect theories tell us, could not cause a detectable change in the earth's climate. But a 20% change—projected to occur around the end of this century if energy-use growth rates continue—would cause a noticeable change. By the middle of the 21st century, CO_2 is projected to double. By then, should the greenhouse estimates prove valid, mankind would become the principal force, albeit by accident, in changing the climate.

Would a change in the global climate be beneficial or detrimental? This would depend upon where you live, what crops you grow, what water supplies you depend on, what diseases you suffer from that are climate-related, and how much flexibility you have to alter crops, water supplies, etc.,

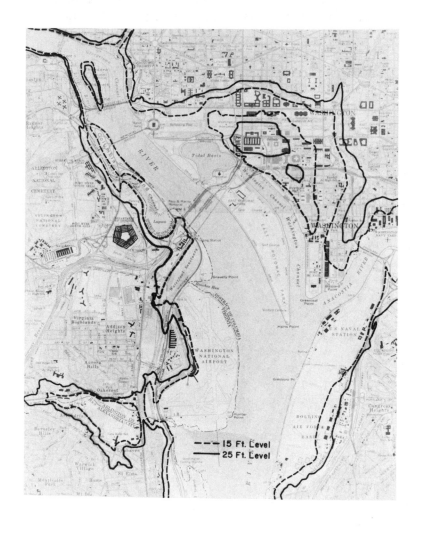

FIGURE 8-6. The increase in atmospheric CO_2 is projected to create a green-house-effect warming that would become significant sometime around A.D. 2000. Should these projections be even reasonably valid, then the warming could, according to a number of glaciologists, destabilize a portion of the ice sheet in the Antarctic continent. If this happened, then sea levels could rise about 8 meters (26 feet). The process could take anywhere from decades to centuries. Despite the uncertainties in the scientific evidence, it is possible to estimate the costs *if* such a coastal flooding were to occur. For the State of Florida, about one third of the land and 67% of the population would be displaced. For the United States alone, the cost of land and structures flooded would be (in relatively uninflated 1971 dollars) about $250 billion. In Washington, D.C., as the figure shows, parts of the Smithsonian Institution would be inundated, and the White House and the U.S. Capitol would become waterfront locations. Whether pursuit of those activities that increase CO_2 in the atmosphere has benefits that justify taking the chance of a sea-level rise is a major value trade-off. Both humanists and scientists must contribute to the process of making the choice. *(From S. H. Schneider and R. S. Chen, "Carbon Dioxide Warming and Coastline Flooding: Physical Factors and Climatic Impact," Annual Reviews of Energy 5, 1980, pp. 107–140.)*

in order to adapt to the new climate. In other words, climatic changes would be good for some, would hardly affect others, and would be dangerous for yet others. It is still a global gamble as to whether you, or your descendants, would win, lose, or draw.

One potential effect of a CO_2-induced warming would be catastrophic for coast dwellers: a sea-level rise. Some glaciologists believe that part of the south polar ice cap is unstable. They fear that a warming of only several degrees could break up part of it, causing it to "surge" into the sea. This surge could raise sea levels by some 15–25 feet (5–8 meters) in as little as a few decades or as much as a few hundred years. The initiation of this process cannot be ruled out as a possibility as early as the end of this century. Figure 8-6 shows what such a sea-level rise would mean for Washington D.C. In the United States alone, some quarter of a trillion dollars (calculated in 1971 dollars) of real estate would be flooded.[17] In 1981 dollars, the figure would be nearer to a trillion dollars.

WHAT IS THE BOTTOM LINE?

All of these projections are no more than rough guesses. We just don't have enough data to draw on to validate theories that permit confident estimates of the precise magnitude, timing, or consequences of many of these human disruptions to the biogeochemical cycles. Even more perplexing, at least from a policy-making point of view, is that few individuals can perceive of something as vast as global climatic changes resulting from their seemingly small tweak to their local environment. The strongest defensible statement we can make from currently available scientific evidence is that no longer are the *collective* environmental impacts of individual human activities limited to local or regional scales. Society is now a major, and growing, competitor with natural factors in determining the future of the global environment. Simply, *we are insulting our environment at a faster rate than we are understanding it*. Major changes are possible, indeed probable, although the details are still sketchy. That is the "bottom line" of human interference in the global cycles of life. The future of the cycles—and those who are tied to them—awaits the outcome. Whether to act to alter our impacts as revealed by present knowledge may hinge more on *ethical views* of our place in nature, than on tentative, present "cost/benefit" analyses.

"I'm in it for posterity."
—TOM STOPPARD

Chapter 9 / THE SOCIAL TITHE

Twentieth-century man has made a world of technological advances and complex social organizations. We rarely think about these structures, though, except to note how they seem to have made us increasingly aloof from Nature. However, the reality is that we are not independent. "We" (as individuals) have enjoyed the use of technology to reduce our vulnerability to many of Nature's hazards. For instance, few of us would go hungry if an early frost wiped out our tomato patch. We would simply pay the grocer for food grown elsewhere, where Nature had been more cooperative. Nearly everyone in society, though, depends on food grown elsewhere. This makes us still dependent on Nature, but our dependence is on Nature's providing sufficient harvests for everyone. *Sufficient* here means the overall food supply's being large enough to meet worldwide demand. If Nature adversely affects food production in one region, the people who live there have to turn elsewhere for their supply. They then need money to buy food and more time to wait for its distribution. It is an insurance step to keep adequate supplies close to home. Local maintenance of food reserves would alleviate these problems.

Without adequate food reserves, entire nations still fall victim to famines. For instance, several million "excess deaths" (increase in death statistics in excess of normal rates) in India and Bangladesh occurred in the drought years of 1972 and 1974.[1] Those droughts cut food production at a time when world grain reserves were being lowered deliberately in order to keep prices up.[2] This combination of bad harvests and human politics was, literally, deadly.

It is easy to blame the famines of the mid-1970s on a malevolent Nature. Yet, the occurrence of drought is highly precedented; only the timing and severity are uncertain. Their effects should have been anticipated. As important as Nature in those tragedies was the lack of proper planning by governments. The cutting of food stocks in the early 1970s is one example of poor planning. Another is the practice of some countries of living too close to the margin. That is, their food demand is allowed to come too close to their food requirements for them to weather a few bad growing years comfortably. Coupling this tight margin between supplies and needs with inadequate food reserves forces these countries to rely on the world grain market or on grain aid to make up for local shortages. In the mid-1970s, with food stocks down and prices soaring, the poorest of these countries that were short of food couldn't afford to buy their way out of the effects of the droughts. In addition, nations rich in grain were reluctant to give away their high-priced commodity. Millions died and tens of millions suffered from acute malnutrition while the world talked about the issue at the 1974 Rome World Food Conference.

The creation of social organizations to regulate food markets, stockpiles, and distribution systems reduces our vulnerability to *local* harvest failures. In the language of the insurance business, we have "pooled our risk," lowering the likelihood of local, individual catastrophes. Even so, we remain dependent on Nature to allow sufficient food production averaged over the entire world (or at least over the large part of it that participates in international food trade). More importantly, we have bought our insurance against individual, local vulnerability to Nature's extremes at a considerable premium: almost total dependence on others to plan for, produce, store, and distribute sufficient quantities of vital materials *at a price we can afford.*

Sometimes, that price is not monetary but political. It can come in the form of threats to a nation's oil imports or even to the safety of its citizens. Some obvious examples include threats to U.S. hostages in Iran in 1979–1980 in exchange for the extradition of the former shah, or the 1973 Arab oil embargo against nations the Arabs considered pro-Israel. The Iranian situation provides a broad example of the dangers of dependence on technology and organization to provide strategic services—in this case, energy supplies in the form of oil. Despite a general world disapproval of using embassy personnel as hostages, few nations dared condone early countermeasures against Iran, because withdrawal of its oil from the world market would be felt by all oil-importing nations, either as a serious shortage or, at best, in a price increase. Since nearly every nation is tied into the world oil-supply system, nearly everyone is subjected to the consequences of a decrease in overall supplies. Ironically, the United States and its oil-importing allies have become hostages to their own dependence on oil imports.

Our civilization's view of its place in Nature underlies the problems we've just cited. It is easy to see how. The Western cultures, for example, have been predominantly dissatisfied with the man/Nature bond. Their active response, as we've already postulated, has been to attempt to control Nature. Oil is a critical element in this attempt to shift the bounds of Nature in our favor. Oil provides energy for housing, industry, and transportation. But it has had its price. We have substituted a growing reliance on oil imports in place of the less mobile societies of the past. This substitution has greatly reduced our flexibility in dealing with any crisis that threatens world oil supplies. In essence, we have created a "social Frankenstein" in our attempt to use oil to improve economic conditions *and* to loosen the constraints of Nature on our lives.

If we are to use technology and organization to create better economic conditions or to alter our place in Nature favorably, then we must also take steps to maintain adequate stockpiles of strategic materials to tide us over the inevitable periods of political instabilities that can interrupt the normal flow of needed goods and services. The need to insure against political crises is no less important than the need to maintain adequate reserves of food to weather the inevitability of some "lean years" in the world's granaries.

We are certainly attempting to detach ourselves from Nature, but we are no more able to achieve that goal fully than were previous civilizations. The continuing paradox is that we are both detaching from and becoming more "embedded" in Nature. "We," as a society, are still dependent on

Nature to allow us to produce enough water, food, and so forth for all of us, as individuals. At the same time, "we," as individuals, have become dependent on society for the delivery of the goods we need to survive.

Another key to understanding this paradox lies in the meaning of the word *embedded*. The planning, producing, storage, and distribution of food, for instance, are accomplished through technologies that use vast quantities of, for example, energy, fertilizers, and chemicals. These, as we have seen, are becoming a growing influence on Nature, upon which we, as a society, are still highly dependent. Just as man depends on Nature, though, Nature also increasingly depends on man. Through technology and organization, we, the society, have pooled our resources to change the bounds of Nature. This action has caused massive alterations in the global cycles. The future stocks and flows of many forms of nutrients will increasingly depend on man. With these clarifications, the phrase "man is embedded in Nature," is consistent with the observation that individuals—in the industrialized countries, at least—are less vulnerable to the local hazards of Nature than their ancestors. Today, whole societies, instead of individuals, are "bonded" to Nature. The social sanction of the use of technology and supporting organizations to detach ourselves individually from Nature has merely forced us into collective dependence on Nature and the need for unprecedented cooperation among people for their necessities.

THE VALUE DICHOTOMY IN CONTEMPORARY ISSUES

Even though we are now discussing a broader kind of dependence, we are still talking about dependence—the very same kind of dependence we discussed earlier in values and reactions to man's place in Nature. We have only returned to the issue of values, but on a larger scale. C. P. Snow suggested, "The scientific process has two motives: one is to understand the natural world, the other is to control it."[3] Although some dangers, mostly military, of applications of science are mentioned, Snow remains firmly convinced that only through more science and technology can humanity, particularly the poor, progress. He comes down firmly on the side of those whose values are to alter the primordial bond for the convenience of man.

Bronowski states, "as a set of discoveries and devices, science has mastered nature; but it has been able to do so only because its values, which derive from its method, have formed those who practice it into a living, stable and incorruptible society."[4] How naive this notion of an "incorruptible society" of scientists must seem to those driven from their homes when their children's health was threatened in the Love Canal area near Niagara Falls. The people suffered because of toxic chemicals created by scientists and carelessly discarded by technical managers a few decades earlier. We could question whether "science has mastered nature" or should even try to.

Bronowski and Snow, like others writing during the Cold War era of the 1950s, were rightly concerned with the increasing worldwide repression of individual liberties that marked that time. However, at the same time, they underemphasized the negative consequences of the very rapid proliferation of science and technology. Among these consequences are environmental degradation and increasing technical complexity in issues, in addition to Snow's "two cultures" split. Along with the information explosion introduced by the growth of science and technology comes a growing disenfranchisement of nonspecialist citizens. The "average person," unfamiliar with the language or arguments of the technological components of major public-policy issues, cannot intelligently apply his own values to problems that he does not understand. Such problems crop up when the complexity of the issues involved vastly exceeds his knowledge of the subject. Such disenfranchisement is an integral part of the growth of science and technology. When the new information generated exceeds the willingness or the capacity of the citizenry to assimilate it, then the people lose control of the decision-making process. Without knowledge of the consequences of policy alternatives, intelligent choices cannot be made. This situation represents the loss of an individual freedom. Ironically, this loss arises from the very protection of the scientific values of freedom to discover and invent that have allowed the information explosion to flourish. "Too much" science and technology can boomerang, reducing individual liberty in a wash of information overload. The advent of this irony was almost wholly unanticipated by many of those who most passionately professed (as many still do) such libertarian or scientific values as the pursuit of truth at all costs.

It is not necessary that the growth of complexity must exceed the rate of education of the people. Undoubtedly, technological and organizational growth during the 19th century led to economic conditions that permitted education to become available rapidly, thereby reducing confusion, not increasing it. Such a situation may still apply in much of the Third World today. But today, in the most advanced countries, where nearly everyone is literate, it is not at all clear that the level of public education is increasing faster than the need to keep current. Quite possibly, if some U.S. national test scores are to be believed, we are steadily losing ground. Walter

Lippmann once remarked that "the movement of opinion is slower than the movement of events."[5]

We do not address these problems with scientific values merely to pick a quarrel with Snow and Bronowski as a counterbalance with our earlier favorable quotations of their views on the "two cultures" problem. Rather, it is our feeling that as the negative consequences of too much reliance on science and technology are more fully felt, along with a public loss of trust in science and technology *per se*, will come a loss of confidence in the concomitant scientific values that give priority to individual freedoms. Some voluntary restraints on the rates at which individuals, enterprises, and governments expand the practice of science and technology now might well prevent a backlash that could lead to much greater restrictions later.[6]

Of course, not everyone is dissatisfied with our place in Nature, and therefore, not everyone advocates alteration to the present balance. There are many who oppose some of the uses of technology to overcome dependence on Nature. They appear closer in belief to the affinity/preservation value set. In ancient China, Lao-tsu advised:

> Do you think you can take over the universe and improve it?
> I do not believe it can be done.
> The universe is sacred.
> You cannot improve it.
> If you try to change it, you will ruin it.[7]

In the last book of J. R. R. Tolkien's trilogy *The War of the Rings*, the wizard Gandalf remarks,

> Yet it is not our part to master all the tides of the world, but to do what is in us for the succour of those years wherein we are set, uprooting the evil in the fields that we know, so that those who live after may have clean

earth to till. What weather they shall have is not ours
to rule.[8]

In a pluralistic society, and even within a particular individual, there is a spectrum of values evident between polar
opposites. The political process attempts to balance differences in values by adjudicating how people may act in specific
instances (e.g., whether to build a dam or a coal-fired power
plant or to conserve energy). However, when the *global* cycles
of life are involved, no one nation or limited consortium of
nations can regulate globally the relationship between man
and Nature. All the world's people who have some power
to pollute, or who are affected by pollution, are involved.
That is just about everyone.

Our political structures, despite well-known problems,
can work to balance the conflicting feelings and values distributed among their citizens and within their boundaries of
jurisdiction. Global pollutants, like CO_2 and N_2O, affect the
carbon and nitrogen cycles *everywhere*, not only where the
disruption occurred. In this respect, we are facing a problem
of a different magnitude from those faced by our ancestors,
where primarily local changes were involved. Today, if one
nation settles on a course designed to control nature through,
let us say, fossil fuel burning, then the resulting carbon dioxide pollution will alter *everyone's* atmosphere and climate. It
even affects those people who accept their present relationship with Nature and whose values lean toward preservation
of the primordial bond as it stands.

If we apply our value dichotomy to the present environmental debate, another dilemma emerges. Those who hold
predominantly fear/control values might not consider the
benefits from the expanded use of some technologies worth
the costs, if only they knew in advance what the costs would
be. The unintended side effects arising from continued al-

teration to the global nutrient cycles could create a worse situation than before, even in the opinion of those holding fear/control values. Their views on actions meant to control Nature might change if they were aware of the consequences.

Our brief examination of human disruption of the global cycles of life demonstrated a direct link between economic activity and our growing potential for modifying climate and other aspects of the global environment. New, perhaps unprecedented, environments may well be in store for humanity as a result. To be sure, there are large uncertainties in present estimates of the consequences of our disruptions of the natural cycles. These uncertainties will probably remain so large in many cases that the environmental changes themselves will occur before the experts agree on the details of their coming, thereby resolving the scientific uncertainties after the fact. Nevertheless, even if it is only *plausible* that some unprecedented, potentially irreversible environmental change might occur as a result of human activities, it is a chance we may not wish to take. If it occurred, humans would have to learn to adapt, if possible, to environmental conditions that could be outside the range of our cumulative experience.

The dilemma is evident: those who fear dependence on Nature and have developed technologies to control it could well be altering Nature. They and others might become vulnerable to a new, unfamiliar environment, one that could be more difficult to cope with than our present environment. In other words, the attempt to detach ourselves from Nature could, if pushed too far, backfire, thereby creating an altered environment potentially worse—at least, for some—than the one we know. An old expression says, "Better the devil you know than the devil you don't." An altered environment, on the other hand, could—at least, for some—be potentially better than the one we know. There are also benefits from the activities that alter the environment. Another homily can be cited, "Nothing ventured, nothing gained." In essence, we are gambling on the outcome.

To be sure, we are not counseling abandonment of science, technology, or scientific values; we do not believe that life in the Stone Age is preferable to our present in the era of space travel. However, as new knowledge leads to the possibility of great new benefits, so does it increase the dangers of the side effects of new technologies. Increasing knowledge of the atom has led from X rays to radioactive dyes up to modern nuclear medicine, which is helpful in treating some cancers. But it has also led from Alamogordo to Hiroshima, and from kiloton atomic bombs to megaton thermonuclear devices. Along with laser surgery come laser weapons. It seems that risks from the applications of new knowledge grow in proportion to potential benefits. The problem is choosing whether the increasing benefits are worth the increasing risks, especially when the risks become large enough to disrupt the global cycles of life—or threaten the existence of life itself. This choice is as much ethical as it is scientific.

Whether we should encourage scientists, detectives, or poets to pursue truth to all corners of the universe is not, to us, a question of principle. It is an issue of degree. We value "truth seeking" very highly, but not infinitely. How far to pursue truth seeking is analogous to the issue of balancing how much individual liberty to sacrifice in order to maintain the common good. A balance of values is needed. None of this discussion, of course, raises a new debate on the issue of individual versus collective values. Its modern traditions in political science date back to Rousseau's *Social Contract* and the writings of Locke and Hobbes or Jefferson and Adams.

What is new in our context is the *scope* of the collective impact on Nature of our relatively unconstrained individual activities.

People have long recognized the dangers of too much individual freedom. Therefore, we have been willing, perhaps implicitly, to enter into a "social contract" that trades some individual liberty for collective gains. However, those gains have been recognizable. For example, despite disagreements over the degree of our participation in any social contract, almost everyone is willing to pay some taxes to raise an army, run an educational system, build hospitals, and even fund scientific research or an endowment for the humanities. We know from experience that speeding is dangerous, and we pass laws that take away our rights to speed because the individual sacrifice is well demonstrated to be worth the collective gains. The gains are clear-cut.

How do we react if the risks we face are not so clear-cut—like those from our disruptions of Nature? The magnitude of our alteration of Nature, long recognized on a local scale (e.g., London smogs), has grown to the point that *Homo sapiens* is emerging as a major force in determining the fate of the global environment (e.g., a CO_2-induced climatic change). Unlike past localized environmental problems, this long-term, global impact is hard to grasp out of recent experience. The greenhouse effect, for example, is difficult to perceive in familiar terms from the perch of an individual, buffeted by immediate crises and limited by a life span of less than a century. Moreover, in many cases, it is unlikely that there will be a clear signal of these long-term impacts (like a killer smog in London, which led to the control of coal burning on a local scale) before we are irreversibly committed to deal with them. It is also unlikely that a scientific consensus will soon develop to pinpoint the distribution among peoples of the magnitude, timing, or consequences of our long-term, global disruptions of Nature. Furthermore, to undo the activities that threaten long-term environmental changes would require an unprecedented array of value trade-offs. These would be needed among an individual's special interests, between individual and collective interests, between present and future generations, among alternative lifestyles, and between our dependence on Nature and our dependence on other people.

WHAT TO DO?

We can apply our values intelligently only if we know enough of what might happen in the case of each available option so that we can choose preferred alternatives. We need to educate ourselves about (1) how much relative disruption our activities might cause in the global cycles of life; (2) what this disruption might imply for the environment and for us; and (3) how we feel about the alterations of Nature, or our relations with other people, that would possibly be affected by the consequences of our options. Works from science are needed to help us evaluate the first two points, and expressions in the humanities can help us deal with the third. We need to reexamine what scientific analyses have revealed about the consequences of our planned actions in light of our feelings and values.

These steps just outlined can—*in theory*, at least—help society to analyze its place in Nature and to choose ways in which to reach and maintain the place it wants in Nature. *In practice*, of course, people often do not have sufficient time, interest, or even education to assimilate all the relevant facts—particularly about questions in which the issues are unfamiliar or complex.

Without a distinction of facts, speculations, and values, decision making becomes haphazard at best, and it is controlled by elites or special interests at worst. This situation recalls H. G. Wells's well-traveled insight, "Human history becomes more and more a race between education and catastrophe."[9] If people don't expend the effort to keep up with what is happening, or what could happen, and if they don't keep in touch with their feelings and values about these events, catastrophe seems likely. Population biologist Paul R. Ehrlich, recognizing the gravity of this race, has called for the "social tithe." If some people are willing to offer 10% of their income to a religious or political organization, he reasoned, then certainly we should consider giving 10% of our free time to the task of keeping abreast of critical issues or in some other way helping society to function. Being informed is a necessity for successful democracy.

Whether to expand those activities that help us to live apart from Nature and take whatever risks follow, or whether to alter or eliminate those activities that are disrupting Nature is, as we have said repeatedly, a value choice. Its dimensions include a major ethical component. Without dictating the answers, we can show the *kinds* of actions we think people should consider when facing our environmental and related technological problems. Several possible areas are:

1. Redesigning our technology and social organizations so that they minimize the disruption of Nature without cutting services to humanity.
2. Curtailing some of our activities that disrupt Nature, even if the services they provide are reduced.

3. Reducing population growth so that less total disruption of Nature will occur for the same level of service that each activity provides to humanity.
4. Being careful to build large margins of safety into the technologies and organizations that provide strategic services to society.

Parts of the first two are already well known. They are called *conservation*. Conservation itself has two components: *end-use efficiency* and *curtailment*. An example of end-use efficiency is better-insulated houses, which provide the same service (climate control) but use less energy, thus producing less disruption of Nature than poorly insulated houses. Other examples include the redesigning of cars to be more efficient in the use of fuel and materials, or the planning of working and living places to minimize commuting distances. In addition to improvements in end-use efficiency, the first option includes the substitution of one technology for another in order to minimize environmental disruption. The use of solar energy collectors to heat or cool homes, for example, is less disruptive of the carbon cycle than burning coal for the same utility.

Conserving soil by reducing its erosion is another example of minimizing our disruption of Nature, and one which promises a significant dividend: higher productivity from our future farms.

Curtailment, a stricter form of conservation, implies the elimination of some service in order to save energy or minimize pollution. It is usually vigorously opposed by those whose services (or income) are reduced when some activity is curtailed. Both coal unions and mining-company managements, for example, are likely to continue to express values that rate the immediate benefits of coal use above the long-term risks of CO_2-induced climate change.

The third option may seem self-evidently a good policy, at least to most of us in the industrialized world. However, cultural traditions, economic conditions, and historical value systems, particularly in less developed countries, may place a higher priority on large families than on future environmental quality.

The fourth option could be restated as "Build resilience." It calls for the implementation of technologies and social organizations that will minimize our vulnerability to political instabilities or to changes in the environment. In essence, this is tantamount to a simple warning: "Be prepared."[10] One could, as mentioned earlier, set up machinery for international food reserves and distribution systems as a hedge against adverse shifts in climate, whether caused by Nature or by human activities. Another way to build resilience involves the diversification of the technological and social systems that prop up our survival. For example, we could invest heavily in solar, wind, or other "renewable" alternative energy-supply systems. A future switch from fossil-fuel–based energy would then be less economically and socially catastrophic, should society decide at some point to curtail the use of fossil fuels (because of their potentially large impact on the carbon, sulfur, and nitrogen cycles). Such a move— for oil-importing nations, at least—would also weaken the grip of OPEC.

All of these options can be designed to reduce substantially both the impact of humans on Nature and its resultant impact on us—but at a cost. Insulation costs money to install, as do solar heaters (particularly on houses not originally designed and built to include them). Resilience to disruption, in the form of either food or water reserves, and alternative energy-systems development, and political agreements to share goods in times of crisis also have costs, as do soil conservation practices. No personal insurance policy comes without premiums. Likewise, insurance for society against environmental and technological crises also must be bought at a cost. Often that cost is borne now and the benefits accrue to our children or to their children.

Finally, curtailment is most obviously a tough value trade-off, often pitting clear and immediate losses of economic or social conveniences to selected groups against less clear, long-term disruptions of the global environment. In cases where demonstrable benefits now come to us but potential harm goes to posterity, people usually serve their immediate interests. However, the preservation for posterity of ample natural resources and a quality environment *is* a basic human value. It is rooted in our ethical traditions.

The debate over solutions to environmental and related technological problems is, necessarily, laced with the vocabulary of scientific disciplines and punctuated with the often conflicting testimony of experts. There is a danger that in the din of scientific and special-interest debates over policy tactics, the essence of the environmental crisis will be lost: it is fundamentally an issue of feelings and values. The values and opinions of scientists, humanists, and, indeed, all other "cultures" are equal—*provided* they have access to the same information. Without scientists to illuminate a range of future possibilities, our judgment cannot be informed. Without humanists to help us understand our feelings, facts and values are likely to be confused. Democracy is, in large part, the informed application of individuals' values to the solution of collective problems. Humanities and science are both needed to allow judgments that are informed applications of values. Ethics and science play equal roles in guiding our actions.

* * *

Those of us in the technologically advanced, "developed" nations have accustomed ourselves to climate-controlled buildings, instant hot and cold running water, electric clock radios, electric blankets and shavers, dishwashers, frozen foods, comfortable cars, X-ray machines, miracle drugs, and so forth. Our devices by now have become "necessities" of life—like food, clothing, shelter, and other basic physical needs. With technology, we are able to overcome hardships otherwise imposed by Nature. However, we do not do this alone. Households today are rarely self-sufficient. We are embedded in a social system through which everyone is connected to everyone else. We are also altering the global nutrient cycles upon which we depend. Thus, we are "embedded," to keep Lewis Thomas' phrase, in a greater, even more intricate cycle of Nature: the biogeochemical cycle of life.

We have come full circle now, back to where we began, with the recognition that Nature is made up of cycles and that man is "embedded" in that structure, even if he does possess the power to alter his place in Nature. No matter what each succeeding generation invents or implements to alter this primordial bond, we remain part of the cycles of life. As T. S. Eliot says,

> What we call the beginning is often the end
> And to make an end is to make a beginning.
> The end is where we start from . . .
> And the end of all our exploring
> Will be to arrive where we started
> And know the place for the first time.[11]

This generation has acquired unprecedented power to alter, perhaps irreversibly, the global cycles of life. Some even believe that mankind has developed the ability to destroy itself. Out of our new power emerges a nagging possibility, a notion often sensed in some recess of the mind. Will our generation break the cycle of life? Will we become the first from whose end there will follow no more beginnings?

We do not accept the proposition that self-extinction is the inevitable legacy of our inventive "genius." Assuming, then, that *Homo sapiens* will survive, we come next to the question that our present actions demand: What kinds of beginnings will be available in our aftermath to those born into future cycles of life? Beyond that, are we willing to analyze our predicaments? Will we act to reduce them? All of us, humanists and scientists alike, should contribute to the answers. To do otherwise is to play dice with the future, having little hint of the odds or the stakes.

REFERENCE NOTES

CHAPTER HEADING QUOTES

PREFACE: Kettering, Charles P., in *Encyclopedia of Science Fiction*, M. Holdstock, editor, Octopus Books, New York, 1978.

CHAPTER 1: Asimov, Isaac, *Science Past—Science Future*, Ace Books, New York, 1977, p. 347.

CHAPTER 2: Novalis, quoted in Udo Kultermann, *Art and Life*, Praeger, New York, 1971, p. 77.

CHAPTER 3: Kylián, Jiří, quoted in *Ballet News*, November, 1979.

CHAPTER 4: Vishniac, Roman, quoted in *Omni*, October, 1978.

CHAPTER 5: Marcus Aurelius, *Meditations*.

CHAPTER 6: Doyle, Arthur Conan, *The Complete Original Illustrated Sherlock Holmes*, Castle Books, New York, 1976, p. 13.

CHAPTER 7: Lovelock, James E., *Gaia: A New Look at Life on Earth*, Oxford University Press, Oxford, 1979, p. 1.

CHAPTER 8: Ehrlich, Paul R., and Ehrlich, Anne H., *The End of Affluence*, Ballantine, New York, 1974, p. 136.
CHAPTER 9: Stoppard, Tom, quoted in *Playbill*, April 1977, p. 4

CHAPTER 1

1. Thomas, Lewis, *The Lives of a Cell*, Bantam, New York, 1975, p. 1.
2. Dubos, Rene, "Symbiosis between the Earth and Human Kind," *Science* **193,** 1976, pp. 459–462.
3. Pope, Alexander, *The Poetical Works of Alexander Pope*, Macmillan, London, 1930, p. 52.
4. Wordsworth, William, "Lines, Composed a Few Miles Above Tintern Abbey," *The Norton Anthology of Poetry*, Norton, New York, 1970, p. 557.
5. Thoreau, Henry David, *Walden*, in *The American Tradition in Literature*, Vol. 1, 3rd edition, edited by Sculley Bradley, Richmond Croom Beatty, and E. Hudson Long, Norton, New York, 1967, pp. 1427–1428.
6. Dubos, op. cit., p. 459.
7. O'Neill, G. K., *The High Frontier*, William Morrow, New York, 1979, is a leading advocate of space colonization. His vision is shared by Governor Jerry Brown of California and was part of his campaign platform for President of the United States in 1980.
8. E. O. Wilson's book *Sociobiology*, Harvard University Press, Cambridge, Mass., 1975, is a landmark work on the nature/nurture debate. It has stirred a rousing controversy, stretching from the halls of academe all the way to several debates played out on U.S. public television on the Dick Cavett talk show. For a short review article on sociobiology by E. O. Wilson and some references to his critics see *The Wilson Quarterly* **3(4),** Autumn 1979.
9. Shakespeare, William, *The Tempest*, in *The Complete Works of William Shakespeare*, Act V, Scene 1, Walter J. Black, New York, 1937, p. 20.
10. White, Lynn, "The Historical Roots of Our Ecologic Crisis," *Science* **155,** 1967, pp. 1203–1207.
11. Ibid.
12. Ibid.
13. Ibid.
14. Yi-Fu Tuan, "Our Treatment of the Environment in Ideal and Actuality," *American Scientist* **58,** 1970, pp. 244–249.
15. White, op. cit.

CHAPTER 2

1. Snow, C. P., *The Two Cultures and A Second Look*, 2nd edition, Cambridge University Press, Cambridge, 1964, p. 4.
2. Crick, Francis, *Of Molecules and Men*, University of Washington Press, Seattle and London, 1966, pp. 93–94.
3. Bronowski, Jacob, *Science and Human Values*, Perennial Library, New York, 1972, p. 10.
4. A summary of some of the issues in the birth-control-versus-death-control debate, plus a list of references for further readings, can be found in Chapters 2 and 8 of S. H. Schneider with L. E. Mesirow, *The Genesis Strategy: Climate and Global Survival*, Plenum, New York, 1976, 419 pp. See also Lester R. Brown, *The Twenty-Ninth Day*, Norton, New York, 1978, 363 pp., and Garrett Hardin, *The Limits to Altruism: An Ecologist's View of Survival*, Indiana University Press, Bloomington, 1977, for strikingly different viewpoints.
5. Bronowski, op. cit., p. 16 and p. 27.
6. Ibid., p. 17.
7. Ibid., p. 20.
8. Bateson, Gregory, *Mind and Nature: A Necessary Unity*, Dutton, New York, 1979, p. 8.
9. For a discussion of the history of various theories of ice ages, including the effects of orbital changes, see J. Imbrie and K. P. Imbrie, *Ice Ages: Solving the Mystery*, Enslow Publishers, Short Hills, N.J., 1979, 224 pp.
10. Thomas, Lewis, *The Medusa and the Snail*, Viking, New York, 1979, p. 28.

CHAPTER 3

1. This Tom Paxton song, "This World Goes 'Round and 'Round," is in his album "Outward Bound," Elektra Records, New York, 1966.
2. *Rig Veda*: Veda X, 18, 10, *The Mind of India*, edited by William Gerber, Macmillan, New York, 1967.
3. Legge, James, translator and editor, *I Ching: Book of Changes*, Bantam Books, New York, 1964, Appendix III, Chapter 5, Line 31.
4. For more details on the symbols of the tarot, see P. F. Case, *The Tarot: A Key to the Wisdom of the Ages*, Macoy Publishing, Richmond, Va., 1947, 214 pp.
5. Parrinder, Geoffrey, editor, *Religions of the World*, Grosset and Dunlap, New York, 1971.

CHAPTER 4

1. T. S. Eliot, *The Four Quartets,* "The Dry Salvages," Harcourt, Brace & World, New York, 1971, pp. 35–36.
2. Rewald, John, *History of Impressionism,* The Museum of Modern Art, New York, 1973.
3. For a review of the debate over the carrying capacity of the earth for humans (and a list of references), see Chapters 2 and 8 of S. H. Schneider with L. E. Mesirow, *The Genesis Strategy: Climate and Global Survival,* Plenum, New York, 1976, 419 pp. See also P. R. Ehrlich, A. H. Ehrlich, and J. P. Holdren, *Ecoscience: Population, Resources, Environment,* W. H. Freeman, 1977, 1051 pp.
4. An interesting short discussion of photosynthetic efficiency limits is given in B. Gilland, *The Next 70 Years: Population, Food and Resources,* Abacus Press, Turnbridge Wells, Kent, England, 1979, Chapter 4.
5. Shelley, Mary, *Frankenstein, the Modern Prometheus.*
6. Chan, Wing-tsit, translator and editor, *A Source Book in Chinese Philosophy,* Princeton University Press, Princeton, N.J., 1963, p. 116.
7. Ibid., p. 207.
8. Ovid, "The Teaching of Pythagoras," *Metamorphoses,* translated by Rolfe Humphries, Indiana University Press, Bloomington, 1973, pp. 372–373.
9. Reich, Charles A., *The Greening of America: How the Youth Revolution Is Trying to Make America Liveable,* Random House, New York, 1970.
10. McLuhan, T. C., *Touch the Earth: A Self-Portrait of Indian Existence,* Promontory Press, New York, 1971, p. 8.
11. Emerson, Ralph Waldo, "The Rhodora," *The Norton Anthology of Poetry,* Arthur M. Eastman, coordinating editor, Norton, New York, 1970, p. 702.
12. Ovid, op. cit.
13. Joyce, James, *A Portrait of the Artist as a Young Man,* in *The Portable James Joyce,* Harry Levin, editor, Penguin Books, New York, 1976, p. 350.
14. Burton, Ian, Kates, Robert W., and White, Gilbert F., *The Environment as Hazard,* Oxford University Press, New York, 1978, 240 pp., discusses the responses of people to natural hazards, including floods.

CHAPTER 5

1. Ovid, *Metamorphoses,* Rolfe Humphries, translator, Indiana University Press, Bloomington, 1973, pp. 372–373.
2. Robinson, John Mansley, *An Introduction to Early Greek Philosophy,* Houghton Mifflin, Boston, 1968, p. 89.

3. Ibid., p. 101.
4. de Santillana, Giorgio, *The Origins of Scientific Thought*, New American Library, New York, 1961.
5. Ibid., p. 49.
6. Frisinger, H. H., *The History of Meteorology: To 1800*, Science History Publications, New York, 1977.
7. Ibid., p. 16.
8. Robinson, op. cit., pp. 157–158.
9. Ibid., p. 292.
10. Ibid., p. 291.
11. de Santillana, op. cit.

CHAPTER 6

1. *Funk and Wagnall's Standard College Dictionary*, Harcourt, Brace & World, New York, 1963, p. 1203.
2. Manheim, Ralph, and John Willett, editors, *Brecht: The Collected Plays*, Vol. 5, Vintage Books, New York, 1972, p. 3.
3. Bronowski, Jacob, *Science and Human Values*, Perennial Library, New York, 1965, p. 62.
4. Ibid., p. 63.
5. Ibid., p. 71. For an alternative view of the proper role of the scientist in governing society, see Joel Primack and Frank von Hippel, *Advice and Dissent: Scientists in the Political Arena*, Basic Books, New York, 1974, 299 pp.
6. Bronowski, op. cit., p. 64.
7. Frazer, Sir James George, *The Golden Bough*, Macmillan, New York, 1972, pp. 824, 825.
8. Nagel, Ernest, *The Structure of Science*, Harcourt, Brace & World, New York, 1961.
9. Rose, H. J., *A Handbook of Greek Mythology*, Dutton, New York, 1959, p. 12.
10. Nagel, op. cit., p. 4.
11. Ibid., p. 9.
12. The "holists" believe that there are structures in nature that are fundamental characteristics of the whole and not merely "the sum of its parts," as reductionists believe. One example, the "Gaia hypothesis" is explored in Chapter 7. Briefly, in the words of James E. Lovelock (author of *Gaia: A New Look at Life on Earth*, Oxford University Press, Oxford, 1979, p. 1), "the quest for Gaia is an attempt to find the largest living creature on Earth," which the author believes could be all of life combined. In the

philosophical literature, holism is also debated. For example, see Chapter 4 of Gregory Bateson, *Mind and Nature, A Necessary Unity*, Dutton, New York, 1979; Lewis J. Perelman, *The Global Mind: Beyond the Limits to Growth*, Mason Charter, New York, 1976, p. 41; Arthur Koestler and J. R. Smythies, editors, *Beyond Reductionism: New Perspectives in the Life Sciences*, Beacon Press, Boston, 1969, 438 pp.; and Ervin Laszlo, *Introduction to Systems Philosophy: Toward a New Paradigm of Contemporary Thought*, Harper Torchbooks, New York, 1972, 328 pp. For a highly mathematical treatment of the issue of "self-organization" in physics, see G. Nicolis and I. Prigogine, *Self-Organization Non-equilibrium Systems: From Dissipative Structures to Order through Fluctuations*, Wiley, New York, 1977, 491 pp.

13. Culler, J., *Structural Poetics: Structuralism, Linguistics and the Study of Literature*, Cornell University Press, Ithaca, N.Y., 1975, pp. 24–30.
14. For an interesting view of science and the scientific method, see M. Goldstein and I. F. Goldstein, *How We Know: An Exploration of the Scientific Process*, Plenum, New York, 1978, 357 pp.
15. Frisinger, H. H., *The History of Meteorology: To 1800*, Science History Publications, New York, 1977, p. 8.
16. Ibid., p. 16.
17. This passage is from Aristotle's work "On Generation and Corruption." We used Richard P. McKeon, editor, *The Basic Works of Aristotle*, Chicago University Press, Chicago, 1941, pp. 522–523.
18. This passage from Aristotle's *Meteorologica* is found in Frisinger, op. cit., pp. 18–19.

CHAPTER 7

1. These abundances are taken from P. R. Ehrlich, A. H. Ehrlich, and J. P. Holdren, *Ecoscience: Population, Resources, Environment*, W. H. Freeman, San Francisco, 1977, p. 20.
2. An authoritative geology book is F. Press and R. Siever, *Earth*, W. H. Freeman, San Francisco, 1974. A readable popularization on geologic subjects is Nigel Calder's *Restless Earth: A Report on the New Geology*, Viking, New York, 1972, 152 pp.
3. For a review of the basic principles of meteorology, see, for example, F. K. Hare, *The Restless Atmosphere*, Harper Torchbooks, New York, 1961. Also see Navarra, J. B., *Atmosphere, Weather and Climate: An Introduction to Meteorolgy*, W. B. Saunders, Philadelphia, 1979.
4. For a good general introduction to the materials we refer to on nutrient cycles, see Chapter 3 of Ehrlich, Ehrlich, and Holdren, op. cit., and Chapter 5 of G. Tyler Miller, *Living in the Environment*, 2nd edition, Wads-

worth Publishing, Belmont, Calif., 1979. For a more technical description of these cycles, see W. Stumm, editor, *Global Chemical Cycles and their Alteration by Man*, Dahlem Konferenzen, Berlin, 1977.

5. Deevey, E. S., Jr., "Mineral Cycles," *Scientific American*, September 1970, pp. 148–158.

6. Commoner, Barry, *The Closing Circle: Nature, Man, and Technology*, Knopf, New York, 1971, p. 18.

7. A description of the early phases of debate over genetic engineering is in Nicholas Wade's article, "Recombinant DNA: NIH Sets Strict Rules to Launch a New Technology" in *Science* **190**, December 19, 1975, pp. 1175–1179. Many popular books on the subject are in the science section of most bookstores.

8. Actually the chemical formulas are far more complex than these simple equations. For more details, see: A. L. Lehninger, *Biochemistry*, Worth, New York, 1970, p. 457.

9. For a discussion of the carbon cycle, see Woodwell, G. M., "The Carbon Dioxide Question," *Scientific American* **238**(1), 1978, pp. 34–43.

10. A review (as of 1976) of the N_2O/ozone issue is given in Chapter 6 of S. H. Schneider with L. E. Mesirow, *The Genesis Strategy: Climate and Global Survival*, Plenum, New York, 1976. However, as pointed out in *The Genesis Strategy*, the chemical reactions that create and destroy ozone are very complex and are not fully understood. Thus, any quantitative results predicting the effects on ozone of N_2O increase are, of necessity, speculative. This is still true today and is likely to remain so for decades. However, uncertainty is not equivalent to no problem. It is sheer gambling whether increasing N_2O would increase, decrease, or not affect ozone. The best that can be said at this stage is that significant connections between ozone and N_2O are possible.

11. The sulfur cycle is reviewed in the references given in note 4 above and also in B. Bolin and R. J. Charlson, "On the Role of the Tropospheric Sulfur Cycle in the Shortwave Radiative Climate of the Earth," *Ambio* **5**, 1976, pp. 47–54.

12. Many popular books on climate are now available in bookstores. Among these are W. O. Roberts and H. Lansford, *The Climate Mandate*, W. H. Freeman, San Francisco, 1979; R. A. Bryson and Thomas J. Murray, *Climates of Hunger*, University of Wisconsin, Madison, 1977, 171 pp.; and S. H. Schneider with L. E. Mesirow, *The Genesis Strategy: Climate and Global Survival*, Plenum, New York, 1976, 419 pp. Less popular, but useful reviews of climate issues can be found in *Understanding Climate Change*, U. S. National Academy of Sciences, Washington, D.C., 1975, and in the testimony before the Congress on the U.S. National Climate Act: *The National Climate Program Act*, Hearings before the Subcommittee on the Environment and the Atmosphere, May 18, 19, 20, 25, 26, 27, 1976, U.S. Government Printing Office, Washington, D.C., 1976, 779 pp.

13. James E. Lovelock and Lynn Margulis, "Atmospheric Homeostasis by and for the Biosphere: The Gaia Hypothesis," *Tellus* **26**, 1973, p. 2. See also the more recent book by Lovelock, *Gaia: A New Look at Life on Earth*, Oxford University Press, Oxford, 1979, 157 pp.
14. In a recent article, Carl Sagan, Owen B. Toon, and James B. Pollack, *Science* **206**(4425), 1980, pp. 1363–1368, have argued that deforestation and other land uses over history have had at least regional impacts on climate. While this may be so, it is difficult to separate this effect from other climatic forcing factors that may have worked with or against such land uses in the past. Now, however, the expanding use of fossil fuels seems to be the most likely pollutant to alter the *global* climate over the next century or so.
15. Ehrlich, Ehrlich, and Holdren, op. cit., p. 33.
16. Ibid., p. 35.

CHAPTER 8

1. The remark has been attributed to ecologist H. T. Odum.
2. The figures we cite for energy use in U.S. food systems come from J. S. Steinhart and C. E. Steinhart, "Energy Use in the U.S. Food System," *Science* **184**, 1974, pp. 307–316.
3. For two contrasting views of the causes and solutions of the world hunger problem, see Sterling Wortman and Ralph Cummings, *To Feed This World, The Challenge and the Strategy*, Johns Hopkins University Press, Baltimore, 1978, 440 pp.; and Frances Moore Lappé and J. Collins, *Food First, Beyond the Myth of Scarcity*, Ballantine, New York, 1978, 619 pp.
4. For two sharply conflicting views of the human predicament, see P. R. Ehrlich and A. H. Ehrlich, *The End of Affluence*, Ballantine, New York, 1974, and Herman Kahn, William Brown, and Leon Martel, with the assistance of the staff of the Hudson Institute, *The Next 200 Years*, William Morrow, New York, 1976, 241 pp. For other viewpoints, see M. Mesarovic and E. Pestel, *Mankind at the Turning Point*, Dutton, New York, 1974; Alvin Toffler, *The Ecospasm Report*, Bantam, New York, 1975, 116 pp.; and Chapters 8 and 9 of S. H. Schneider with L. E. Mesirow, *The Genesis Strategy: Climate and Global Survival*, Plenum, New York, 1976, 419 pp.
5. P. R. Ehrlich, A. H. Ehrlich, and J. P. Holdren, *Ecoscience: Population, Resources, Environment*, W. H. Freeman, San Francisco, 1977, p. 393.
6. *Energy and Climate*, U.S. National Academy of Sciences, Washington, D.C., 1977, 158 pp., discusses the question of human impacts on climate. See also Chapter 6 of *The Genesis Strategy*.
7. For a general discussion of air pollution effects, see Chapter 10 of Ehrlich, Ehrlich, and Holdren, op. cit.

8. The possible health and economic costs of air pollution are explored in detail in L. B. Lave and E. P. Seskin, *Air Pollution and Human Health*, Johns Hopkins University Press, Baltimore, 1977, 368 pp.
9. For a review of the acid rain problem, see G. E. Likens, R. F. Wright, J. N. Galloway, and T. J. Butler, "Acid Rain," *Scientific American* **241**(4), 1979, pp. 43–51.
10. "Acid from the Sky," in *Mosaic* **10**(4), 1979, p. 36.
11. Carson, Rachel, *The Silent Spring*, Houghton Mifflin, Boston, 1962.
12. For a discussion of the effects of sulfur dust veils on climate, see C. Mass and S. H. Schneider, "Influence of Sunspots and Volcanic Dust on Long-Term Temperature Records Inferred by Statistical Investigations," *Journal of the Atmospheric Sciences* **34**(12), 1977, pp. 1995–2004; B. Bolin and R. J. Charlson, "On the Role of the Tropospheric Sulfur Cycle in the Short-wave Radiative Climate of the Earth," *Ambio* **5**, 1977, pp. 47–54; and H. Stommel and E. Stommel, "The Year Without a Summer," *Scientific American* **240**(6), 1979, pp. 176–186.
13. R. A. Bryson and T. J. Murray, *Climates of Hunger*, University of Wisconsin Press, Madison, 1977.
14. These numbers are only approximate. For a more complete discussion, see W. Stumm, editor, *Global Chemical Cycles and Their Alteration by Man*, Dahlem Konferenzen, Berlin, 1977.
15. For reviews of the role of the biosphere in the CO_2 problem, see W. Seiler and P. Crutzen, "Estimates of Gross and Net Fluxes of Carbon Between the Biosphere and the Atmosphere from Biomass Burning," *Climatic Change* **2**(3), 1980, pp. 207–247, and the *Report of AAAS/DOE Workshop, Annapolis, Maryland, April 2–6, 1979*, on "Environmental and Societal Consequences of a Possible CO_2-Induced Climate Change," CO_2 Research and Effects Program, U.S. Department of Energy.
16. W. S. Broecker, T. Takahashi, H. J. Simpson, and T. H. Peng, "Fate of Fossil Fuel Carbon Dioxide and the Global Carbon Budget," *Science* **206**(4417), 1979, pp. 409–418.
17. For a review of the CO_2 question, particularly the issue of sea-level rise and coastal flooding, see S. H. Schneider and R. S. Chen, "Carbon Dioxide Warming and Coastline Flooding: Physical Factors and Climatic Impact," *Annual Reviews of Energy* **5**, 1980, pp. 107–140.

CHAPTER 9

1. Lester R. Brown, *The Twenty-Ninth Day*, Norton, New York, 1978, pp. 86–92.
2. See Chapter 4 of S. H. Schneider with L. E. Mesirow, *The Genesis Strategy: Climate and Global Survival*, Plenum, New York, 1976.

3. C. P. Snow, *The Two Cultures and a Second Look*, Cambridge University Press, Cambridge, 1964, p. 67.
4. Jacob Bronowski, *Science and Human Values*, Perennial Library, New York, 1965, p. 67.
5. Walter Lippmann, *The Public Philosophy*, New American Library, New York, 1955, p. 24.
6. The accident in 1979 at the Three Mile Island nuclear power plant dealt a serious blow to public confidence in the safety of nuclear power. Investigations showed that faulty procedures and poorly trained staff were a large part of the problem. Had extra time and expense been expended *in advance* to bolster safety, irreparable "public relations" damage to this technology might have been averted. The case illustrates the need for voluntary restraint in the rate of implementation of new, complex, or potentially dangerous technologies.
7. Lao-tsu, *Tao Te Ching*, Vintage Books, New York, 1972, Poem number 29.
8. J. R. R. Tolkien, *The Return of the King*, Ballantine Books, New York, 1965, p. 190.
9. H. G. Wells, *The Outlines of Human History*, Vol. 2, Macmillan, New York, 1921, p. 594.
10. This is what one of us has previously termed the "genesis strategy" (see note 2, above).
11. T. S. Eliot, "Little Gidding," *The Four Quartets*, Harcourt, Brace, & World, New York, 1971, pp. 58–59.

BIBLIOGRAPHY

Works marked with an asterisk (*) were principal references.

Asimov, Isaac, *Science Past—Science Future*, Ace Books, New York, 1977.

Bateson, Gregory, *Mind and Nature: A Necessary Unity*, E. P. Dutton and Sons, New York, 1979.

* Bronowski, Jacob, *Science and Human Values*, Perennial Library, New York, 1972.

Bronowski, Jacob, *The Ascent of Man*, Little, Brown, Boston, 1973.

Burton, Ian, Kates, Robert W., and White, Gilbert F., *The Environment as Hazard*, Oxford University Press, New York, 1978.

* Burtt, E. A., *The Metaphysical Foundations of Modern Science*, Doubleday, New York, 1954.

* de Santillana, Giorgio, *The Origins of Scientific Thought*, New American Library, New York, 1961.

Dubos, Rene, "Symbiosis Between the Earth and Human Kind," *Science* **193,** 1976, pp. 459–462.

Eastman, Arthur M., coordinating editor, *The Norton Anthology of Poetry*, W. W. Norton, New York, 1970.

* Ehrlich, Paul R., Ehrlich, Anne H., and Holdren, John P., *Ecoscience: Population, Resources, Environment*, W. H. Freeman, San Francisco, 1977.

* Frazer, Sir James George, *The Golden Bough*, Macmillan, New York, 1972.

* Frisinger, H. H., *The History of Meteorology: To 1800*, Science History Publications, New York, 1977.

Glimcher, Arnold B., *Louise Nevelson*, Dutton, New York, 1972.

Goldstein, M., and Goldstein, I. F., *How We Know: An Exploration of the Scientific Process*, Plenum, New York, 1978.

* Grant, Michael, *Myths of the Greeks and Romans*, New American Library, New York, 1962.

Hardin, Garrett, *The Limits to Altruism: An Ecologist's View of Survival*, Indiana University Press, Bloomington, 1977.

* Janson, H. W., *History of Art*, Prentice-Hall, Englewood Cliffs, N.J., and Harry N. Abrams, New York, 1969.

Jellicoe, G., and Jellicoe, S., *The Landscape of Man: Shaping the Environment from Prehistory to the Present Day*, Viking, New York, 1975.

* Jung, Carl G., editor, *Man and His Symbols*, Dell, New York, 1973.

Lippmann, Walter, *The Public Philosophy*, New American Library, New York, 1965.

Lovelock, James E., *Gaia: A New Look at Life on Earth*, Oxford University Press, Oxford, 1979.

MacKown, Diana (taped conversations with), *Dawns and Dusks: Louise Nevelson*, Charles Scribner's Sons, New York, 1976.

McLuhan, T. C., *Touch the Earth: A Self-Portrait of Indian Existence*, Promontory Press, New York, 1971.

* Miller, G. Tyler, Jr., *Living in the Environment*, 2nd edition, Wadsworth, Belmont, Calif., 1979.

Nochlin, Linda, *Realism*, Penguin Books, New York, 1975.

Parrinder, Geoffrey, *Religions of the World*, Grosset and Dunlap, New York, 1971.

* Robinson, John Mansley, *An Introduction to Early Greek Philosophy*, Houghton Mifflin, Boston, 1968.

Rose, H. J., *A Handbook of Greek Mythology*, E. P. Dutton, New York, 1959.

* Schneider, S. H., with L. E. Mesirow, *The Genesis Strategy: Climate and Global Survival*, Plenum, New York, 1976.

Schneider, S. H., and Chen, R. S., "Carbon Dioxide Warming and Coastline Flooding: Physical Factors and Climatic Impacts, *Annual Reviews of Energy* **5,** 1980, pp. 107–140.

Snow, C. P., *The Two Cultures and a Second Look*, Cambridge University Press, Cambridge, 1964.

Thomas, Lewis, *The Lives of a Cell*, Bantam Books, New York, 1975.

Toffler, Alvin, *The Ecospasm Report*, Bantam, New York, 1975.

Tuan, Yi-Fu, "Our Treatment of the Environment in Ideal and Actuality," *American Scientist* **58**, 1970, pp. 244–249.

White, Lynn, "The Historical Roots of Our Ecologic Crisis," *Science* **155**, 1967, pp. 1203–1207.

INDEX

Page numbers in *italics* refer to illustrations.

Acid rain, 257, 260–261
Aeschylus (Greek), plays by, 100–101
African deities, 64, 65
Air, the Element, 190–192
Air pollution
  effect on health, 256–259
  sulfur injection, 264–265, 268
Amino acids, 208
Anaxagoras (Greek), Aristotle's
  criticism of, 171, 172, 224
Architecture, as control of Nature,
  112–113, *114*
Aristotle (Greek), 136–141, 142,
  168–174, 182, 224
Ashanti deity, 64
Asimov, Isaac, quoted, 2
Astrology, 59

Astronomy
  cycles in, 34–35
  Galileo's observations, 149–150
Atomic particles, 180

Bacteria
  in nitrogen cycle, 207, 211, 215
  phosphatizing, 218
  in sulfur cycle, 220
Bali, Indonesia, Hindu funeral on, *52*
Bateson, Gregory, quoted, 28
Baucis and Philemon myth, 59, 63
  in art, *62*
Beowulf (character), 112
Bible, flood tale in, 77–78
Black bodies, radiative, 229
Bolin, B., 267

Boulding, Kenneth, quoted, 25
Brahma (Hindu god), 51
Bramantino (Bartolomeo Suardi),
  painting by, 62
Brecht, Bertold, play by, 149–150
Bronowski, Jacob, 23, 24, 26–28,
  151–152, 153, 288
Brueghel, Pieter, painting by, 111
Bryson, Reid, 265
Buddhism
  and art, 101
  mandala, 55
  prayer wheels, 57, 58
  stupas, 54, 57, 58
  zodiac, 59

Calorie, definition of, 248 note
Carbon cycle, 200, 202–203, 204
  disruption of, 270–271, 273–278
  graph, 272
Carbon dioxide, in carbon cycle,
  202–203, 205, 225
  annual oscillations, 202–203, 272, 273
  long-term increase, 270–278
Carbon soot, sulfates combined
  with, 268
Carrying capacity of land, 82, 84
Carson, Rachel, 262
Case, Paul Foster, quoted, 61
Cathedrals
  Gothic, 113, 114
  paintings of, 31, 32, 33
Cave paintings, 93–94
Cayuse Indian, quoted, 97, 100
Charlson, R. J., 267
Chartres, France, cathedral at, 114
Chekhov, Anton, play by, 106–107
Chemical pollution, 261–263
Chen, R. S., 277
Chicago, Ill., World's Fair (1933), 11
China (country)
  recent history, 153
  traditions, 15, 51, 59, 95, 131–132,
    290
  in art, 101, 102, 104–105
Christianity, view of Nature in,
  13–15
  fire, 132–133
  life/death cycle, 47

Chuang Tzu, quoted, 95
Climate
  current knowledge, 172–173
  effects of, 246–247
  and global cycles, 221–231, 239
  Greek interest in, 136, 143, 168
  Aristotelian theory, 171–172,
    224
  human influence on, 244, 253,
    255
  CO_2 concentration, increase in,
    270–278
  sulfur injection, 264–265
  hydrologic cycle and, 194, 196
  modification, 118
  volcanic influence on, 265–266
Coffee growing, climate and,
  246–247
Coleridge, Samuel Taylor, 26–27
Collective unconscious, evidence
  for, 64–65, 68
Colonization movements, 11, 12
Commoner, Barry, quoted, 199
Communal living, 96–97
Confucian teachings, 51, 95,
  131–132
Conservation, 297
Continental drift theory, 181–183, 184
Contrails, 16
Crick, Francis, quoted, 22–23
Cultural determinism, 12, 13
Curtailment, 297, 299
Cycles, 29
  definition, 30–31
  life/death, 46–47, 50–54, 62, 63,
    69, 134–135
  in nitrogen cycle, 208–209
  See also Nature: cycles in

Daedalus (mythological figure),
  107–108
Daedalus, Stephen (character), 109
Debussy, Claude, 78, 81
Deductive reasoning, 137, 155,
  156–157, 165
  examples, 166, 167
Deevey, Edward S., Jr., 198
Deforestation, and CO_2
  concentration, 274

Demeter (Greek goddess), 45–46, 124
Dentistry, outdoors in Nepal, 250, 251
de Santillana, Giorgio, 133, 144
Dickinson, Emily, 96
Dillon, Lake, Colo., 88, 89
Doyle, Sir Arthur Conan, quoted, 145
Dubos, Rene, quoted, 5, 7, 9 note, 11

Earth, 178–181
  continental drift, 181–183, 184
  cycles. See Nutrient cycles
  orbit, 34
  rotation, 35
  satellite photos, 226, 244
  transport of materials, 183, 185–186, 187, 188, 189
  as woman, 66, 233
East Anglia, England, landscape architecture in, 5, 6, 7
Eastern cultures
  cycles, role of, 50–52, 54, 55, 57, 58
  Nature, views of, 14–15, 95, 131–132, 288
  in art, 101, 102, 103, 104, 105
Ecological crisis, components of, 24 note, 245
Education, rate of, 289
Egyptian deities, 64
Ehrlich, Paul R., and Anne H., 184, 187, 195, 259, 296
  quoted, 235–236, 237, 241
Einstein, Albert, 148
Elements
  ancient Greek, 128–135, 138, 139, 141–143, 167–170
  modern understanding of, 178–196, 234–235
  rarification of, 178–179
  in modern science, 179–181
  air, components of, 190
  cycles based on, 200–221, 264–278
  in living beings, 198–199
Eliade, Mircea, 126–127
Eliot, T. S., quoted, 76, 300

Emerson, Ralph Waldo, 96, 100
Empedocles of Arigentum, 134–136, 167–168
End-use efficiency, 297
Energy
  alternative sources, 298
  amounts produced and used, table of, 254
  dependence on, 247–248
  foreign oil, 285–286
  disruption of natural flow, 245, 253, 255
  in laws of thermodynamics, 235–237
  nuclear, debate over, 151
  See also Fossil fuels; Radiant energy
England, landscape architecture in, 5, 6, 7
Environmentalism, 11
  economic development versus, 4, 17
Epidemiologists, work of, 257
Epimetheus (mythological figure), 92–93
Epiphyte (plant), 232
Erosion, 185, 188
Eumenides (Furies, Greek gods), 100–101
Evaporation, 192, 195, 223–224

Famine, 1970s, 284
Feedback mechanism, in nitrogen cycle, 212
Fire
  and nitrogen oxide production, 206, 210, 268
  views of, 132–133
  current, 234–235
Fish, effect of acidity on, 260
Flatirons (foothills), Boulder, Colo., 189
Floods
  biblical, 77–78
  Johnstown, Pa., 78
  from sea-level rise, possible, 276, 278
Food system
  energy use in, 247–248

Food system (*cont.*)
  worldwide differences, 248–249
  sufficiency problem, 249,
    283–285
Fossil fuels
  and carbon cycle, 225, 274–275
  imported oil, dependence on,
    285–286
  and sulfur, 221, 264
France
  cathedrals, *114*
  paintings of, 31, *32, 33*
  Versailles, *8*, 112–113
Frankenstein (Shelley), 91
Frazer, Sir James, 155
  quoted, 156
Friends of the Earth, 11
Frisinger, H. H., 136, 139, 168–169,
  172
Fuller, R. Buckminster, 11
Furies (Eumenides, Greek gods),
  100–101

Gaia (Mother Earth goddess), 66
Gaia hypothesis, 231, 233
Galileo (Italian), 149–150
Garfunkel, Art, 155
Gases, 190, 191–192
  nitrogen, 206–212, 215
  See also Carbon dioxide
Genetic determinism, 12–13
Genetic engineering controversy,
  13, 150, 200
Geology
  continental drift, 181–183, *184*
  sedimentary cycle, 185–186, *187*,
    188, 190
Géricault, Théodore, painting by,
  78, *79*
Giorgione (Italian), painting by, *116*
Global cycles
  of air, 191–192
  See also Nutrient cycles
Gothic cathedrals, 113, *114*
Great Spirit, Indian belief in, 97,
  100
Greeks, ancient, 95
  concept of time, 13
  mythology. *See* Mythology: Greek

Greeks, ancient (*cont.*)
  natural philosophy, 87, 90,
    123–144, 167–172, 182–224
  rarification of, 178–179
Greenhouse effect, 211, 229
  increase in CO_2 concentration
    and, 270–278

Hades (Greek god), 45, 46
Hail, Aristotle's theory of, 171–172
Helen of Troy, 66, 67
Hemingway, Ernest, 112
Heraclitus (Greek), 130–134
Hercules (Mythological character),
  112
Hesiod (Greek), 87, 90, 126–128,
  130
Hinduism
  funeral, *52*
  life/death cycle in, 50, 51, 52, 54,
    63
  mandala, 54, *55*
  Upanishads, 64
Holdren, John P., 187, 195, 259
  quoted, 25 note, 235–236, 237
Homer (Greek), 126
Hooker Chemical Company, 262
Hsun Tzu (Confucian writing),
  quoted, 95
Human predicament, 252
Hydrologic cycle, 192–194, *195*,
  196, 223–224, 225, 227, 228

I Ching (Confucius), quoted, 51
Icarus myth, 107–109
  in art, *111*
Impressionism
  music, 78, 81
  paintings, 31, *32, 33*, 78
Indians of the Americas
  affinity with Nature, 86, 97, 100
  Navajo sand painting, *56*
  Toltec deities, 64
Indonesian funeral, *52*
Inductive reasoning, 155, 165
  examples, 166–167
Information explosion,
  consequences of, 288–289
Ionian philosophers, 131–136

Iranian hostage crisis (1979–1980), 285

Jaffe, Aniela, 63–64
Japanese art, 101, 105
Jet airplanes, contrails from, 16
Johnstown, Pa., floods, 78
Joyce, James, 109
Judeo-Christian tradition, 13–14, 64
life/death cycle in, 47
Jung, Carl, 63
Jupiter (Roman god), 59, 62, 63, 66

Katmandu, Nepal
outdoor dentistry, 250, 251
stupa near, 57
Kettering, Charles F., quoted, v
Kylián, Jiří, quoted, 41

Lan Ying, painting by, 104
Lao-tze (Lao-tsu, Chinese
philosopher), 290
Leda and the swan, myth of, 65–66
in art, 67
Léger, Fernand, painting by, 10
Legumes, 207
Le Nôtre, André, 8
Life, chemistry of, 198–200, 201
Likens, Gene, quoted, 261
Lippmann, Walter, quoted, 290
Louis XIV, King (France), 8, 112–113
Love Canal, N.Y., chemical
dumping at 262–263
Lovelock, James E., 231, 233
quoted, 175
Lungs, normal versus diseased, 258

Mandala, 54, 55
Marcus Aurelius, quoted, 121
Margulis, Lynn, 231, 233
Mauna Loa Observatory, Hawaii,
CO2 concentration at, 272, 273
Metamorphoses (Ovid)
myths from, 59, 63, 66
in art, 62, 71
quoted, 95–96, 109, 128–129
Meteorologica (Aristotle), 138, 140,
168–169, 171–172

Michelangelo Buonarroti, painting
by, 201
Miller, G. Tyler, Jr., 205, 215, 217
Moby Dick (Melville), 112
Monet, Claude, paintings by, 31,
32, 33
Mutations, 35
Mythology
Greek, 45–46, 65–66, 68–69, 91,
92–93, 100–101, 107–109,
112, 124–125
in art, 48, 67, 70, 111
Hesiod's approach to, 127
use of, in modern science, 231, 233
hard science versus, 154, 156, 157
Roman, 59, 63, 66
in art, 62

Nagel, Ernest, quoted, 157, 158,
161–162
Natural philosophy, ancient Greek,
86, 90, 123–145, 167–172, 182,
224
Nature
alteration of, 81–82, 83, 88
literary examples, 91, 107,
108–109
unintended side effects, 91,
118, 291–292
See also Nutrient cycles: human
disruptions of
bounds of, 82–83, 84
cycles in, 31, 34–35
in hard science, 154–155
humanistic expression, 43–72,
124–125
in natural philosophy, 127–143
See also Nutrient cycles
definition, 30
dependence on, 246–247,
278–279, 283–284
feelings about, 75–119
affinity/preservation, 86,
93–103, 104, 290
fear/control, 87, 88–89,
103–114, 117, 291–292
water, 76–78, 79, 80, 81
versus nurture, 12–13
religious attitudes toward, 13–15

Nature (*cont.*)
  restraint of, 5, 6, 7, 8
  Romantic view of, 7, 9, 94–95
  separation from, 3–4, 9, 11,
    250–251
    example, 245–246
Navajo Indian sand painting, 56
Nepal
  outdoor dentistry, 250, 251
  stupa, 57
Nevelson, Louise, sculpture by, 36
Niagara Falls, N.Y., chemical
    dumping at, 262
Nitrogen cycle, 206–212, 214
  disruption, 268–269
  acid rain, 257, 260
Nitrogen fixation, 206–208
Nitrous oxide, 211–212, 215, 269
Novalis (Friedrich von
    Hardenberg), quoted, 19
Nuclear energy, debate over, 151
Nutrient cycles, 177–240
  carbon, 200, 202–203, 204
    disruption, 270–271, 274–278
  climate and, 221–231, 239
  definition, 197
  human disruptions of, 231,
    243–279
  of energy flows, 244, 253, 255
  global, 263–278, 291–292,
    294–295
  higher standards and, 249, 252
  local, 256–263
  minimization, 296–298
  hydrologic, 192–194, 195, 196,
    223–224, 225, 227, 228
  interconnectedness, diagram of,
    238
  nitrogen, 206–212, 214
    disruption, 259–261, 268–269
  phosphorus, 212–213, 216, 218
  sedimentary, 183–186, 187, 188,
    190
  sulfur, 218–221
    disruption, 259–261, 264–268
Nutrients, 186, 197

Occult art (tarot), 54, 60

Oil imports, dependence on,
    285–286
O'Keefe, Georgia, paintings by, 97,
    98
Oparin, A. I., 199
Orbit, earth's, 34
Oresteia (Aeschylus), 100–101
Oriental cultures. *See* Eastern
    cultures
Ovid (Roman). *See Metamorphoses*
Ozone, 190, 212

Pacific Ocean, 189
Pandora's box, legend of, 92–93
Paxton, Tom, quoted, 43–44
Penicillin, as symbol of science, 25
Persephone myth, 45–46, 124, 125
  in art, 48
Philosophy. *See* China: traditions;
    Natural philosophy
Phosphorus cycle, 212–213, 216, 218
Photosynthesis, 200, 202–203, 204,
    271
Plates, continental, 182, 184
  interfaces, 183
Plutonium
  release into environment,
    261–262
  as symbol of science, 25
Pollution
  chemical, 261–263
  See also Air pollution; Water
    pollution
Pope, Alexander, quoted, 7
Prayer wheels, 57, 58
Pre-Raphaelite painting, 48
Prometheus (mythological figure),
    91, 92
Pygmy deity, 65
Pyramids, 113
Pythagoras (Greek), 128–130

Rackham, Arthur, painting by, 80
Radiant energy, 228–230, 239
  solar, 222–225, 228, 229
    ultraviolet, 193, 211–212, 222–223
Rain
  acid, 257, 260–261

Rain (cont.)
    and epiphytes, 233
    personification of, 65, 66
    and weathering, 185
Reductionism, 157, 162
Reich, Charles, 97
Religion
    cycles, belief in, 47, 50-54,
        55-58, 59
    value conflict with science,
        149-150
    views of nature, 15-17
    fire, 132-133
    and Oriental art, 101, 104
    personification, 64-65, 94, 103,
        106, 127
    See also Mythology
Rhizobium (bacteria), 207
Rig Veda (Hindu book), quoted, 50
Robinson, John Mansley, quoted, 131
Romans, ancient, 95
    See also Metamorphoses (Ovid)
Romanticism, view of Nature in, 7,
    9, 94-95
Rose, H. J., 157
Rossetti, Dante Gabriel, painting
    by, 48
Rotation, earth's, 35
Rouen cathedral, France, paintings
    of, 31, 32, 33
Rousseau, Jean Jacques, 96

Sand painting, Navajo, 56
Schneider, S. H., 277
Science, 147-174
    advances, 29-30
    art compared to
        common ground, 26-28
        polarization, 21-24
    cycles, 34-35, 154-155
        See also Nutrient cycles
    dictionary definition, 147
    growth, consequences of,
        288-290
    hard versus speculative, 148-149,
        150, 154-157
    method, 164-167
        Aristotle's lack of, 140, 170, 172

Science (cont.)
    method (cont.)
        contrast with speculative
            science, 154-157
        degree of exactitude in,
            158-162
        imaginative component, 158
        levels of description, 160-163
        speculative. See Speculative
            sciences
        symbolization of, 25
        and values, 149-153
Sea-level rise, possible, 276-278
Sedimentary cycle, 183-186, 187,
    188, 190
Shakespeare, William, quoted, 12
Shelley, Mary, book by, 91
Shelley, Percy Bysshe, quoted, 72
Shintoism, 104
Simon, Paul, 155
Sistine Chapel, Rome, Italy,
    painting from,
    201
Sisyphus myth, 68-69
    in art, 70
Siva (Hindu god), 51
Snow, C. P., 22, 24, 26, 288
Social contracts, 293-294
Social tithe, 296
Sociobiology, 12
Socratic method, 156-157
Solar energy, 222-225, 228, 239
    in photosynthesis, 202, 204
    ultraviolet, 193, 211-212, 222-223
Space colonization movement, 11,
    12
Speculative sciences
    hard sciences compared to,
        148-149, 150, 154-157
    natural-cycle motif in, 44-71
    See also Mythology; Natural
        philosophy; Religion
Stoppard, Tom, quoted, 281
Storm control, 118
Structuralist school of poetry, 163
Stupas (Buddhist temples), 54, 57,
    58
Suardi, Bartolomeo (Bramantino),
    painting by, 62

Sulfur cycle, 218–221
  disruption, 264–265, 266, 267–268
  acid rain, 257, 260–261
Sun. See Solar energy
Sweden, and acid rain problem,
  261

Taoism, 95
Tarot, 54, 60
Thales of Miletus, 141–144, 148, 182
Theogony (Hesiod), 87, 90, 127
Thermodynamics, laws of, 235–237
Thermonuclear reactions, of sun,
  222
Third World countries, 249, 252
  food system, 246–247
  higher standards, prospect of,
  248–249, 250
Thomas, Dylan, quoted, 50
Thomas, Lewis, 4, 35
Thoreau, Henry David, 9, 96
Tides, 35
Titian (Italian), paintings by, 67, 70
Tolkien, J. R. R., quoted, 290–291
Toltec deities, 64
Transcendentalism, 96
Transmigration of soul, belief in,
  51, 52, 63
Transpiration, 192, 195
Trial by fire, 112, 133
Tuan, Yi-Fu, 14–15
"Two cultures" dichotomy, 21–24,
  288
  common ground, 26–28

Ultraviolet radiation, 193, 211–212,
  222–223
"Unity in variety" concept, 26–28,
  37
Upanishads (Hindustani writings),
  64
Urban heat-island effect, 244, 253,
  255

Value judgments, 18, 26, 81, 91,
  167, 295–296, 299–300
Value sets
  affinity/preservation, 86, 93–103,
  104, 290
  fear/control, 87, 88–89, 103–114,
  118, 291–292
Versailles, France, 8, 112–113
Vishniac, Roman, quoted, 73
Vishnu (Hindu god), 51
Volcanoes, sulfur compounds from,
  264–265

Water, 192
  hydrologic cycle, 194, 195,
  196, 223–224, 225, 227, 228
  loss into space, 193
  views of, 76–78, 81
  by Thales, 141–143
  in visual arts, 78, 79, 80
Water pollution, 257
  acid rain, 257, 260–261
Waterfall, in art, 105
Weather, See Climate
Weathering, 185
Wells, H. G., quoted, 296
Wheel of fortune, 54, 60
White, Lynn, 13–14, 15
Wilson, E. O., 12
Wordsworth, William, poem by, 7,
  9, 94–95
World's Fair, Chicago, Ill. (1933), 11

Yeats, W. B., 65
Young Chief (Cayuse Indian),
  quoted, 97, 100

Zeus (Greek god), 46, 65–66, 67,
  69, 71, 92, 233
Zodiac, 59